Capitalism and the Limits of Desire

ALSO AVAILABLE FROM BLOOMSBURY

The Reasoning of Unreason: Universalism, Capitalism and Disenlightenment, John Roberts
The War against Marxism: Reification and Revolution, Tony McKenna
Challenging Power: Democracy and Accountability in a Fractured World, Cynthia Kaufman
Marx: An Introduction, Michel Henry
How to Be a Marxist in Philosophy, Louis Althusser

Capitalism and the Limits of Desire

John Roberts

BLOOMSBURY ACADEMIC
LONDON • NEW YORK • OXFORD • NEW DELHI • SYDNEY

BLOOMSBURY ACADEMIC
Bloomsbury Publishing Plc
50 Bedford Square, London, WC1B 3DP, UK
1385 Broadway, New York, NY 10018, USA
29 Earlsfort Terrace, Dublin 2, Ireland

BLOOMSBURY, BLOOMSBURY ACADEMIC and the Diana logo are trademarks of Bloomsbury Publishing Plc

First published in Great Britain 2022

Copyright © John Roberts, 2022

John Roberts has asserted his right under the Copyright, Designs and Patents Act, 1988, to be identified as Author of this work.

For legal purposes the Acknowledgements on p. vi constitute an extension of this copyright page.

Cover design by Ben Anslow
Cover image: Barbell from coins (© lcs813 / iStock)

All rights reserved. No part of this publication may be reproduced or transmitted in any form or by any means, electronic or mechanical, including photocopying, recording, or any information storage or retrieval system, without prior permission in writing from the publishers.

Bloomsbury Publishing Plc does not have any control over, or responsibility for, any third-party websites referred to or in this book. All internet addresses given in this book were correct at the time of going to press. The author and publisher regret any inconvenience caused if addresses have changed or sites have ceased to exist, but can accept no responsibility for any such changes.

A catalogue record for this book is available from the British Library.

A catalog record for this book is available from the Library of Congress.

ISBN:	HB:	978-1-3502-1494-1
	PB:	978-1-3502-1495-8
	ePDF:	978-1-3502-1496-5
	eBook:	978-1-3502-1497-2

Typeset by Integra Software Services Pvt. Ltd.

To find out more about our authors and books visit www.bloomsbury.com and sign up for our newsletters.

Contents

Acknowledgements vi

Introduction 1

1 Capitalism, *jouissance* and subjective ruination 21

2 Individuation, egoism and social reproduction 61

3 Self-Love, *jouissance* and desire 93

4 Perfectionism, individuation and self-realization 137

Conclusion 189

Notes 214
Bibliography 235
Index 247

Acknowledgements

Thanks to Chris Gomersall for our continuous dialogue on politics and philosophy, during the writing of the book, to Keti Chukhrov for our many discussions on shared interests, to Liza Thompson at Bloomsbury for the support of the project and to the three anonymous reviewers for their insightful comments on the manuscript.

Introduction

Capitalism and the Limits of Desire addresses the long-standing and complex question of people's practical, intellectual, emotive and affective investment in capitalism as a system. In this it draws on the new Marxian writing on libidinal economy and social reproduction (Frédéric Lordon, Samo Tomšič, Endnotes, Bernard Stiegler, Tristan Garcia), in the wake of the growing post-Deleuzian literatures on digital 'control societies' and the value form. However, it makes a crucial distinction that this literature rarely makes: that capitalism's vast production of *jouissance* for the producer and consumer succeeds, as a condition of this investment, insofar as it is perceived as a form of self-development that acts in the interests of rational enlightenment. Capitalism then does not reproduce itself simply through illusion and managed consent, but through the *active investment* of producers and consumers in a pragmatic, if evolving, ideal version of capitalism, which – irrespective of the subject's doubts, scepticism and criticisms about capitalism as a system – is assumed to be in the (immediate) best interests of producers and consumers alike. This process may generate false expectations based on misjudgements about the 'real nature of capitalism', but it also produces a rational acceptance of 'least resistance' as the best way of maintaining pleasure and its continuity. Crucial to this process, therefore, is how capitalism produces what I call 'the love of the love of the self' as an *enlightened* investment in the desire for desire or surplus jouissance (Jacques Lacan). This is the pragmatic 'reason of pleasure' of libidinal economy, insofar as the pursuit and maintenance of the love of the love of self is constitutive of, and driven by this ideal version of capitalism as an unconditioned realm of self-optimization-beyond-need, what I refer to as the 'demonic-infinite'.

But this book is not the familiar story about narcissism, individualism and social fragmentation under mature capitalism. Much of the new writing on libidinal economy fails to address how the obvious disaggregation of collective labour and the destruction of the older social and cultural unities and attachments, provide the conditions for *new affects and attachments*, and therefore the possibility of new unities. In this sense the 'love of the love of self' is not in and of itself an irredeemable pathology of mature capitalism – its narcissistic core – even if it operates in many instances pathologically and destructively. But rather, it is a claim, explicitly or implicitly, on the production of the transindividual, in as much as the escape from or resistance to, old unities, old attachments, recalls 'self-love' and the pursuit of individuation to the social and collective conditions of self-realization within the universal and normative demands of the perfectionist philosophical tradition (self-realization as an 'all rounded' flourishing of human capacities and interests) (Jean-Jacques Rousseau, Karl Marx and recently Thomas Hurka). Self-love and self-affection form the basis of the socialized development of 'all-roundedness'.

Hence 'self-love' (*amour-propre*) is split under capitalism: it is easily attached to processes of de-individuation and as such to a narrow and repressive range of affects and interests, but in its residual connection to self-autonomy it reconnects self-realization to the struggle for *new forms* of socialization; the struggle for autonomy and socialization are indivisible. Hence my critique of the love of the love of self doesn't stop at a critique of 'individualism' and the mourning for lost collectivities – how capitalism captures individuation for particular repressive ends – but, rather, moves on to discuss the parts self-love, self-affection and 'care of the self' play in the emancipatory legacy of perfectionism as the production of human 'all roundedness' – what I call 'non-repressive self-governance'. But before we embark on this discussion we need to provide a diagnostics of the political landscape of the new libidinal economy and the crisis of capitalist social reproduction. For it is here we'll see why, and how, 'self-love' and 'non-repressive self-governance' have become increasingly central to emancipatory politics and to the normative demands of political philosophy, not only obviously in relation to neoliberal accounts of 'well-being', but also in relation to various de-subjectivizing positions on the left attached to accelerationist defences of new technology and post-agential theories of change in the wake of 'post-work' political theory and the deepening ecological crisis.

There are three theoretico-political models on the radical left, which cover the present 'state of emergency':

1) A parliamentary, party-based radical social democracy that is post-labourist, in which electoralism and extra-parliamentary alliances serve to produce a new 'commons' based on the new network technologies and digital economy, and, which in turn, provides the space for a new 'intersectional' identity politics. The objective being: to assimilate workers and the petty-bourgeoisie into a new democratic capitalist consensus, based on the re-nationalization of public services, the further expansion of renewable energies and 'green policies' and the protection and development of local economies against globalization.

2) An extra-parliamentary, 'post-work' alliance of radical and activist groups, research centres, consultancies, which sees the technological and technical drivers of the new advanced machinic productive forces, as the basis for a world without scarcity. This is supported politically and socially by the disenchantment of the majority with waged labour. As such, automation serves as a Promethean defence of the capacity of the forces of production to 'exit' their contradictions, freeing up the 'communistic' tendencies inherent in the digital economy, that will provide a wide variety of low cost or zero cost goods and services available to all.[1] This position can be divided into two periodizations: a weak accelerationism (the rational and democratic capture of new technologies and big data), in which the building up of a 'post-work', fully automated society, is continuous with the technocratic achievements of capitalism; and a strong discontinuous, or even apocalyptic, accelerationism, in which a nihilistic overidentification with the liberatory possibilities of 'post-work' and post-human tendencies and data mining, forces capitalism to the point of social collapse and ungovernability and the possible release of new relations of production and a new world.

3) And an extra-parliamentary 'progressive anti-progressivist' and anti-technocratic extra-parliamentary alliance of revolutionary political groups, based on the re-composition of workers' struggles, in the wake of the strategic and cultural impotence of the old workers

movement. Fundamental to position this is a recommitment to the questions of *subjectivation, history and memory* – of the creation of new affects and desires – as the basis for a new emancipatory politics and collective struggle. In this respect, crucially, there is a political and social recognition that capital remains *at war* with labour and those forces that would weaken or destroy the rule of capital. Indeed, this position derives from a classical martial conception of politics.[2] The ideological success of neoliberalism since the 1970s has, effectively, been its pursuit of a global war *as* politics, as a low-level civil offensive against labour and peoples in struggle, demolishing and demobilizing the workers' movement's capacity to sustain its own 'counter-warfare', that certainly before the 1950s workers took for granted as a matter of class self-discipline. The success of neoliberalism's 'civil war' against labour, however, has been based on the democratic management and dissolution of the martial and conflictual character of this ongoing civil war, under the pacifying and coercive rationalizations of cost-effective financialization and creative competition in all areas of the economy and social life. This is because capital has had to find ways of governing the destabilizing effects of the would-be creativity of capitalism, distinct from incorporatist and welfarist democratic options. This is based on a cost/creative coefficient: The social injuries and divisions of capitalism are the price that people must bear if the creativity of capitalism is to bring about its global benefits, particularly when this creativity is attached to the unprecedented expansion of new forms of social individuation and freedom. Labour, then, has had to confront an unforgiving condition of late capitalist modernity: It is hard to maintain the martial identity of the workers movement, when, creative solutions appear to define the future and the promises, real or not, of the expanded individuation of social reproduction.[3] And, therefore, it is hard to connect the reach and power of capital with the notion of 'war', when day-to-day governance in the Western economies appears distinct from the obvious realities of actual wars themselves. The United States and the UK, for example, may be governments involved in external imperialist wars, but they do not appear to be governments *of* war involved in a war against their own people. The aim of this 'progressive anti-progressivist' position, consequently, is to rebuild the strategic, cognitive and imaginary 'war machines' of emancipatory politics in face of the suppressed actuality of war-as-capital and capital-as-war (accumulation by dispossession; the looting of resources from weaker globally exposed economies; the increasing expansion of fictitious capital in order to protect paper titles to wealth[4]), as a condition of a new offensive solidarity, and, crucially, new processes of radical subjectivity; new affects and desires. But, this rebuilding is to be pursued on the *other side* of the workerist attachments of the old workers movement; if the mass agency of the old workers' movement established workers' collective power on a 'war footing', the unified character of this agency based on stable industrial identities is no longer available. Unity is now a condition of separation, in the wake of both social individuation and the weakening of collective and ethnographic class identities.[5] In this respect, the 'post-work' and disaggregative realities of labour power under the new capitalism, will determine the strength and weakness, perspicacity and opacity of these strategies, although directed towards very different immediate and long term ends than the two models above.

These three models obviously assume different philosophical positions on agency and the political subject in the current crisis and state of emergency. In this they directly inherit all the fundamental problems attached to the questions of class decomposition and re-composition, class representation, subjectivity and subjectivation since the 1950s. Indeed, the question of class *re*composition and agency has been the great problem of revolutionary political theory and practice over the last sixty years: that is, the radical contraction of the industrial working class as an emancipatory force and the delinking of working-class identity from ethnographic attachments to a progressive 'workers culture'. The list of proactive 'revisions' of this condition in the wake of this contraction since the 1960s is endless: Herbert Marcuse's 'new subjects'; Félix Guattari's 'marginalities'; André Gorz's 'post-industrial' working class; Toni Negri and Paulo Virno's 'multitudes'; Ernesto Laclau and Chantal Mouffe's 'counter-hegemonic' identities; Alain Badiou's 'movementist' alliances; Slavoj Žižek's and Bernard Stiegler's 'universal proletarianization' ('we're all proletarians now'); Endnotes' generalization of the 'consciousness of capital'; The Invisible Committee's generalized 'insurrectionism'; and Jodi Dean's networked and motile new communist party as a 'drop-in' centre for the activist and non-engaged multiple.

The three models inherit and reshape the problems and horizons of this party and post-party legacy, agency and representation. Unsurprisingly, therefore, the first model, given its electoral basis, accepts the need for a pragmatic class reconciliation between labour and capital that is highly familiar from post–Second World War twentieth-century parliamentary politics.[6] That is, it accepts, as a constitutive reality of a would-be post-revolutionary epoch, that the defence of workers' material interests is primary, over and above, questions of equality. Accordingly, its politics remain based on the fundamental assumption that workers have too much to lose in any revolutionary struggle with capital, and, therefore, are prepared to accept short-term gains – in the long run – against any long term and broader gains. But, it gives this process a radical twist, insofar as it revives the notion that labour can make capitalism – in the way social democratic state planners, economists and technocrats assumed in the 1950s – work better than the absolutist market defenders of capitalism, without the subjective destabilizations of neoliberalism, through retraining and work sharing. In this respect, from the radical left inside the parliamentary party this new social democracy borrows strategically from the 'post-work' theorists of the second model a primary commitment to a technocratic solution to the 'state of emergency', particularly given the global ecological crisis and the necessary pursuit of renewable energy. It is the new technologies and the new sciences under the control of a new democracy and the socialized investment in 'green energy' (A New Green Deal), that will lead capitalism out of the neoliberal nightmare; the issue of agency, of securing popular power in order to implement these urgent changes is secondary. As such, there is a general appeal to a new social-technocratic *reordering* of the market and democracy; green imperatives will restrict the predatory forms of financialization, enlarging the flow of loanable capital into production and the creation of a new regime of public use values. Similarly, in model two, weak accelerationism relies on a new relationship between market allocations and democracy to push open up the ongoing crisis of the system; but, in this respect, with a notional attachment to working class agency. Through the vigorous development of automation, in alliance with a progressive system of basic income for all, workers will be in a position to exert some control over the labour process; workers themselves will decide how much labour power they will provide and to what ends. In a situation, therefore, where there is no full employment as a measure of value production, the political mediation of workers interests as a collective confrontation with capital, disappears, enabling progressive continuity, without fruitless wage-based conflict. Moreover, an automation driven 'post-work' economy, freely incorporates the disabled and domestic labourers and the previously long-term unemployed into the workplace on equal terms.

In this book I take my critical point of departure from model three, given what I believe to be its more exacting account of the limits and possibilities of emancipatory politics in this epoch of 'feudalistic' and 'anti-modern' retreats globally. In this I reject both the ultraleftist fantasies of accelerationism (and its emancipatory-technist, anti-subjectivist tendencies[7]) and all the current attempts electorally to 're-enchant' social democracy through advanced technology – a doomed project, insofar as capital remains on a continuing violent course of confrontation with workers, in which accumulation by dispossession and resource looting, reveals in all its foreboding starkness, the fundamental and moving contradiction of capitalism: the irresolvable conflict between capital's need to capture living labour and living labour's inexorable expulsion from the system in the interests of competitive 'efficiency'. In this sense, an emancipatory post-capitalist politics has to emerge through the conflictual and subjective energies of this fundamental contradiction. A post-capitalist politics is not simply the objective consequence of the irresolvable nature of this conflict between living labour and machines (and therefore an invitation for the Technocratic Solution to step in), but must be constitutive of the critical *working through* of the opportunities for autonomy that this contradiction between living labour and machines presents – with all its vicissitudes. Model two accelerationism fails to do this. Consequently, there is some leverage in Endnotes' notion that the 'consciousness of capital', must prevail as the basis for new forms of unity and agency. That is, consciousness of the function of capital and the value form must prevail over attachment to economistic and ethnographic class identities and wage-based struggles. This is quite different then from both the new social democracy's pragmatic insistence on the 'greening' of waged labour and the expansion of consumption in a jobless market, and by extension, accelerationism's emancipation 'without' subjects.

Significantly and importantly, model three establishes continuity with Marx's systemic critique of political economy – first and foremost his contestation of bourgeois class power supported by parliamentary democracy – and with the cultural legacy of critical theory (social philosophy as a theory of negation) and psychoanalysis. In this it provides a working framework in which the critique of notions of capitalist progress is challenged by the unmet *needs* of the majority of workers and humanity, as a collective means of self-transformation. Emancipatory politics has more than ever to move beyond the immediate interests of the working class's relationship to capital, what the early Marx attacked as the mere 'class interests' of workers; in other words, emancipatory politics has to reconnect with the unmet needs of the working class as the *universal* needs of all.[8] However, this is not an abstract politics of hope. If the 'consciousness of capital' clears away some of the tired progressivist sentiment of 'collective class consciousness' still hanging around on the left, it is not in and of itself, the mantra for a new praxis. On the contrary the 'progressive critique of progress' is the opportunity for a radical assessment of the post-workerist and 'post-work' space of politics as the working class exits the old assurances and identities. It, therefore, requires more than a shift in perspective or flag-waving solidarity with model two, as if the demise of the old reformist workers movement carries with it the promise of things now being, if not exactly back on track, at least open again for business. Yet, conversely, neither does it mean that we are swept back unceremoniously to 1848, and to the origins of the workers' movement, as Badiou sometimes assumes melancholically.[9] Rather if we do need to 'return' anywhere, we need to go 'back' to where Marxism, critical theory and psychoanalysis dropped us with a bump methodologically in 1945: the requirement to *see through* a radical diagnostics of self, agency and the pathologies of social reproduction, as the means by which emancipation might function *as* praxis and not as a technological gift or ideational promise. That is, fully immersed in a world of conflictual 'mortal' social conditions, in which theory and practice are released from both the idealist philosophical tradition (from René Descartes to Edmund Husserl and Martin Heidegger) and Stalinist and orthodox Marxist objectivism and teleology. Thus, this 'mortal' horizon is necessarily framed within an account of agency in which the question of unmet needs is mediated and shaped by the continuing antagonistic realities of the subject (class compromise) under capitalist social reproduction. This is why Endnotes' notion of the disaggregation of the collective worker is crucial here as a radical rectification of present illusions.

As they say in their important essay, 'A History of Separation' (2015), in the twentieth century only:

> *A portion of the proletariat ever identified with the programme of the workers' movement.* That was because many proletarians affirmed their non-class identities – organized primarily around race and nation but secondarily around gender, skill and trade – above their class identity. They saw their interests as adding up differently, depending on which identity they favoured ... That meant that the workers' movement came to include always a fraction of the working class.[10]

Consequently, the workers' movement emerged delimited by its internal demographics. And one of the outcomes of this was that workers' links with other workers lay mostly outside of the factory and office: 'on the roads, in electricity lines, in the supermarket, on television'.[11] The anticipated expansion of the collective worker under the growth of waged labour was stillborn. '*The atomized worker revealed itself as the truth of the collective worker*. Here was the unity-in-separation of capitalism, corroding the bases of workers' solidarity.'[12] The social democratic and state socialist 'advances' of the post-war period, then, have turned out to be 'strange victories', that is only 'temporary respites from the ravages of capitalist society'.[13]

Indeed, between 1945 and 1975 the workers' movement was assumed to take on a partnership role in the Western democracies, as well as a leadership role in the Peoples Republic of China and the Eastern European states. In East and West increased production and the growth of industrial society was held to be a measure of workers' success and the unfolding – if gradual – penetration of collective values and workers' consciousness into the state, East and West. Through the 'collective worker' this was a nascent 'workers' world', even if workers were not directly in control, or, indeed, failed to see themselves actively as part of the workers' movement at all. But this class representation begins to break down by the late 1950s–60s as the varied experiences and cultural interests of workers begin to diverge dramatically from the corporate character of the workers' movement, given the fact that labour power was increasingly becoming detached from the *productive power of the collective worker*; science and technical – machine-based – expertise takes over the collective integrity of workers' skills, and as such, workers' self-identity as producers – as we have noted. The outcome is that workers' resistance, resentments and refusals were beginning to be set adrift from values, attachments and institutional resources, establishing some distance, or an alternate space, from capitalist practice and thinking; unions today, for instance, are no more than facilitators of 'joint partnerships' with management and enablers of flexible working practices. They may still seek, as a primary commitment, the protection of low-paid workers; they may even continue to provide a moderate schooling in class politics,[14] but the logic is fundamentally one of 'petitioning' as opposed to negotiation from a position of class solidarity. So, the actions of unions are no less defined by the disaggregative effects and experience of workers today as any other workers' organization or party; under this 'petitionist' regime workers are seen as clients and 'professionals' in search of economic justice, before they are seen as class representatives. Indeed, this is the fundamental political consequence of the disaggregative dissolution of collective labour: it is increasingly difficult to bring the notion of injustice under the concept of exploitation, when the concreteness of 'rights' overshadow the indeterminacies of 'collective struggle'. The issue, therefore, is not that unions continue to betray the collective interest of workers, but rather that unions now function primarily to contain the subjective ruination of the worker, in order to maximize his or her access to the enlightened reason of the market: 'the more workers' lives [in the twentieth century] were imbricated in market relations the more they were reduced to the atomized observers of their own exploitation',[15] – increasingly exposing the workers' movement as a fictive unity. Unions are now, consequently, no more than feint cheerleaders for this fictive unity. Hence, overall, even though proletarianization and immiseration grow on a global scale swallowing up sections of the petty bourgeoisie, 'workers find themselves wandering in an immense infrastructure, that of modern life, which reflects back to them not their growing power, but rather, their impotence.'[16]

The subjective ruination of workers as workers, consequently, is evidence of the fact that in the twentieth century, far from the workers' movement giving rise to the collective worker as a transformative unity, the opposite has in fact occurred under the expansion of the commodity form: an increasing separation between the reproduction of class relations and class consciousness. One of the self-evident outcomes of this is the separation of class identity from the ethnographic identifications and symbols of industrial labour. Indeed, this is reflected today in the extremely low levels of trade union membership and mass voter abstention globally (e.g. a staggering 18 million people choose not to vote in the UK; that is, a majority of low-paid working-class voters, the unemployed and the low-paid petty bourgeoisie, would rather withdraw all consent, than attach their name and interests to centre-left parties that, for all their political limits, could nevertheless easily, electorally swamp, the voter base of conservative and bourgeois parties). The issue here, then, is not that there exists an absentee majority of voters that are holding out for a more 'radical option', but, rather, that the relationship between politics and class identity, offers so little to those who might be best placed to see its advantages. In this sense this is not simply evidence of a new post-reformist realism: the recognition that workers' interests are not in the system's interests. Rather, as Endnotes say: 'being a worker is no longer one's essence, even if one is poor.'[17] And this requires as Adorno noted presciently in the mid-1950s, not abjuration and forbearance, but critical re-engagement and new forms of emancipatory practice. 'If a worker no longer notices that he is a worker, this has important implications for theory.'[18]

So, any radical diagnostics of the 'state of emergency' has to recognize first and foremost the huge barriers that remain subjectively and objectively in the way of the production of new anti-capitalist use values post the old workers' movement, certainly given the benignly ameliorative ways in which the new 'post-work' social democrats and 'weak accelerationists' imagine the future – confronted, as emancipatory thought is today, by the multi-accented realities of a global anti-Enlightenment reaction. From this perspective the accelerationist 'post-work' theorists are classic post-agentists. They assume technology and technicians, given the historical absence of a self-consciously unifiable emancipatory agent, will do the heavy lifting of emancipatory transformation. Indeed, both 'weak accelerationists' and 'strong accelerationists' see the new subject–technology interfaces as a pathway out of the objective and subjective crisis of the labour–capital relation; in releasing the worker from all the old attachments to the 'integrity of labour', technology will not only free the worker from the tedium of work, but also remove the anxiety of collective praxis; all the subjective investment in the struggle of the 'collective worker' to control the means of production will be demoted to negotiations about the lightest of technical monitoring, for, on the other side of a 'post-work' world, the popular control of production will offer limited passionate attachments. In fact, for accelerationism we have already effectively 'arrived' in a 'post-work' world; the global unemployed and underemployed are the impending social vanguard of the fully unemployed[19] under 'post-work' conditions and therefore will be better placed to pursue 'post-work' values and horizons than those still in full-time employment, or those still striving for full-time employment. The favelas, shanty towns and immiserated peripheries of metropolitan centres are the new experimental hubs and 'training centres' of future 'post-work' practices and forms of self-affection.[20]

Under the dictates of model two, then, the capitalist post-human technists and the accelerationists share a certain ambition: under mass post-work conditions, it will be technology that will define socialization and self-realization given its functional hold already in the lives and pleasures of the majority. On this basis, the accelerationists share with the subject-intrusive programmes of the doyens of the new interactive technologies a faith in the utopic extension of self-identity into the machinic. For accelerationists and post-human technists alike this offers a 'perfect' means of adaptation of the mass loss of skills amongst 'surplus populations' to machinic use values. Linked to the enlargement the cognitive and affective attachments of the subject, access to knowledge and communication platforms are uploaded as a new skill set for everyone. But if all this energetic interfusion between body and machine, self and the collective intellect, provides a new regime of participatory 'use-values', it is also just another cover for the *disappointments and impotence of agency and desire*, another way of deflating or offsetting desire and self-realization through capitalist solutions: the technological distribution of facility. And, in turn, this is why, despite the anti-workerist and anti-historicist politics of accelerationism, accelerationism ironically is strikingly reminiscent of the techno-evolutionism of Second International Marxism; history, subjectivity and workers' and non-workers' struggle are secondary to technological progress and its (projected) guarantees of material well-being.

The first priority of model three, therefore, is an assessment of subjective conditions under which the transformation of the relations of production in a 'post-work' economy may occur. On this basis, models one and two fail to recognize – or limit the recognition of – how the 'post-work' reduction in necessary labour time may establish new forms of re-attachment to capital (a greened capitalism), and an affective reinvestment in the long-term democratic flexibility and adaptability of the capitalist market. If capitalism can continue to provide some modicum of leisure and autonomy in a world in which some of the problems of the ecological crisis have been solved technologically, why is there any pressing need for equality and popular control over resources, given the fact that the destabilization of the situation could make things much worse? Hence, one of the fundamental problems with the new 'post-work' emancipatory discourse across models one and two is their indifference to ideology and subjectivation. Weak accelerationism may certainly talk about the need for 'building a mass political movement',[21] but the technocratic optimization of automation tends to override this; there is an undeclared assumption that automated (big data) transition from full-time waged labour to universal basic income and part-time labour, releases the burden of the subject from ideology and passivity. Or, more precisely, it acts as a faucet through which the forces of autonomy will flow.

Thus, my reading of model three, in contrast, is framed within a conflictual account of agency, in which the unmet (emancipatory) needs of the majority are mediated and shaped by the realities of social reproduction and subjectivation. For weak accelerationism social reproduction and class subjectivation appear as inconveniences in the light of the prospect of ending artificial scarcity ('our technology is already making us gods').[22] Indeed, this rolling over of subjectivation is particularly acute in the absence of any substantive discussion of the parliamentary class compromise that has overwhelmingly defined social democratic and reformist politics since 1945. The key question, accordingly, is how class compromise under capitalist social reproduction intersects with the growing realities of a 'post-work' capitalism, and therefore, what this opens up for the critique of waged labour and the possibilities of self-transformative practice and autonomy and the release of new (unmet) needs as a political and cultural strategy, and not, how automation can provide a necessary pathway to 'post-work' emancipation. We cannot expect automation alone to either produce an emancipatory 'post-work' discourse, and, therefore, dissolve the worker's and non-worker's attachment to capitalist reason. This is why the third technological revolution ('The Third Disruption' as Aaron Bastani calls it) is not simply a parallel 'precursor' along with the advent of 'collective struggle' to a new emancipatory politics.[23] The conflicts of ideology immanent to capitalist subjectivation will determine this outcome, not the technology. This is why the new social democracy and the new accelerationism leap over the facticities of social reproduction in a period of deepening reaction, in a kind of Promethean face-off with the political inertia of this conservatism, as if the future is already decided ('In one sense, it's like the future is already written ... ').[24] Present conflicts over automation and new technological use values (human–machine interfacing; deskilling/reskilling; self-autonomy and community), however, are not simply 'culturalist choices' based on a neutral notion of practical efficiency. On the contrary, they are grounded in a system of adaptive preferences that are shaped by the value form, and, therefore, attuned consciously and unconsciously to already familiar user attachments to capitalist reason. And this, inarguably, is the basis by which the compromises and negotiated pleasures of the libidinal economy of mature capitalism are formed, that is the material–ideological terrain on which the subject reproduces itself as a productive, desiring and sapient being. Reason, agency and desire fall under and are shaped, therefore, by a range of material and ideological constraints: the electoral consent to exploitation in order to increase welfare in the present or immediate future or to defend a notion of 'community', the assumed neutrality of technological change, the acceptance of adaptive preference as the basis for 'realistic' political agency, the pursuit of pleasure as a release from the immiserations of social life and the political process, the subordination of abstract reason to the reason of pleasure and affect, and the cultivation of social identities that emphasize individuation and self-realization over and above labour-based collective and social-ethnographic identities.

In this sense, my position here derives its strategy from the conflictual realities of the *subjectivation of the subject,* as the material of emancipatory practice. Indeed, my primary concern in this book is a reflection on the relationship between self, identity and social reproduction as the basis for an analysis of what critical theory and psychoanalysis recognize as the *constitutive embedding of individuation within the processes of capitalist subjectivation.* Thus, in any substantive account of economic reason, reason and *jouissance* are to be seen as thoroughly enmeshed. Indeed, as Axel Honneth argues, individuation has, under contemporary processes of capitalist subjectivation, lost its old promissory and qualitative content (specifically its attachment to the emancipatory aspects of the aesthetic judgement in the eighteenth and nineteenth centuries), to become co-extensive with economic reason itself; self-realization is so limited and shaped by the modalities of industrialized libidinal identification today that individualization might be construed as having fallen, in fact, into reverse. The processes of adaptive individuation 'have so definitely become a feature of the institutionalized expectations inherent in social reproduction that the particular goods of such claims are lost and they are transmuted into a support of the system's legitimacy'.[25]

Unlike Honneth, however, I take a path quite different from the institutionalization of 'individuation' school. That is, if the crisis of individuation under mature capitalism is not solely about *individual* pathologies, as Honneth rightly recognizes, neither is it simply the abstract, adaptive, coercive work of the commodity form, in Georg Lukács' sense: vis: 'reification is ... the necessary, immediate reality of every person'[26] – which leaves neither space for negation or transformation and conflict nor the analysis of pleasure; in short as de-subjectivized abstraction, it removes reflection and action altogether from the category of intentionality. If this understanding blocks off moralism and subjectivism, nevertheless, at the same time it makes it incomprehensible that workers might take pleasure *from* failing to act in the name of their own best interests, or, indeed, that they might offer good reasons for doing so. Thus, the loss of the emancipatory link between unmet needs and modern processes of individuation, needs, accordingly, more than a 'crisis of reason' and all the familiar shibboleths of 'cultural decline' to understand the efficacy of capitalist processes of subjectivation, that Honneth, with his own version of Lukács' de-rationalization thesis, falls into.[27] In other words, we need a social-psychic aetiology of individuation, in which individuation is seen at the same time both as the work of subjectivation (and institutional capture) *and* resistance (as desire–pleasure), on the basis that the relations of domination are produced not passively, but through an active, indeed phantasmatic, investment in the libidinal drive of self-realization. Hence, we require an aetiology that follows the spitting of the subject as a *political* reality, specifically derived from Jacques Lacan's insistence on *jouissance* as constitutively attached to an unconscious economy of *pleasure as unpleasure* and *unpleasure as pleasure*. That is, it is imperative to examine individuation as the *conflictual substance of social reproduction*, and not simply evidence, in the abstract, of de-rationalization and pacification. Thus, the best way of addressing this is expressly through recognizing the deep ambiguity and conflict the subject experiences under the regime of capitalist subjectivation, insofar as the subject is always testing his or her investment in the pleasures of capitalist individuation against the coercive and constraining realities of the drive to self-valorization. In one sense this obviously leads to the pleasures of 'voluntary servitude' and 'adaptive preferences'. Yet, it also leads to non-identity and resistance. No matter how much the subject is shaped and constrained by the processes of libidinal predetermination and their unpleasurable–pleasurable, pleasurable–unpleasable affects, the subject is not coextensive with these processes; subjectivity displaces, resists, invades subjectivation; that is, at some point the unpleasurable–pleasurable switch breaks down; the unpleasurable finds its expression as non-compensatory desire–pleasure.[28]

My version of model three, therefore, derives its understanding and strategies from a normative understanding of the conflictual realities of subjectivation, but without any of the old critical-theoretical machinery that assumes capitalist subjectivation is a *reason without reason*. As such, we need a reason of desire, pleasure and *jouissance* derived from psychoanalysis and the vicissitudes of late capitalist social reproduction, that takes questions of adaptive preference – and what I've called elsewhere – the *jouissance* of the 'reasoning of unreason' seriously, as a means of understanding why there remains a terrible cognitive gap between the vast growth in post-capitalist theory currently, and the values and expectations of the majority, *irrespective of people's disappointments in capitalism*.[29] It is this interlink between agency, pleasure, subjective ruination and subjectivation, consequently, that I explore in this book, *on the terrain of the 'post-work' future, and the present anti-Enlightenment hegemony*.

Understandably I do this work expressly through what determines the present conditions of subjectivation: the expansion of individuation as the ineradicable language of capitalist freedom. Capitalism's release, confinement, control, enabling of self-individuation, is both capital's fundamental *raison d'etre*, and equally, the thing that continues to tie the subject, affectively, emotively, ideologically, to the conflicts of social reproduction. This is why there is a pressing demand for a repositioning of the questions of libidinal economy on the terrain of 'post-work' and the critique of waged labour. For, if under capitalism the value form in its advanced digital aspects captures individuation for a narrow range of affects and attachments, the question of individuation, nevertheless, is re-posed by the new culture as a political and transformative problem: what will secure my flourishing and powers of self-development under these new conditions?

In this respect, my thinking here follows a growing philosophical and political literature on the constraints and immiserations of individuation and libidinal economy today (Stiegler, Garcia, Lorden, Tomšič and Endnotes). This body of writing has generated a penetrating analysis of the pathologies of libidinal economy, drawing on a powerful post-Kantian and psychoanalytic range of reflections on pleasure and affect. As Lordon says: 'The task of enlisting powers of acting ... is a matter of suitable desires (suitable to the master-desire). Capitalism must therefore be grasped not only in its structures but also as a certain *regime of desire*.'[30] However, my analysis of 'master-desire' has a particular focus: namely, the issue of self-love and the 'love of capitalism' as key elements of this productive and reproductive power.

The notion of the 'love of capitalism' is particularly contentious for those 'post-work' theorists who see little evidence for this given the way neoliberalism has stripped out what remains of the residual attachments to 'work-pride' at the place of work.[31] Realistically where is this love of capitalism in the workplace? Such a notion would appear to collapse individuation into identity, that is clearly at odds with most people's experience of waged labour. Half of the world's population currently available for employment are unemployed; and in a recent global survey only 13 per cent surveyed considered themselves happy with their job.[32] Similarly, there is a growing disparity between educational achievements and the availability of suitable employment. In 2013 the US Bureau of Labor Statistics reported that 753,000 workers in the US fast food industry graduated from college with a bachelor's degree or higher.[33] But the 'love of capitalism' does not exist primarily in the workplace (this is where Lordon is open to criticism, as we will see) – although I would say, despite neoliberalism, indeed, *because* of neoliberalism, it nevertheless holds its own in certain sectors of the economy. The 'love of capitalism', rather, is functionally attached more generally to what individuation promises inside and *outside* of the workplace: what I define more exactly as the '*love of the love of self*'. This is mature capitalism's great collective ecstasis. Hence in examining issues of *amour-propre*, *amour de soi* and the 'love of capitalism', my primary concern is to examine in what ways *jouissance* is captured by capitalism as a (pleasurable) substitute *for* the radical unmet needs of producers and non-producers. But at the same time, self-love also grounds resistance – albeit in weakened from – to capitalist individuation. That is, more precisely, self-love is always being mobilized to conflictual ends under the pressure of self-realization: it is both an opening up to the fantasy of individuation as a resistance to knowledge and action (to pleasure free from normative value formation), and, conversely, an opening up *to* worldly knowledge, self-affection and action (to normative value formation). My engagement with self-love and *jouissance* is not, therefore, the basis for a theory of social decomposition alone, as if all I'm interested in is identifying self-love with the pathological effects of 'individualism' and 'narcissism'. On the contrary, the love of the love of self has a very different meaning and agency when we recognize that self-love also provides a barrier (a connection to autonomy) *against* 'individualism' and 'narcissism' as coercive internal externalities, and, therefore, has a very different role to play in the debate on class decomposition and mediation. To love oneself is paradoxically to also love selflessly, insofar as 'loving oneself' is loving things disinterestedly for their own sake, that is without external and heteronomous pressures. But this is not a love which is purely *self*-grounded; one cannot love oneself disinterestedly unless one loves other things; to love oneself is to love *other* things. Indeed, I see self-love in these terms as crucial to the universalizing issues of human flourishing and self-realization in the debate on individuation that are central to the Enlightenment perfectionist tradition (Rousseau, Marx), and, therefore, philosophically distinct from 'narcissism' in the usual pejorative sense. Consequently, my concern here is to open up the debate on *jouissance* and social reproduction and political agency to this classical legacy of perfectionism (the maximalization of rational and creative capacity), as something which is mostly conspicuous by its absence in recent debates on the crisis of individuation, social reproduction and the question of autonomy.[34]

In this respect, the increase and diversification of the processes of individuation in the late twentieth century and early twenty-first century is not a pathological process in and of itself; rather, these pathologies that shape these processes heighten the desire for forms of individuation that are *not* compulsive and self-constraining. Hence, I foreground the notion that the production of individuation under digital capitalism (however illusory), opens up a real and determinate space for thinking the limits of this individuation as a constitutive part of a new emancipatory 'post-work', post-capitalist politics. Questions about what constitutes real autonomy and self-realization, therefore, should be part of any new mediation between the singular and the collective, individuation and transindividuation, that is currently being forged under digital 'post-work' conditions, not in order to revive compensatory notions of individualism (a dead concept), but to advance an understanding of the mutualities of autonomy, as the basis for the free development of all. Indeed, without these mutualities of autonomy, a new emancipatory 'post-work' politics is lost to the reactionary conflict between collectivism and individualism, long-term macro-change and short-term ameliorations, and to the chronic tyranny of capitalist 'creativity'.

I want to begin in the first chapter, then, by stripping back diagnostically, the conditions under which individuation, social reproduction and subjectivation are currently taking form. This means looking at the fundamental intersection between subjective ruination and *jouissance*, and pleasure and unpleasure. For here lie the core (heteronomous) materials for our theorization of emancipation, perfectionism, individuation and autonomy.

Chapter 1
Capitalism, *jouissance* and subjective ruination

What the present crisis tells us

It has become one of the clichés recently on the radical left – perhaps best represented by some of Slavoj Žižek's *bon mots* – to say that it is far easier to imagine the end of the world than the end of capitalism.[1] Indeed, in this hypertrophic extension of Freud's death drive to humanity as a whole, this position possesses a dirty little secret: it sees the end of the world, in fact, as infinitely more *pleasurable* than the actual end of capitalism, because, then, there would be no possibility of feeling any direct sense of loss. In other words, there would be no possibility of people experiencing the dire and uncomfortable pathos that invariably accompanies the absence of certain habituated pleasures – pleasures, in this instance, that capitalism has consistently provided for exploiters and exploited alike: namely, the *jouissance* associated with the fantasy of individual autonomy and self-sufficiency. These are the pleasures of knowing that what happens 'out there' doesn't affect me, or need affect me, or when it does affect me, is of little purchase. This sense of autonomy is of course extremely relative, yet despite its relativity it has amazing powers of subjective plasticity, even in the face of the deepening social, political and ecological crisis of our carbon-based economy.[2] This is what Jacques Lacan once called the tyranny of I-cracy under capitalism,[3] and what Jean-Jacques Rousseau once described – talking, more specifically, about the vested professional interests of bourgeois artists and their bourgeois audience, rather than specifically the subjective machinery of a nascent capitalism – as *amour de soi*, self-love.[4]

One of the unnamed paradoxes of the critique of capitalism presently on the left, therefore, is how little the contemporary passionate critiques of capitalism are transformed into a discourse *on* the end of capitalism. When capitalism is not being invested with remarkable powers of recovery and extension, the very critique of capitalism seems to be more captivating and engaging than the actual cessation of the capitalist system itself. Maybe, realistically, this luxuriating in critique is to be expected, a transition state truly conditional of a proto-revolutionary situation, when workers, activists and intellectuals begin to move from supposition and wishful thinking to actually act on the assumption that a new world is not just possible, but is in the first stages of being made. Maybe. Maybe, these pleasures of critique, then, are our first faltering steps into the transitional void. Yet, in reality, presently, this is hard to see; there is no transition state to talk of in any realistic sense, or at least, it is not self-evident in ways that might be constructed as a politics from below, or more concretely, as various *techniques* of transition; the vanguard of neoliberalism presses on, hitched to various authoritarian and neo-fascist forms or to the stultifying remnants of a technocratic social democracy. And, depressingly, recent 'real-utopian' and critical pragmatist assessments of the situation largely testify to this impasse; possible techniques of transition from a fossil-based to post-carbon economy are still routinely tied to democratic market 'solutions',[5] that is, tied to a version of model one (paradoxically driven by a green underconsumptionist anti-austerity politics, as if we can ecologically *produce* our way out of the crisis).[6] As a result, activists and theorists in models one and two talk sanguinely about institutional redesign as a radical cornerstone for an 'alternative social world',[7] without any discussion of the interlocking character of climate change and capital: namely, for post-capitalist transition to function coherently it has to be holistically and radically systemic, given that there is a fundamental *integration* between increased energy use and the production of value. There is no gentle 'give and take', pragmatic exit route from this reality. Thus, it is no surprise, therefore, on present evidence, that capital is prepared to manage climate change in defiance of this reality, even if global unemployment may rise to 3 billion, and a third of the earth may either be incinerated or drowned. In fact, 'manage' is slightly misleading here:

> For the capitalist economy climate change ... also opens up entirely new markets, due to the melting of the arctic ice, the burning of the Amazon, and the drying up of the world's freshwater sources, providing new realms

for the extraction and sale of fossil fuels and other natural resources. There are trillions of dollars still to be made on fossil fuels, which is what counts from the perspective of profitability.[8]

This is the Great Fault Line, then, inside the present ecology movement: on the one hand, the broadly mitigationist struggle for a New Green Deal (which would include much of the Extinction Rebellion movement), and, on the other, the revolutionary mobilization *against* fossil capital. In this sense, the representatives of fossil capital will do all they can to take the mitigationist route, for capital 'in general' now is absolutely clear about what is at stake in protecting the system as such, that is, the attack on fossil capital potentially is the weak link that capital 'in general' has for a longtime feared, insofar as it offers to the enemies of capital a revolutionary destabilization of the political–economic order.[9] As David Harvey has noted: it is evident how capital is responding to this crisis, how capital is currently seizing 'the environmental mantle for itself as the legitimate foundation for the big business environmentalism of the future. In this way it can dominate ecological discourses.'[10]

Yet, it's hard to avoid the fact that although we are living through an extraordinary period in which leftist critique, anti-capitalist rhetoric and civic resistance proliferate, little of it actually sticks, or wants to stick. That is, little of it makes any kind of subjective headway or sense, beyond mere posturing or short-termism or humanist empathy and the cultivation of beautiful souls, travelling in hope. One might say there is nothing new in this; of course. There is no particular moral shortfall in contemporary radical politics; just as crises do not automatically presage the desire for change. But today there is an unprecedented disconnect between the palpable structural crisis of capitalism and any viable countermeasures, that is, forms of self-directed action that are both popular and transformative. This is because today in the heartlands of capitalism it is incredibly hard to imagine and act on an *alterior* set of values and possibilities that, in redressing current ills, might lie graspable *in advance of, and as a break with*, present social and political arrangements. For, to act consistently for such an outcome is to act, more than ever, in the name of systemic critique outside of the parliamentary process, mass political parties and the trade union movement. Not because parliament, political parties and the trade unions are finally exhausted as a moral or intellectual home to the left, but, rather, that, however, well-intentioned contemporary leftist electoral politics are – on the basis that these are still the institutions where 'the majority think and act' – it is impossible to break through the wall that links democracy *to* capital, particularly when parties of the centre-left act as the resolute guardians of the capitalist–democratic process. Parties of the centre-right and far right today are in a way profoundly grateful for the way in which parties of the centre-left are currently so deeply invested in maintaining democratic procedure (as a stick to beat the importunity and corruption of the right in power), because it at least shows that the parliamentary process is still working and has some legitimacy, even though their own allegiances and alignments lie transparently with capital and *not* democracy, certainly when parliamentary democracy threatens capital, as in some instances it vainly tries to do. It is no surprise that centre-left politics today in the absence of a martial imagination remains a mixture of liberal piety and kum-bah-yah 'socialism', particularly under the network techniks of digitalization, that the Schmittian right can run rings around.

In this respect, both of the radical theoretico-political models two and three I discuss in the introduction share a certain implacable horizon: they both act systemically to break the link between capital *and* democracy of model one, on the grounds that mass participation for change has to pass through processes and forms that destroy this link. Indeed, they both recognize that any proper political act has to connect action to a new Naming of Things – a new positive Master-Signifier, as opposed to a simply a subversive rupture. Hence the construction of this new connection between popular action and a new Naming of Things cannot exist without a conception of disinvestment from what defines the reason of capital, and this means, necessarily, imagining a world in which action and thought and being are crucially external to this reason. The new Naming of Things therefore has to connect this sense of externality to praxis. But it is precisely this sense of externality that remains constitutively weak, given, how capital and democracy define the limits of legitimate praxis and political reason. This pinpoints the nature of the current crisis: the parliamentary indivisibility of capital and democracy delivers exteriority over to the realm of abstraction and ineffability. This is why, therefore, all models of action on the left have to confront this loss of exteriority as a historical reality. And this is why, consequently, despite the widespread proliferation of critique and concern about inequality, ecological crisis and the social democratic revival of the desire for the nationalization of social utilities, certainly in Europe and recently the United States, all practice on the ground is confronted with a preset fatigue about the costs of radical change. Even the impending catastrophes of climate change, the arrival of peak oil and eco-disaster have been unable to shift this stalled or suspensive condition.

Exteriority and crisis

The loss of exteriority is a common theme in post-war critical theory. In this, at its high point (Max Horkheimer and Theodor Adorno's *Dialectic of Enlightenment,* 1946)[11] it assumes the character of post-Thermidorian structural impasse, in which monopoly capitalism and Stalinism cohere to produce a world of instrumental reason and counterrevolution without egress. This loss of exteriority today, however, is no longer obviously shaped by the specificities of this détente, even if over the long-term the post-Thermidorian defeat of the workers' movement remains key to the diminishment of the imagining of an 'outside' to capital. This is because the loss of exteriority today is grounded precisely in the loss of consciousness of the proletariat's sense of 'exteriority' *inside* capitalism. Because the proletariat is no longer a political entity able to think itself as a lived 'exteriority' to capital internal to capitalism, it is also, therefore, unable to act in the name of, or even memory of, the destruction of this internal 'exteriority' as the destruction, externally, of itself as a class. In other words, the proletariat's seeing and acting on 'interiorized exteriority' is fundamental to the displacement of capitalism's self-understanding as a totality and, consequently, capitalism's continuous self-defence against all notions of interiorized exteriority that would define its limits as a system. Today, though, the absence – as a political reality – of the sense of the proletariat's internal exteriority as an immanent critique of totality means that the critique of totality has to be found elsewhere, principally through a collective consciousness of the political crisis of value and the growing ecological breakdown, and, as such, through a political recognition of the vast systemic implications for the reproduction of the system through the increasing expulsion of living labour. Capital is finding it increasingly difficult to dissociate the social effects of the crisis of the value form from the breakdown of nature and the reproduction of capitalism – insofar as capitalism can only guarantee waged labour for a relatively small number of those available to work globally. Consequently, the system is desperate to reincorporate the internal exteriorities of the expulsion of living labour and the metabolic breakdown of the natural world inside a *re-expanded capitalist totality*: these crises, it says, are not substantive, threatening externalities, but anomalies, exceptions, that can be brought back into the totality and expansiveness of capitalist relations, and therefore in reach of capitalism's capacity for creative solutions. The relentless attack on the science of 'climate change', particularly by representatives of US capital, has been, in these terms, a *Real Politik* way of philosophically fending off attacks on the legitimacy of capitalist totality and creativity. But, climate denial is no longer a realistic option for fossil capital and the banks. The social costs are too great, the political costs too destabilizing. The mitigationist route, therefore, is the best way forward for capitalism, given it can recalibrate a new regime of accumulation on the basis of a New Green Deal. Capital 'in general' recognizes, then, that the New Green Deal will undoubtedly come and accordingly wants to be able to determine the new boundaries of the system against any destabilizing and expanding threat of any 'internal exteriority'.

Exteriority and creativity

In response to this historical crisis of exteriority, Cornelius Castoriadis at the beginning of the millennium talked in terms borrowed from Max Weber and Georg Simmel about the increasing loss of, or indifference to, 'relation' (what he called the emergence of 'insignificance') given the perceived view of emancipatory discourse as an externalizing, coercive and a self-alienating process: 'people have become so much more critical, much more skeptical, which also inhibits them from acting.'[12] In other words, the divorce of action from exteriority inhibits people from freely acting in dianoetic ways; that is, resistance, non-compliance, disaffection, have not disappeared, but, rather, in the absence of emancipatory discourse as the realization of 'interiorized exteriority', actions find other, personal, identity-driven objects to cathect to. Action finds its expression in an overidentification with the promises of self-management, self-identity and individual ambition as places of minimal security and achievable ends. This is because these subjective rewards appear to be confirmed and advanced by the undaunting 'creativity' of capitalism itself. And this is why in the period of neoliberalism's rise to hegemony the repeated crises of capitalism present and past have become imaginatively connected to an invigorating uncertainty and exciting unpredictability, identifiable, with the corrective 'energy' and 'problem solving' capacities of the system as a whole, what Joseph Schumpeter once famously called, of course, the 'creative destruction' of capital, but more generally now is defined simply, as capitalism's unbounded 'creativity', destruction being too impolitic for politicians and CEOs.[13] Thus, if crisis-as-opportunity is not exactly a new ideology for the executive defenders of capitalism, this hyper-valorization of uncertainty-*as*-creativity certainly is. Claims to creativity have now entered all aspects of the production and distribution process; the only (good) solutions are 'creative' ones; the happy consumer is the consumer whose intelligence and creativity is respected and encouraged. The rise of 'creativity' as measure of capitalist efficacy operates, therefore, not as an illusory desideratum, but as a *productive ideology*, that appears to cohere with what is required of workers when they are encouraged to use their own initiative or, in relation to what workers would like to think best of themselves when they are doing what is asked of them. 'Creativity', then, possesses ideological charms, certainly, but not because the CEOs and managers who endorse it believe that its powers of self-motivation dispel or veil the realities of work. Highlighting the 'creative' inputs and outputs of work does not remove the uncreative, boring and routinized content of most office or factory labour, or diminish the brutal reality – where notions of creativity obviously appear the most risible – of exhausting, extractive labour. However, under the self-motivational dictates of the neoliberal digital and cognitive economy 'creativity' achieves a facticity and resonance that appears to define the inclusive logic of the new economy more broadly: namely, that we are all now – workers and managers alike – able to freely imagine ourselves as self-determined agents, and, therefore, free from the hierarchical and exclusionary excesses and horrors of the old workplace and capitalism's past. The substance of this, of course, is not an illusory desideratum either: the 'creative' inputs or, lack of access to such inputs at work, are underwritten by, and connected to, the universal creative continuum of digitalization itself, that subtends and shapes the meaning of work, routinized or not, under the communicative demands of the new economy. And this is where the ideology of 'creativity' lands and produces its interpolative enticements, so to speak, irrespective of whether the specificities of work match, or don't match up to, to a viable and realistic notion of creativity.

'Creativity' at work is part of the general creativity that capitalism secures as the flow-through of communicative and affective energy within the system. This is what many theorists in the new millennium have described as the increasing indivisibility of work from non-work, and the increasing sense, in turn, that those experiences that don't fall within the bounds of this 'creativity' are not worth noting or attending to. The work/non-work interface, accordingly, is a *ductile* world. And this is why this energy has a particular libidinal force: the networked ductile world comes to diminish and override counter-realities and those experiences that fall outside of its demands. For to participate in this work/non-work continuum is to be seen and judged as creative; to not participate fully is to be seen as judgemental, incurious and inefficient, and therefore, uncreative. This takes us to a place slightly different from Guy Debord's society of the spectacle. The ameliorative overriding of the realities of capitalism as a consequence of the ideology of 'creativity' is not because the real is magically suppressed and made 'unknown' by these new ductile conditions, but because it is hard for the real to be internalized and *acted on* without placing the subject in a great deal of stress and in a high state of anxiety, for the dianoetic appears to be neither 'efficient' nor 'creative'; under these ductile conditions acting on truth becomes a distressing luxury, best left alone, unless it can be harnessed to individual attainment, that is to 'creativity'. Hence, the self is increasingly attached to the interests of economic reason in ways that it overwhelms those affects and identities that resist or de-rationalize the creative assumptions of uncertainty and destruction, that is, non-market affects and identities that were once supported by the workers' movement and civil institutions. The creative self is increasingly allied with the constant and renewed *failed mastery* of these ductile conditions.

In this way, the character of possessive individualism in bourgeois society as the prudential outcome of economic reason – 'I am my own master, despite my feelings of powerlessness, despite everything' – has changed.[14] The notion of the self as an autotelic interiority no longer sees or feels its sense of self-directed individuation as an economic subject as under constant threat from those external and would-be inchoate forces of pleasure and moral dissolution that would weaken its power of self-assertion and endeavour. Indeed, it is the moral and virtuous content of self-possession that has weakened since the nineteenth century, given the diminishment of the social role of church, craft institution, trade union and the family as the key sources of socialization and the moderation of the passions. Thus, whereas in the nineteenth century possessive individualism was shaped by 'duty' and 'good conduct' and a fear of the loss of mastery of the self, in the latter part of the twentieth century and twenty-first century, self-possession has become a form of autolatry, a process in which individuation is defined by the worship of the self as a mode of passionate self-scrutiny. Self-possession has undergone a profound split under the vast libidinal transformation of the subject as producer and consumer. Whereas the 'parsimoniously' constructed self of the nineteenth century saw the passions and their narcissistic optic, as delimiting the powers of self-possession under advanced capitalism, in which secularization and consumption act as a profound extension of individuation beyond 'duty' and 'good conduct', the self sees self-possession now as thwarting and weakening individuation and pleasure. Self-possession becomes the very thing that holds individuation back. This is because pleasure now overwhelmingly defines the pursuit of individuation and the virtue of an intense life. In fact, the intense life achieves a kind of moral perspicacity in which the pleasures of individuation and self-development seem more exactingly real than the challenges of social and political experience. This is why Castoriadis's crisis of relation and dianoetic action appears, from the vantage point of the neoliberal libidinal subject, less of a burden than it might – certainly for those, who see intensity and pleasure as moral correlatives of creativity. As Tristan Garcia argues: '*external* morality has been replaced by a sort of *internal* ethics ... The intense person distrusts thought, knowledge, and language because they all reduce living variation to stable entities or quantities and end up making the world unliveable.'[15] It is little surprise, therefore, that the self 'without' moral self-possession seeks and is willingly shaped by neoliberalism's invitation to the 'new economic subject' to find the intensity they desire at work and in consumption. The language of intensity is the language of 'creative uncertainty' itself. In this respect, the shedding of a traditional self-possession is the shedding of those notions of 'delay', 'qualification', 'withdrawal', 'postponement', 'long-term assessment', that hinder the expansion and renewal of individuation, that limit spontaneity. This produces a subject that seeks reason in intensity and pleasure, not as a compensation for what routinely or inconveniently prevents these outcomes, but as the practical work of the ductile self; in short, we might call this a dianoetics *of* the self. This is why possessive individualism may not be newly invented under capitalism in this period of neoliberal ascendancy, but its newly constructed modes of ideological incorporation and subjective invitation certainly are, and as such, it can be argued, these modes of incorporation and invitation, are *qualitatively* different than those available to the 'parsimoniously' distracted (and morally constrained) late-nineteenth-century and early-to-mid-twentieth-century worker stolidly linked to trade union, craft association, church (and revolutionary tradition).

Now, admittedly, uncertainty and unpredictability are not uniformly acceptable to the defenders of the present system; there are practicable limits to this uncertainty and unpredictability beyond which the market must not trespass, even for the anti-statist and neoliberal libertarian right. Yet, nevertheless, overall, uncertainty and unpredictability tend to be seen as good or potentially good things, because they encompass and capture the would-be stochastic energy of producer and consumer alike, stochasticism here being the veritable motor of ductile renewal under neoliberal conditions of accumulation. This leads to the notion that any fundamental alteration of these arrangements would dangerously diminish the individuation of the 'unmastered' creativity that supposedly comes with and shapes uncertainty and unpredictability, despite the pitiful anxiety and distress and wretchedness it brings. This is why perhaps, not so strangely, out of the political defeat of the left over the last fifty years even the far left has recently developed a taste for uncertainty and unpredictability itself in the current revival of an affirmation of the speed, dislocation and disruption of capitalism's powers of recovery-through-crisis.[16] This is what strong accelerationism embraces: the only way the system can be purged and transformed is through actually accelerating its stochastic tendencies to the point of system collapse in a critical overidentification with capital, for then the system will be finally exhausted and exposed to its limits (and immanent alternatives). But collapse is utterly relative here; capitalism still has a huge amount of capacity for dislocation and speed still left in it (through war if necessary), if, that is, this speed and dislocation don't *outpace* workers' skills and capacities completely and, as such, remain compatible with *amour de soi* and creative I-cracy.

Capital, in these terms, is forever dreaming of fully absorbing subjectivity into its model of competitive and destructive 'creativity'. Yet capital cannot leave subjectivity completely behind in the interests of technocratic and technological control and development. This is the great risk of the creative destructiveness of the new network economy and culture, and the expansion of Artificial Intelligence and robotics: *it threatens a de-subjectivized world of labour and leisure that disconnects the productive self from creative affirmationism itself.* So, affirmationism, as a force for self-transformation – as Manfredo Tafuri noted in the early 1970s[17] – is the very lifeblood of capital's self-identity and therefore cannot be completely subsumed under the demands of 'efficiency' and cost-effective accounting. That is, for capitalism as an economic system to fulfil and meet the 'logic of capital'-as-desire it has to reproduce itself as a system of *individuated* dynamism, *of* creative subjects, even as technology drains productive labour and subjectivity of this possibility and 'surplus populations' grow globally. Consequently, if the fundamental moving contradiction of capitalism, as Marx insists, is between living labour and the machine,[18] its living contradiction under mature capitalism is that between the drive of capital to lock individuation into production and consumption (as the constitutive subjective force of 'creative destruction' and renewal) and machinic objectivity. This is why belief in, or tacit acceptance of, creative affirmationism as the inexorable motor of capitalism is hard to shake off, even amongst the critics of its excesses. Dynamic individuation is held to be a moral virtue that capitalism requires above all other virtues if it is to render its phantasies of I-cratic self-transformation workable and the inequalities and exclusions of the system liveable.

The catechisms of uxoriousness

Accordingly, much current anti-capitalist critique hides an additional dirty little secret: critique may be built on the hoped-for exit from the inequalities of capitalism – or the worst of them – but not at the expense of the 'dynamism' of the system as such. This oxymoronic position loosely is what used to be called blandly market socialism; namely, the introduction of controls on capital exchange and the pursuit of systematic state intervention, as opposed to radical free trade and the free movement of workers. Indeed, this is the usual default position of the non-revolutionary left's critique of capitalism: let us accept what is best in capitalism and control what is worst, thereby making the need for fundamental change unnecessary: 'We can control capitalism!' rings down the ages, with dreary familiarity, and, not surprisingly, has doggedly reattached itself – as we have noted – to model one and the new social democracy.[19]

As such, there is a fundamental aporia here. If there remains an excessive love for capitalism amongst capitalism's most ardent defenders (what I call here, metaphorically, uxoriousness) there is a comparable secret (unconscious) uxorious love for the damaged and twisted pleasures and pathologies of capital's spirit of renewal, that haunts the popular critiques and acceptance of capitalism, and much of the centre-left's zeal for 'change through stability'. For, in concert with capital's more passionate advocates, manifest here is the fear that without the market, economic life would become inert and passive and the 'creativity' of the majority would merely limp along and eventually dry up. Hence the continuing and overwhelming consensus on both centre-left and right, critics and defenders of capitalism, about capitalism needing to 'work better', 'flow better', 'eradicate' its glitches.

In this light Slavoj Žižek has noticed how capitalism, subjectively at this level, constantly produces the pleasures of denial: capitalism is destructive, produces deep and abiding inequality, destroys communities, destroys species, excludes, eradicates ecologies and habitats, inoculates, fractures, denudes and enervates, *but*.... This he says 'is the material efficiency of capitalist ideology: even when we know how things are we continue to act upon our false beliefs'.[20] But if there is an acknowledgement of falsity here, there is also the *jouissance* of self-rationalizing accommodation, underscored by the powerful and reassuring *jouissance* of self-correction: capitalism is 'not perfect', it makes mistakes – many mistakes – yet it does its best given the difficulties it encounters in its pursuit of the 'maximization' of efficiency and profit.[21] Consequently, capitalism as a self-correcting system *delivers* – despite its travails and human cost – historically despite slavery, racism, child labour, World War, the seventy-hour week for manual workers, illiteracy, violence against women, colonialism, imperialism, religious oppression, global unemployment, mass cultural immiseration, and the loss and pollution of the environment. It delivers precisely, therefore, because across the generations these problems and horrors have been slowly corrected, prevented, ameliorated, eradicated in the interests of material progress, discernible in the rise of wages globally and improved 'life chances' for the majority; there is no glory for capitalism in slavery, racism, imperialism, the oppression of women and child labour; there is glory, however, in the continuing advance political, culturally, economically of the majority. So powerful is this fable of self-correction that social democrats and parliamentary and extra-parliamentary leftists have continued to offer their own, albeit less, sanguine – if no less assured – versions of this unfolding story of capitalist progress in order to 'stay in the game', as we have noted in our discussion of models 1 and 2. 'Things have been difficult, but we're on track!' 'Technology will get us out of this mess.' Thus, if this story of self-correction wobbled in the aftermath of the Russian revolution in the 1920s and the Great Depression in the 1930s, since the rise and fall of Stalinism in the East it has, assuredly, gained a new authority, in a refulgent attachment to a combination of technological determinism and social evolutionism. Indeed, the crisis and disappearance of an alternative narrative – whether illusory or not – has strengthened this resurgence, in fact, given its historicist self-confidence, demonstrating a hubris out of all proportion to global realities.[22]

This means that subjectivizing the possibility of radical change is always caught up with the desire to first make amends on these terms, that is, to make tolerable that which is intolerable as a condition of not *forfeiting* expected pleasures that appear to be de facto given, and as such crucial to social reproduction and continuity and the maintenance of 'creative' order. This, indeed, is fundamental to the conventional rhetoric of parliamentary stabilization of the political process and the rhetoric of progress, and touches on a substantive question: Why give up palpable pleasures and habits for abstract imponderables?[23]

Thus, presently there is a demonstrable psychological dimension to the left and right's adherence to the notion of the need for capitalism to 'work better' that underlies a discernible shift in support for the system. That is, if capitalism needs to 'improve its performance', this means less the defence of stable growth – as though capitalism was precipitously 'out of balance' – than the assimilation, and crucially, *toleration* of the system's creative waywardness, glitches and 'foibles', as if capitalism was a particularly difficult child that needs loving care and correction and understanding. This is the familiar 'progressive' rhetoric of contemporary world leaders, CEOs, bankers and technocrats: 'we are the people disposed to care for the system, so let us do our job'. One doesn't need to be crassly subjectivist, then, to recognize why at present 'care for capitalism' appears so reasonable, and therefore, why there is a subjectively weak investment in the possibility of critique and disappointment turning into radically systemic transformation; or, indeed, why the need for what both Žižek and Bruno Bosteels have called the production of a new communist 'ordering' against capitalist disorder, appears, unfortunately, so recherché.[24] Firstly, capitalism still appears to the majority essentially benign in its systemic capacities (and its disappointments); and, coextensively, despite the exponential rise in inequality and social dislocation, capital's macro-powers and reach are seen as essentially neutral; capital just needs more enlightened controls, better fiscal adjustments, less avariciousness on the part of fund managers and MNCs, more social cooperation from CEOs, and as a result better technological solutions to ameliorate the fallout from 'creative destruction' unmoored, reflected, most alarmingly in the current technocratic faith in the chemical 'quick fix' reduction of CO_2 emissions, fronted up by Bill Gates amongst others, as the corporate vanguard of the New Green Deal. Even the new social democracy has a few positive words for this logic, placing their faith firstly in an underconsumptionist renewal of a new ('clean') productivism, in defiance of the catastrophic expulsion of living labour from the system, and secondly, in the hope that the state under anti-austerity direction can curtail 'billionaire power' in the interests of the many. This is why under this current global regime class has lost its focal power, because with the loss of an imagined exteriority to capitalism the link between working class experience and struggle and systemic transformation appears incoherent, or inconsequential, as a negation of the present state of things.

And thus, crucially, there is nothing to suggest that if there was a global upturn in class struggle (in the major industrial sectors for instance) that this political perspective would in fact change, given the weakening aggregate role of labour under these conditions and the fact that the 'winning back of decent jobs' is no longer possible, and therefore incapable of stabilizing the system for reformism. This is because increased productivity through technological development diminishes the value of living labour relative to that of past labour, and hence overall reduces the quantitative and qualitative place of labour power in the production of value.

Thus, the reality of this diminishment of the political force of collective labour is not the work of would-be 'prosperity'. The current loss of workers' power is not an updated version of that hoary old sociological saw from the 1960s, namely that and TV, cars and washing machines, etc., have 'bought off' the working class after the Second World War – which so preoccupied the 'commentariat', conservatives and labourists in this period. Rather, the moving contradiction between living labour and machines continues a fundamental secular trend, certainly since the 1950s: the reshaping of the consciousness and actions of workers in the interests of the subordination of labour power to machinic knowledge. In essence the moving contradiction between living labour and machines continues to *de-subjectivize* the labour–capital relation, insofar as the skills of the worker – as part of the life of the collective worker – are increasingly evacuated from working class identity. This is precisely what Marx meant by proletarianization in the 1860s: not the reduction of workers to mere labourers, but the *subjective ruination* of workers and occasional workers as collective workers through the subjugation of workers as an appendage of the labour process. The increasing gap between labour and collective class identity – as consequence of this disaggregation – is, therefore, not the result of any idling increase in the comforts of affluence – ill health and poverty remains on the rise amongst the working poor and median wage earners as much as the unemployed – but, the outcome of the fact that labouring and non-labouring bodies are now subject to a process of proletarianization as a lethal combination of deskilling and class dis-identification, crucially, underwritten by exposure of these bodies to an unprecedented expansion of post-industrialized *pleasures* into the interstices of all aspects of everyday life, which enables the class relation to reproduce itself.

Capitalism, then, has been fomenting a fundamental problem for itself since the 1950s: the conflict between the increasing subjective ruination of workers as workers and the constant call to workers to invest creatively in the system as producers and consumers.[25] Yet, this contradiction has failed to produce a crisis of legitimacy. On the contrary, the interstitial expansion of pleasures has, in fact, diminished class identity at the expense of the worker as consumer, by overwhelmingly connecting pleasure *with* reason, not with the erosion of reason. The outcome is that workers are increasingly disinterested in *being* workers, so to speak, irrespective of their objective, if residual, class attachments; for wage struggles offer a diminished valence as class struggle and as such limited scope for transformative social outcomes. This is not to overplay the intercessory power of these technological and somatic pleasures as sources of *conscious* control, or to stress either their local or global uniformity. But rather, in both the immiserated/marginal zones and core zones of the global market, there are in place – without borders or constraint – innumerable pleasures that tie the exploited body (in work and out of work) to capitalism's I-cratic logic, that as a result, constantly weaken class solidarity as the agent and sign of a *different* sets of pleasures, affects and bodily expectations (what was once called the 'workers' movement'). It is easy to sound bleak here. But we forget at our peril how much contemporary capitalism reproduces itself not simply through ideological misrepresentation and the dull and coercive compulsion of the economic, but through the *jouissance* of individuation as the rationalization of 'creativity' at work and in consumption. This is the affective, endo-colonizing work of real subsumption, insofar as real subsumption as the 'completed' internalization of labour power into production is the production of relations and subjects and not simply 'things'. Or more precisely, under real subsumption the production of subjectivity is no longer marginal to production, but *is constitutive of production itself*. This is quite different, then, from assuming that workers' failure to act on the 'truth of the system' is the *repression* of trauma. Rather, capitalism 'survives' because it generates new forms of liveable and rational solidarity *from and from within* the phantasmagoric capitalist factory of pleasure.

The new Libidinal Economy

It is hardly surprising, therefore, that we have seen the rise today of a new Marxian literature on libidinal economy, in which the vicissitudes of 'joyful alienation' play a far more systematic role in the critique of the reign of the commodity form and economic reason than hitherto (Lordon, Stiegler, Garcia, Endnotes, Tomšič).[26] As such 'joyful alienation' takes on a particular affirmative valency in the production of subjectivity: to see reason at work in 'joyful alienation' it is necessary to see it oxymoronically as a discourse of freedom, insofar as, in the light of capitalism as a 'factory of pleasure' any diminishment of pleasure appears particularly grievous for the subject's sense of autonomy.

Thus, what distinguishes this writing is precisely the theorization of the production of subjectivity in ways that adequately analyse the advanced conditions of real subsumption today. Crucial to this is a rejection of two political orthodoxies on the critique of political economy: an orthodox anthropological position on the forces of production, in which workers' interests remain external to the capitalist production of subjectivity (as an ethnographic expression of class solidarity), and the philosophical reflection on the production of subjectivity – as the production of the self – separate from the valorization process, best represented by the later work of Michel Foucault and Julia Kristeva.[27] Marx's work, of course, at points draws on both positions. But at other points, questions of subjectivity and production radically intersect, as in the *Grundrisse* (1973).

> Production thus produces not only the object but also the manner of consumption, not only objectively but also subjectively. Production thus creates the consumer. Production not only supplies a. material for the need, but it also supplies a need for the material ... Production thus not only creates an object for the subject, but also a subject for the object ...

Consumption likewise produces the consumer's *inclination* by beckoning to him as an aim-determining need.[28]

In the twentieth century as formal subsumption retreats under the onslaught of real subsumption, methodologically this opens up a space for the emergence of social reproduction theory in critical theory (social philosophy) and psychoanalysis. But critical theory and psychoanalysis present their own problems in the early decades of the twentieth century: Western Marxism and the Frankfurt School development of a version of the Enlightenment de-rationalization thesis, and psychoanalysis's general adoption, between Freud and Lacan, of a psychic-cultural determinism, closed-off Marx's dialectical insight: that subjectivity is not simply reproduced by the forces of production, but is made directly productive, and therefore situated not in some external space of decline (of reason) under real subsumption, but at the centre of the struggle around individuation. Lacan, to his credit, in the later writings, fully acknowledges this through his explicit identification between surplus value and surplus *jouissance*. In this respect the new work on libidinal economy has internalized this in its critique of labour as an anthropological constant, irrespective of whether Lacan's thinking plays a direct role or not in this work. The key change in this writing, therefore, is that Marx's insight becomes the basis for a systematic interaction of the psychic and material, desire and production, desire and pleasure, identity and affect. Yet, if the capitalist mode of production is re-functioned here as a mode of the production of desire, this writing is not a late Deleuzianization of Marx. Gilles Deleuze, overall, has of course, left his mark on the critique of libidinal economy and production as the production of desire and modes of life, but in the new writing on libidinal economy there is conceptual retreat from Deleuze's vitalist propulsion of this production-as-desire as the vector of actions and passions that will smash through capitalist valorization. On the contrary, the new writing is far less sanguine about capitalist *jouissance* as a potential counter-capitalist energy; an energy that has the capacity to exceed – in transgressive a-signifying ways – the heteronomous limits of capitalist desire. This is precisely because this writing turns expressly to the pleasurable-affective and active–passive forces of subjectivation in the light of neoliberalism's onslaught against living labour. As Samo Tomšič stresses, psychoanalysis shares with the Marx of the *Grundrisse* an emphasis on the *labour* of subjectivity. But following Lacan, Tomšič's concern is less the surplus of individuation that escapes subjectivation, than 'the production of the relations of domination by means of the production of enjoyment',[29] the way in which individuals' production of enjoyment, 'compulsively sustain and reproduce the established socioeconomic order even in its most exploitative aspects'.[30] 'Enjoyment is never purely subjective (the subject's private matter) or voluntary (the subject's private choice). In their seemingly private enjoyment, subjects work for the system.'[31] And this is what concerns me in this book and my engagement with the conflictual dynamics of 'self-love', subjectivation and desire. It is hard to talk about the counter-production of desire when the resistance of subjectivity to subjectivation is unconsciously and consciously attached to the monetary and ideological credit forms of capitalism, that is, the way in which the struggle for individuation is converted into an identification with, or love of, capitalism. The requirement therefore from the critique of libidinal economy is what affective forces are at work under real subsumption that realistically provides the space for the subject to challenge capitalist subjectivation? But to do this we must first establish the ways in which capitalism in the name of creativity and freedom, as Jason Read argues, in, *The Micro-Politics of Capital* (2003) 'must fetter' this subjective potential, 'tying it to particular modes of subjection, particular ways of living'.[32]

> In real subsumption social conflict no longer passes between the singular and the abstract, rather, conflict is immediately over the singular and common. As singular forms of life become directly productive of capital-producing styles, fashions, tastes, and conditions for more production it is also these singular conditions of existence that becomes grounds for resistance ... Capital no longer tries to subordinate the singularity and commonality of social relations to the abstraction of labor time and the wage, but instead tries to directly appropriate the singularity and commonality of existence.[33]

And this is why the neoliberal flourishing of monetary and ideological credit forms of capitalism are so important in naturalizing 'creativity', and consequently why the majority of those on the immiserated pleasure margins of the global market imagine their future as based on a greater participation in the pleasures of the market, not less, indeed, see it as an exit point to the recovery of their humanity and social individuation. Similarly, the erosion of forms of collective orientation in the core capitalist zones feels less like a loss in these terms and more of a relief from onerous social obligations. As

Fredric Jameson has noted on this score: the drift from public and collective values post the early 1970s, to consumerist pleasure as a ubiquitous and interstitial force of the 'general good' and self-worth 'does not seem to be a particularly painful or stressful prospect' for the majority.[34] Or, as Lordon asserts, in a more brutal fashion, the growing intersection between pleasure, the market and sophisticated practices of marketized governmentality invoke a spectacle of the 'happily dominated'.[35] As I outline in detail in Chapter 3, Lordon's notion of the 'happily dominated' revives the debates on 'voluntary servitude' and 'adaptive preference' from the late 1970s and 1980s. As such, this link remains crucial to the debate on social reproduction, *jouissance* and the libidinal economy, precisely because the questions of 'voluntary servitude' and the 'happily dominated', define, at its most stark, the capture of *jouissance* by economic reason and the fettering of subjectivity. The issue is not whether the 'happily dominated' is a convenient sociological fiction or not in these circumstances (in some sense it is a fiction, and as such problematic), but rather, how subjectivation works today, what new affects it announces and consequently the part 'happiness' plays in this.

The key point is not that the majority has no access to values and resources other than those of capitalist subjectivation; non-capitalist values. We know these arguments on the left, well (Marx, Luxemburg, Gramsci, Mao, Debord, Dunayevskaya, Tronti, Negri, Virno etc.). Power produces resistance, negation; in a world of 'insignificance', uxoriousness and 'joyful alienation' the resistance and negation of capitalist subjectivation act as a kind of continuous, uneven, residuum to collective action by workers and the dominated. As Howard Caygill explains, in *On Resistance* (2013), his historical account of the modalities of resistance from the French Revolution to the Black Panthers and Zapatistas:

> The capacity to resist [emerges] reactively in response to a predicament of oppression, manifesting itself in spontaneous acts of violence that defy insufferable conditions. Yet the specific subjectivity of the violent resistant lashing out at repression remains shaped by the enemy and is initially a resistance of *ressentiment* ... [As such reactive resistance] needs in some way to metamorphose into an affirmative, inventive resistance that does not just react to an intolerable predicament.[36]

But something else has entered this historical process under mature capitalism: this residuum is currently vulnerable to its *rational* devaluation politically, given the greater powers of rationalization attributed to pleasure over that of dianoetic action and knowledge, i.e. the *jouissance* of alienation under commodity production and exchange secures pleasure as the appropriate form of reason expressed as the *limits* of reason, certainly emancipatory reason. This is why to experience the diminishment of one's access to pleasure feels like an attack on reason itself, and therefore anything that weakens this pleasure is easily rationalizable as a misappropriation and misdirection of the will; and this, in a sense, is what Castoriadis means by 'indifference'. This redirects our attention – however egregiously – to the idea that the social and cultural immiserations of mature capitalism possess *overt and covert pleasures*, causing these overt and covert pleasures to produce extraordinary affective attachments that continually deflect from the rational critique and rejection of the nugatory rewards of these pleasures.[37]

Indeed, at some level we might say that twentieth-century de-rationalization theories of Western Marxism and critical theory distinguished themselves from orthodox Marxism precisely in these terms: that is, the critique of orthodoxy is haunted by the threatening efficacy of pleasures that escape working-class identity. Lukács' theory of reification, for example, was haunted by the *jouissance* of worker self-abnegation, bringing his early writing on reification notionally, at least, into alignment with psychoanalysis, as was Antonio's Gramsci's work on hegemony in the 1930s, a theory that at one level is about how workers are happy to find pleasure in 'fitting in', when not 'fitting in' appears such a difficult prospect.[38] But post the 1970s this 'fitting in' is no longer attached to the collective *proletarian memory* of not 'fitting in', with the decline of the workers' movement as a shared culture, and the loss of a sense of class exteriority. This essentially is the theme of Jean-François Lyotard's early work on the unburdening pleasures of self-alienation in *Libidinal Economy* (1974), and his insistence on the increasing naturalization of 'joyful alienation' – one of the first attempts to confront the subjective realities of real subsumption and the capitalist dynamic of the pleasure–unpleasure dyad after the Second World War. Indeed, if in 1974, Lyotard's 'evil book' as he called it, appeared jejune in its amoral exposure of capital's libidinal forces, today it reads like a prescient neoliberal manual written by an astute manager-philosopher, outlining in gruesome realist detail how capital produces a truth of pleasure that is ruinous of its revolutionary enemies. If workers

> [B]ecome the slave of the machine, the machine of the machine, fucker fucked by it, eight hours, twelve hours, a day, year after year, it is because

they are forced into it, constrained, because they cling to life? Death is not an alternative to it, it is a part of it, it attests to the fact that there is *jouissance* in it, the English unemployed did not become workers to survive, they – hang on tight and spit on me – *enjoyed* [*ils ont joui de*] the hysterical, masochistic, whatever exhaustion it was of *hanging on* in the mines, in the foundries, in the factories, in hell, they enjoyed it, enjoyed the mad destruction of their organic body which was indeed imposed upon them, they enjoyed the decomposition of their personal identity, the identity that the present tradition had constructed for them, enjoyed the dissolution of their families and villages, and enjoyed the new monstrous *anonymity* of the suburbs and the pubs in the morning and evening.[39]

One might call this the *concupiscent exit back into capitalism*, as if, in a move of undying love, one is being asked to take back an abusive lover as an act of rational forgiveness; and it is this, more than ever, that defines the current moment and represents the ontological ground, more crucially, of the contemporary critique of the commodity form and libidinal economy. The question of counter-hegemony, then, seems if not quaint, inoperative under conditions of class disaggregation; and this is exactly the point Jameson, Lordon, Tomšič and others are making; there is little to counter-hegemonize on the basis that workers, when they do act, invariably act alone, or find that wage struggles have only the weakest sectionalist impact and political life. Even the courageous wave of big strikes amongst young workers in China, India and South Africa in the new millennium – in the new Fordist factories and extractive industries – against the extension of the working day, have left the barest of traces on new forms of local and international solidarity. This is largely because, given that they represent a form of frontline struggle against the violent effects of primitive accumulation, they take on the appearance to other workers – certainly in Europe and North America – of an older stage of the workers' movement and therefore distant from the 'non-class' non-unionized workplace struggles in the new knowledge industries, that currently determine the shape of labour–capital relations. These big factory struggles in China and India appear to be peripheral to the struggles over new life–work relations that dominate the new economy in the West, even though the labour in the electronic sectors of these economies provide the very *matériel* for the new economy and digital workplace. This is one of the many internal tensions within the global division of labour today that is heightened as a result of the radical cultural unevenness of the forces and interests of workers' struggles. Outside of trade union affiliations, workers make little symbolic investment in the struggles of other workers. This, of course, at one level, is the result of a continuing and long-standing period of rebarbative anti-trade union legislation across the globe, that has destroyed the active power of trade union representation in the workplace and labour contractualism, and, therefore, contributed to the destruction of the international language of solidarity as the cultural form of workers' lives. (In 2009, for example, only 12.3 per cent of US workers were unionized.)[40] But it is also the result of the wider symbolic disconnection between workers, given workers' disinvestment from working class self-identity on a historically invested basis. Most workers become workers briefly in struggle; a small minority continue to struggle *as* workers. In fact, these conditions coalesce to form a perfect vicious circle: most workers have no interest in acting consistently as workers, because there is no good reason to act consistently as workers, particularly, when, the libidinal rewards of not acting consistently are greater than acting consistently.

Proletarians against proletarians

But if workers find little reward in the symbolic attachments of working-class self-identity, or find little solidarity with other workers, particularly, when, issues of class consciousness, seem irrelevant to 'personal development', the struggle to be a worker, 'consistently' or not, is one of the overwhelming aims of millions of people out of work globally who want to become wage earners and full-time workers, if they could. This produces another tension deep inside the vastly uneven division of labour globally: that is, between the systemic brutality of the exclusion of living labour from the system and the libidinal investment on the part of millions of the unemployed and those scraping a living outside of the exchange economy, capitalism, especially Western capitalism holds a place open for all, as in for instance, the mass emigration from the immiserated and war-torn zones of the Middle East into Europe and the United States, on the grounds of a 'better life' for exiles and economic migrants. Crucial to this perspective is what I called earlier capitalist ecstasis: namely, beneath the conventional narrative of improved life – or the left version of this, that migrancy is the very mobile function of labour under capital and therefore congruent with the logic of capital itself: migrancy *is* capitalism under capital's law of motility[41] – is the hope of a *fulfilled* capitalist body presently weakened by exclusion and division, in this case, through imperialist war and regional 'underdevelopment'. The capitalist body in the immiserated zones is not just a body under duress that rightly wants immediate relief from this violent and barbarous threat, but a body also starved of *jouissance* that wants without respite to participate in the creative superfluities of a capitalism that can provide the conditions for sustained consumption. Every year, for instance, around 300,000 young workers enter the labour market in Syria with little hope of full-time employment. The outcome of this is that few migrants in the country want to travel to 'underdeveloped' capitalist states (even if they were allowed to), for this, unconsciously at least, feels like a weakening of *jouissance*. The failed or underdeveloped zones of clientalist capitalism in the Middle East, then, produces a hyper-investment in the phantasy of the core capitalist zones as places where capitalism 'works' or 'works better'; escape and flight becoming attached to the dream of enchanted market participation. The fundamentalist and religious reaction to this in the immiserated zones themselves is the desperate and self-violating negation of this convergence between the underinvested capitalist body and the superfluity of capitalist pleasure in the core zones. This is why the rise of fundamentalist reaction to these unassailable attractions is the *ressentiment* not of those who ascribe to a religious rejection of modernity per se, but the actions of those who are the disappointed sons and daughters of a failed modernity, a modernity that didn't quite work. Paradoxically political Islam's violent attack on the 'infidel' is also attack on capitalist Islam in these terms, a perverse lashing out against cultural and economic subjection. Hence in escaping this version of modernity migrants are not assured allies in any anti-capitalist project in the West or elsewhere. As Friends of the Classless Society have noted about the immigration crisis in Germany in 2017:

> That the marginalised living in the greatest misery are the most likely to rise up is a myth of the New Left. Refugees have no inherent interest in an uprising; for many, crossing the border will be their first and last subversive act. This is to be expected, since those still hoping to be admitted to the system have more to gain through conformity.[42]

Thus, to be *in* the West and working or not working is to aspire towards feelings of true capitalist belonging and self-respect, irrespective of the realities of poverty and violent racism. We have the strange spectacle, then, of migrancy as an instrumental category of social inclusion – a process of market and multicultural adaptation, without full economic integration – rather than a possible *transcultural* transaction between host culture and other cultures, in a remaking of global culture and modernity itself, in which the migrant worker – particularly the Muslim worker – is the welcome proletarian agent of global change. But, again this is no surprise: migration today is obviously at the very centre of the moving contradiction between living labour and machines and as such brutal evidence of the systemic antagonism between surplus populations on a global scale. Common class interests are thereby further fractured presently by this reality, making it very difficult for the left to organize collective values around the shared demands of wage labour, when (stable) full-time wage labour is no longer a viable horizon for the many, East, South, North *and* West. This is why intra-proletarian competition currently in the wake of the migrant crisis makes it hard for workers to create a new international, aracial and transcultural workers' culture on these terms: neither native workers nor most migrants themselves in the core zones see shared struggles as viable or workable – for both sets of workers there is too much to lose – hence the global rise of the populist right and the reinforcement of the still powerful attractions of identity politics and nationalism as compensatory attachments in the face of such division. There is a sense, therefore, paradoxically, that successful migrancy from East and South to the West functions abstractly more like a capitalist 'healing' process, in which the traumatized migrant body rushes towards a beneficent democracy; migrant and Western host country meeting each other, irrespective of poverty and economic exclusion for the worker, in a gladdening stabilization of market-led affects. Consequently, the crisis of the migrant is not simply a 'human crisis' and cannot be 'healed'. Expelled from the Southern and Eastern countrysides, and blocked at Europe's city gates, the economic migrant is the constitutive living political economic form of the present crisis, insofar rural migrancy is where the dots that connect ecological crisis, the expulsion of living labour, surplus populations, the pathologies of social reproduction and libidinal economy are joined up. This is because *there is no* feasible mass assimilation of the migrant into global industrial production; the rural migrant accordingly is the stark reminder of what the expulsion of living labour's proletarian exteriority actually means critically today on a global scale: that is, the need for the dismantling of growth-based capitalism as a narrow, urban, Western metropolitanism. Thus, lying behind the ecological crisis, the expulsion of living labour, the immiseration of surplus populations, the pathologies of social reproduction and the libidinal economy are the fundamental problems of twentieth- and twenty-first-century capitalism: the unresolved 'agrarian question', the question, in fact that Stalinism, orthodox Marxism and capitalist developmentalism (Third Worldism) believed that it had solved, or was solving in the twentieth century, and that yet now defines the very immiserated core of the system and the lives of the vast majority of humanity. As Loren Goldner argues:

> Only in 2010 did the world's rural population drop below 50 percent of the total. The great majority of those remaining in the countryside are petty producer peasants, artisans and rural proletarian labourers. Considering only India and China, with close to 40 percent of the world's population between them, it is clear that the 'agrarian question', on a world scale, remains central to any possible creation of a renewed communism. This is all the more urgent in light of the one million people a *day* who arrive from the countryside in the world's cities, as capitalism increasingly makes their way of life unviable and draws them into a dubious future in the world's shantytowns, or China's 270 million migrant workers.[43]

In this sense, the rural global proletariat is not the agent of a new and equitable industrial modernity, in which the borders of advanced capitalism are eventually opened up to include everyone, but the traumatized point where the presumed rational and 'working' totality of capitalism is violently exposed, and as such the productive and conflictual site where a 'progressive anti-progressivism' (or a non-developmentalist modernity) can do its radical, global work in the production of an emancipated 'post-work' world.

Love unlimited: The demonic-infinite

If we do truly live in a period of capitalist uxoriousness – and this book offers an open reflection on this question – in key respects uxoriousness and 'healing' would appear to be close to religious belief and subservience. Indeed, if uxoriousness is a form of excessive and misplaced love, a love without reflection or a love in denial, its concupiscent pleasures are easily framed by the needs of religious experience in a global culture where presently spiritualized affirmation and national belonging trumps ideological de-legitimation every time. Capitalism as religion was a common theme in philosophy, critical theory and sociology in Germany in the early decades of the twentieth century in response to the new mass politics and mass culture. Lukács, Simmel, Weber and Walter Benjamin all were influenced by this connection, particularly the early Benjamin; all recognizing how feelings of submission and passive observance shaped the spirit of self-reliance of *homo economicus*; and how belief in the naturalism of capitalism produced a theodicy of capitalist reason: *all is for the best, despite all setbacks*: 'capitalism essentially serves to satisfy the same worries, anguish, and disquiet formerly answered by so-called religion', as Benjamin declared.[44] This Weberian-Marxist approach to ideological interpellation has been revived recently in the writings of Michael Löwy and Georgio Agamben[45]: capitalism, they assert following Benjamin, is a system in which fetishism and primitive magic combine to provide the renewable pleasures of unending (and importantly) *real* solace. That is, the question of solace has its basis not in an effervescent and abstract hope, but in real material, economic efficacy. If capitalism sustains the possibility of a prospective future and self-realization, it does so through the consolation and endless faith in the seeming 'gift' of credit. 'The capitalist religion, consistent with Benjamin's thesis, lives in a continual indebtedness, which neither can nor should be paid off.'[46] Credit, for Agamben, in other words, is the *medium* of capitalist reason, the source of the self's ductile self-validation, and the basis, concretely, of capitalism's claims to 'creativity'. However, if easy credit releases the indebted from the shame of debt, it also, conversely, weakens the power of the indebted to escape the conditions of financial bondage and confront the power of the creditor. It is far more comfortable on the part of the debtor to remain in debt and service the interests of the creditor given that this is precisely what easy credit encourages and enables, defying the idea that one should remain poor even if one is poor and will remain poor. Credit on these terms offers a kind of 'luxuriant' bondage, as opposed to being the first step to immiseration. We can see, in these terms, then, how uxoriousness might function religiously as one of the stabilizing props of I-cracy: namely, uxoriousness is another way of talking about how the comfort and consolation of I-cratic self-realization are attached to capitalism's endless powers of 'reparation' as a kind 'maternal' credit.

However, if I-cracy and 'joyful alienation' rings out with religious fervour, and must define at least in broad outline, the libidinal nature of social reproduction today, there are innumerable problems with the notion of capitalism as religion in any strict sense for a theory of uxoriousness and 'joyful alienation'; if the *jouissance* of capitalism provides continuous comfort and solace, the majority of workers and consumers don't *worship* capital or relish the possibility of war, poverty, racism, low wages, exile and unemployment as acts of 'just punishment' or 'just constraint'; they also don't seek spiritual redemption through submitting to its 'economic' laws, as if the desire to 'fit in' (through extended credit) always follows the terms dictated by the financial bondage of capitalism.[47] Nevertheless, the naturalization of credit does operate according to the demands of the religious imaginary as a form of *secular* hope: *believe against all the odds, fortified by credit and despite setbacks you will be rewarded*; and this, obviously, is extremely flexible, and like the gambler's self-justification for seeing riches on the horizon, enticingly uncertain. Indeed, capitalism 'works' in these terms because it invites and promotes the pleasure of unrealistic expectations.[48] Or rather, flexible adaptation to capitalism 'works' not simply through adaptation-as-rational assessment, but through the *overidentification* with its ideal expectations; overidentification, in other words, *induces and captures* the pleasures of unrealistic expectations. One might say then, that uxoriousness as a bridging of the concupiscent with the wifely, maternal Other, is the experience of capitalism as something in these terms that *never stops giving*, despite the system's abjections, destructiveness, divisions, exclusions, mass racial incarcerations and cultural regression. In this way, the stochastic defence of capitalist creativity as the motor of individuation has its roots in the notion of capitalism as a source of endless maternal beneficence, even when this beneficence is postponed or even denied. And, consequently, this sense of beneficence is actually closer to the demonic, the demonic being here not equivalent to the satanic in the obvious and crude sense, but in Paul Tillich's intriguing reading of the value form in the 1920s, as the destruction of sociality through the 'desire for infinity' (1926).[49] In this respect, there is a notional link to Lacan's concept of surplus *jouissance*. *Jouissance* is not the name for pleasure savoured and conserved, but that, which is produced continuously out of the impossibility of satisfaction. This is why Lacan was keen in the late writings to identify surplus *jouissance* with the production of surplus value itself.[50] And this is why it makes no sense to talk about capitalism as suppressing desire and the drive: surplus *jouissance* 'repeats the imperative of satisfaction beyond the need'.[51] In other words, the creative destruction inherent to capitalism is precisely the infinite-maternal embrace that never says 'no', that can always accommodate the desires of its offspring, however destabilizing and corrupting.

Thus, the notion of the demonic is helpful here in understanding the anxious attachment of the self to ductility and the 'rationality' of creative destruction. For, the power of the demonic lies precisely in its integration of the negative (the self-destructive) *and* the creative. The social body of capitalism not only absorbs all the destructive energies of those who live inside its boundaries, but also teleologically as it turns this destructive energy into an act of creativity under all unpropitious circumstances. The realities of division and exclusion remain weak or ambiguous as defining markers of the de-legitimation of the system when faced with the *continuity* of pleasures – or continuity in pleasure – that the system generates out of destructive creativity. That is, banally, as long as the avocadoes and pizzas still arrive in the supermarkets, and in moments of leisure my electronic self can move freely throughout the world, then, the system has the capacity and will to resolve its problems, for the 'order' of *these* pleasures, graspable in a finite time frame, overrides the actual or threatening disorder and inchoateness of division and exclusion, and destruction over the long term.

The continuity of immediate pleasures possesses, therefore, a greater perspicacity and common sense – or realism – than the continuity of pain and loss experienced by oneself and others and future generations. This is what Baruch Spinoza calls the intoxicating power of affect to dissolve all memory of the reality of causation.[52] Indeed, it is not stretching plausibility to say this is why almost 58 million people in Brazil in 2018 voted for the successful neo-fascist presidential candidate Jair Bolsonaro as a claim on a 'better' future, despite the violence and oppression of Bolsonaro's Brazilian fascist forbears; and this is why in the immiserated war zones in Middle East the call for the 'end of capitalism' – where one would assume it would be at least a palpable option of some kind, something, indeed, linked notionally to anti-imperialism – is presently so weak, insofar as the brutal destruction of families, homes, communities and habitats appears to be the tragedy of regional capitalist *underdevelopment*, irrespective of who is in control at home: native Islamist insurgents, secular nationalists or pro-imperialists. In this sense, only a *better* capitalism can successfully rebuild the ruins.

These 'diabolic' investments and compensatory comforts, then, are not to be underestimated, in either the core capitalist zones or the immiserated peripheries, in tying the present ductile economic self to the system. Yet, to underline my remarks above, this is why we should be particularly wary when talking about pleasure and *jouissance* of attaching the appeal of these 'infinite-demonic' powers of capitalism to those old (Freudian-Marxist) shibboleths from the 1960s and 1970s about the post-1960s rise of the 'narcissistic' self (Christopher Lasch)[53] distracting itself to 'death' under the new media conditions of capitalist individuation, as if humanity and the labour–capital relation were subject under these advanced conditions of consumption and creative destruction to a kind of veil of distraction. There are no *veils* of distraction under capitalism, as if the demonic power and uxoriousness of the commodity form is defined by mass delusion. On the contrary, the internalization of capitalism as the *rational and creative* solution to its own degradations and horrors represents an *active investment* in the *jouissance* of the system, *irrespective of its oppressive outcomes*; and it is this understanding of this *active* acceptance of capitalism, that has, essentially, to be the core of any critique of 'joyful alienation' and libidinal economy now (and the rise of the new right), in order to avoid all the political and philosophical pitfalls of the de-rationalizing of the contemporary libidinal subject as someone who fails the test of reason, given the fact that *self-ascriptive claims to rationality are constitutive of all beliefs*. In other words: the key libidinal politico-economic issue is not the rise of distraction, solace or consolation per se under mature capitalism (as a delusional, self-pleasuring break from the constraints of labour, reason and family), but of the fluid interpenetration of subjectivity and economic agency as the site of the ongoing crisis of the subject's creative investment in capitalism as a form of *pragmatic enlightenment*, or, the 'best reason' available. That is, we need to be clear that under I-cratic mature capitalism the logic of surplus *jouissance* is attached precisely *to* the claims of enlightened reason, that is, speaks in its name.[54] *Jouissance* is reason made to work *in the name of jouissance*.

Surplus-*jouissance*-enlightened reason

In this respect, understanding the social logic of contemporary digital neoliberal capitalism has an important part to play in the contemporary critique of social reproduction and the production of the capitalist subject. One of the reasons that social individuation, pleasure, ductility, uxoriousness, *jouissance*, autolatry and the demonic-infinite have become a knot of issues today is that digital capitalism has ameliorated one of the problems of social reproduction of mature capitalism under its chronic long-term cultural and social decline: the introjection of the self into networks of knowledge and collective approbation in ways that further inculcate feelings of autonomy and self-control as part of imagined or real shared experience of creative reason. In other words, the ductility of the economic self is given an unprecedented *living plasticity* in digital culture, based on an increased sense of autonomy and subjective control through the consumption of things and signs; things *as* signs. As such, one of the outcomes of this is digital capitalism's intensification of enjoyment without restriction – without participatory boundaries or moral judgement. And this is what I mean by qualitatively new forms of subjective invitation: digital capitalism inaugurates a new freely I-cratic subject of pleasure and freedom: a subject that disarticulates the drive of endless *jouissance* from *conspicuous shame,* as the motor of personal intensity. Individuation, self-display and self-ascriptions of reason coalesce in the drive to be the 'best I can be' as a rational expression of self-interest. Indeed, the question of credit here takes on explicit psychological dimension: the rise of personal and household indebtedness under neoliberalism has both enabled and legitimized this erosion of shame, insofar as being a personal debtor has lost the worst of its social stigma.[55] Credit, therefore, has a particular psychological outcome: it erodes the link, as Marx once noted of the significant social character attached to shame, between shame and the formation of political consciousness, strengthening the ethics of intensity and self-realization. Thus, the rise in personal debt is not the new capitalist 'magic dust' that gets people to consume beyond need, but, rather, evidence of the *normalizing economic through-flow* of surplus *jouissance.* It thereby gives everyday material support and psychological weight and coherence to the separation of the 'truth of the system' from pain and its social consequences. As Tomšič says in an echo of Jameson and Lyotard:

> [The] masochist would indeed be the perfect subject of capitalism, someone who would enjoy being a commodity among others, while assuming the role of surplus labour, the position of the object that willingly satisfies the systemic demands. The capitalist regime demands from everyone to become ideal masochists and the actual message of the superego's injunction is: 'enjoy your suffering, enjoy capitalism'. [56]

Capitalism did not develop network culture, the smart phone and smart technology in order to alleviate the problems of social reproduction in these terms, as if it imagined, teleologically in the 1960s how such forms might eventually act as libidinal drivers of the ductile self. Similarly, masochism is certainly not a word you find in neoliberal management discourse or on the factory floor or in the office, when the question of 'work and enjoyment' and personal development comes up. Nevertheless, the new avatars and visionaries of computer technology recognized that the 'old' analogic technologies were blocking the flow of capital and desire (*jouissance*), and thus, digitalization presented a vast opportunity for new linkages and relations, new points of connection and adaptation, new social networks, that could '*re-subjectivize*' producer and consumer as active and demonically 'creative', and as such be presented as the democratic fruits of I-cracy and the new forms of digital production and consumption. In fact, against all practical evidence, 'creativity' is now thoroughly naturalized as a correlate of digital capitalism's networks and 'infinite' virtual expansion, *radically offsetting* the subjective ruination of producers as workers.

In the light of this shift and the fundamental contradiction between ruination and creativity, the critical literature on the technologies and techniques of the new libidinal economy is now vast, reviving what is left of Marxian critical theory in the academy in the Western democracies. There is now a growing literature on technology, subjectivity and the pathologies of digital culture, which at least recognizes the cultural force of the new order of economic reason; a relinking of subjective ruination (in Honneth's sense) with libidinal economy, social reproduction with pleasure; the subject as anthropological constant has been thoroughly excised.

This is what makes Tomšič's revaluation of the critical links between Lacan and Marx on the production of subjectivity particularly pertinent. It also points to the value of Bernard Stiegler's work on the technological crisis of individuation. Stiegler has developed a powerful dissection of the crisis of individuation on the grounds of what he calls the hyper-industrial production of symbolic misery: namely, with the global expansion of libidinal forms of 'engaged-disengagement' through digital culture, 'the mental, intellectual, affective and aesthetic capacities of humanity are massively threatened.'[57] This is because a huge proportion of humanity is now subject to the sensuous compliance of aestheticized marketing (across all areas of social and cultural life), separate from the experience of aesthetic or cultural investigation, or attentiveness. The resulting symbolic misery leads to the loss of what he calls 'primordial narcissism,'[58] that is, the ability to form aesthetic attachments to singularities and the production of critical judgements that are backed up by independent practice and non-algorithmically derived forms of analysis: 'my past [and interests, as they come to framed by consumption, are] less and less differentiated from other people. [My self-proclaimed pursuit of individuation] loses, therefore, its singularity.'[59] Stiegler's recognition of the increasing libidinal powers of capitalist subjectivation, and as such the adaptive pleasures of 'control society', is not, however, a post-Heideggerian, anti-Enlightenment screed against advanced technology. Emancipatory struggle lies not in the struggle against technology as such, but against the weaponization of technology as part of the proletarianization of skill, affect and attention released by real subsumption, what I called above, more sanguinely, technology's libidinal offsetting of the producer's subjective ruination. One thing stands out here that we will explore in detail later: cultural proletarianization affects all of humanity, insofar, as it works to control the range, horizons and possibilities of individuation, through delimited processes of discernment and the mass synchronization of public and individual memory. We might say, therefore, that the processes of proletarianization (principally the loss of independent capacity and singularity) intersect to form a triadic structure, on a global scale: cultural and affective proletarianization through digitalization; the proletarianization of the permanently excluded from production (the global rural poor and the occasional worker); and the disaggregated, proletarian mass of part-time and full-time workers in the West. Proletarianization, consequently, as it was imagined to be the case within the workers' movement in the first decades of the twentieth century, as the progressive incorporation of the majority of humanity into a unified mass of wage earners, has suffered a catastrophic reversal; the processes of proletarianization have indefatigably become the processes of waste production and exclusion. The relentless focus in Stiegler's writing on deskilling, de-sensitivization and de-individuation, hence, captures what is crucial to contemporary libidinal economy and to my understanding of model three: that is, libidinal economy's destruction of primordial narcissism represents a *war* against autonomy, and not just a loss of institutional civic bearings and democratic proportionality on the part of a refulgent capitalist populism.

In *Wars and Capital* (2016), Éric Alliez and Maurizio Lazzarato reframe this reality by expanding Gilles Deleuze's concept of 'control societies' to the notion of a fully integrated political economic war on individuation and autonomy.[60] This returns us to the model of symbolic and cultural violence, developed broadly by critical theory from the 1950s: capitalism produces an inherent destruction of all civilizational values as a consequence of the production of value. The authors, however, push this one step further, by putting this destruction of civilization on an explicit 'war footing'. On the one hand, they make clear, like Stiegler (and Adorno), that the pleasures of de-individuation are formulated and delivered on an industrial scale. But, on the other hand, they also insist that such industries – these industries of the moment – are part of a large-scale and long-standing process of radical continuity between, war, economy and politics. Capitalism's history of emergence, triumph, expansion and libidinal re-composition is characterized not just by the chronology of colonial and imperialist wars of conquest and intervention, but by a multiplicity of *non-martial* wars: wars of race and sex; wars of subjectivity; wars of culture and civilization; wars against immigrants and refugees; and wars against foreigners. War on this basis, then, functions as the hegemonic principle of internal and external order, transforming Carl von Clausewitz's famous formula, 'war is the continuation of politics by other means', into politics as *war* continued by other means, covering both interstate war and generalized 'civil war'.

Without these external and internal war machines capitalism would not have emerged and sustained its power and reach. In this respect, the authors prefer 'civil war' to 'class struggle', because the reality of this war falls daily under the radar, even though it is axiomatic of modern power and the exercise of democracy. This 'civil war' now reaches totalizing proportions: it exercises its power against society as a whole through the money form and commodity form, and is, thereby, first and foremost, a relentless war of subjectivation. The production of subjectivity, consequently, is the fundamental organizing principle of this 'civil war' machine. However, the politics of liberalism, the centre-left and the centre-right, are built precisely upon the opposite, that is on the separation of the economy from the ideological (Carl Schmitt's great preoccupation in the 1920s), and where they do touch, they are assumed to be purely contingent. We are in period, as such, where the dissociation between subjectivity and production is maintained as a condition of 'market reason' and democratic governance, further heightening the notion of capitalist relations as the free association of producer and consumers. So, the denial of the existence of this 'civil war' raises the definition of political economy as the technical management of markets to a new level of historical naturalization. Accordingly, as a total war this 'civil war' should be understood as concerted mobilization of all the productive, social, technical, cultural and subjective forces of society – the post-war success of this integration lying in the pacification of collective desire and the mobilization of the majority against itself. Politically, this has been underscored, since the 1970s by the fact that proletarians and their allies have no access to a viable 'war machines' that could compete collectively with this successful process of endocolonization. Moreover, as a general principle, the authors take their distance from capitalism's 'creative destruction' as something specific to the macro-economic. *Creative destruction organizes the relentless and restless war of subjectivation itself* and therefore is the propulsive force of the 'civil war' machine. Capitalism remains on a war footing whether particular states are engaged in interstate warfare or not. Peace after interstate warfare is one thing; release from 'civil war' is another. Indeed, after the Second World War, the peace after interstate conflict – a 'pseudo-peace'[61] – has enabled capital to transfer an increased part of its resources to the maintenance of the 'civil war' machine. The success of neoliberalism is an indication of this shift, with its intensification of non-punitive and affective modes of subjectivation.

The coercive lens of 'civil war' is, however, too methodologically unstable for our analysis of pleasure, desire and social reproduction, given that the majority find it hard to see the 'war for pleasure' as war: endocolonization therefore needs a theory of subjectivation that is equal to the pleasure invested in 'least resistance' and individuation-de-individuation. Otherwise it is easy to detach the production of subjectivity from the pleasures of 'least resistance' and slip, melancholically, into the 'de-rationalization' thesis from an older Marxism and critical theory and psychoanalysis, as it does in the case of Jonathan's Crary's spirited, but tragederian, post-Adornian critique of our post-digital condition, in *24/7: Late Capitalism and the Ends of Sleep* (2013).[62] Alliez and Lazzarato admittedly don't fall into this trap, and in fact, Lazzarato has devoted much of his work to the contemporary conditions of subjectivation and subjectivity. Their notion of a continuous 'civil war' is designed to avoid narratives of de-rationalization. But if the 'war for pleasure' falls under the broader designation 'civil war', the 'war for pleasure' needs to retain its relative autonomy; otherwise there is diminished sense of how much of humanity, now living and producing inside this compressed world of subjective ruination have no qualms, indeed, relish its speed, instantaneity and opportunity for endless self-display and connectivity, for fear of social annihilation and a rapid de-pleasuring of their status as untrammelled consumers of things and signs, and as such 'masters' of *jouissance*. As Byung-Chul Han notes in this respect, the 'war for pleasure' is a friendly one: '*Friendly* power proves *more powerful* ... than purely repressive power.'[63] Or as Lordon puts it: 'Contradictory as it may sound, tyrants would rather be loved! ... [They act to promote] imaginaries of desire that better align with their own particular plans.'[64] Han, thus, may severely underestimate how the repressive power of neoliberal 'control societies' continues to underwrite friendly power, making his version of libidinal economy far more sanguine than is helpful in the need to understand how the 'business of friendliness' is also the 'business of war'. (In this we should certainly look to Alliez and Lazzarato.) But the substantive issue remains: Why has the intensification of these non-punitive modes of subjectivation been so successful? Why is this war for pleasure – this 'civil war' for 'individuation' against individuation and autonomy – not recognized as a war? It is only in answering this question that we can produce the resources to oppose these forces. Thus, Han rightly makes the point – as others do – that the new digital technologies of power are not simply involved in the *managing* of consent, but rather in the expressive exploitation of self-individualizing choice, as we will examine in detail later. And this argument, accordingly, is far more suasive as a legitimating force than simply the consensual administration of difference, let alone the threat of direct repression. The notion of 'friendly' power is able to add a plausible affective dimension to uxoriousness and 'joyful alienation' and therefore provides further evidence of how pleasure accompanies and shapes the active investment in capitalism.

Thus, there are two significant things here that can sharpen up our critique of libidinal economy and understanding of *jouissance* and 'joyful alienation' now without falling theoretically into a submissive mode, doomsday moral condemnation or sanguine or inflationary accounts of 'network culture' and as such diminishing our powers of understanding. Firstly – less importantly – there is no doubt that this networked individuation appears 'thrilling' to the majority in its friendly expectancy, insofar as it invites the user to take unending pleasure from the 'new', and, therefore, one should not underestimate its subjectivizing and supervising powers for capital in ways that make an older kind of capitalist cultural interpellation (sedentary TV, popular magazines and street advertising, for instance) appear almost modest, timid and distancingly inefficient by comparison. In this respect one would want to note Georg Franck's now familiar notion of changing 'economies of attention' as crucial to this logic and the production of the neoliberal subject.[65] And second and more significantly, it is hard to deny that this relentless production of individuation across technological platforms, and as such, a process that is internal to everyday exchange produces a love of the self that, in fact, undergirds what I have been calling uxoriousness. For to give one's love to capitalism today – or more precisely to feel the deepest connection to its identitary pleasures and investments, *irrespective of one's particular criticisms of it or exclusions from it* – is to also give one's love to oneself as a discerning lover of capital's 'endlessly giving' 'individuation', in the hope of receiving love in return from its entreaties. 'Please recognize me; please confirm my love for the love of self.' This is where the subjective split in neoliberal I-cracy occurs: *the majority of people do not love capitalism as such, under all conditions; rather, they love the love of self that capitalism provides and enables*, either at their place of work or in the multiple domains of consumption. Or as Richard Gilman-Opalsky notes perceptibly: 'In a sense nobody really desires real capitalism ... What most people desire is the spectacular form of capitalism where every person is on the road to personal empowerment and relative wealth, or can get on that road if they wish.'[66] As such capitalism produces an ideal version of itself at the symbolic level, that producers and consumers willingly contribute to, shape and adhere to (or critically adjust), in order to make bearable the endless disappointments of the promises held out by love of the love of self; what Louis Althusser once called, in a very different language, the lived illusions of capitalism. In these terms, the subject's (political) attention to externalities and sense of agency passes through the phantasmatic-relation of this 'spectacle' as a *rational* corrective to the threat of un-*jouissance*, a modern version of *ataraxy* (the avoidance of unpleasure). But this rational corrective provides no harmonious barrier against the reality of the commodity form and the loss of *jouissance*. This is because the love of the love of self represents the subject's *internalization* of the objective externality of the commodity and its demonic infinitude. And this is why, more precisely, the love of the love of self is the manifestation of surplus *jouissance* as a continual state of anxiety.[67]

The love of the love of self does not simply ask: what does capitalism want from me? – as a response to a finite set of responsibilities as producer and consumer – but rather, how can my love of the love of self be consistently equal to the desire for desire that capitalism demands. And this demand is radically non-specific. That is, anxiety here is not a definable emotional state but a free-floating affect or feeling, something as Lacan says, that is, 'unfastened ... drifts about'.[68] And it drifts about because it exists, for Lacan, in a suspensive state between desire and *jouissance*. Anxiety is found 'suspended between, on the one hand, the pre-existent form, so to speak, of the relation to the cause – the *What is there?* which will go on to be formulated as cause, namely *embarrassment* – and, on the other hand, the *turmoil* that cannot get a hold on this cause because, primordially, anxiety literally produced it'.[69] In this sense, anxiety refers expressly to the subject's relation to the indeterminate function of the object *a*: 'anxiety is bound to the fact that I don't know which object *a* I am for the desire of the Other,'[70] and therefore relates directly to the subject's realization of the 'impossibility of finding his cause within himself at the level of desire'.[71] On this basis, anxiety is, in fact, the *truth* of desire, that is, it is that which emerges as the inescapable encounter with the subject's endless seeking out of the object with all its 'phases of abeyance, its wrong turns, its false trails, its side long drifting, which makes the search turn endlessly around and around'.[72] So, anxiety is that which crucially *fails* to deceive, that 'which deceives not,'[73] as Lacan puts it, in the endless and elusive pursuit of the object of desire, making its unambiguousness as an experience the very truth of desire's 'drama',[74] indeed, it is the very thing that is *not* mediated in the production of desire. The implication here for subjectivation under the strictures of libidinal economy is that as an affect or feeling, as opposed to an emotional state, anxiety represents that unstable, temporal mode of pleasure in which the *desire for desire* (as pleasure) secures its valency, providing, in turn, the necessary affective space for the relentless entrepreneuralization of the self. Indeed, anxiety is precisely the name for surplus *jouissance*.[75]

Love of the love of self and the feminization of neotony

Hence the love of the love of self produces an anxious process of discernment as a self-votive endorsement of one's better demonic self, as a good capitalist subject. The subject is always betting on the prospect of *jouissance* as an expression of discernment and creativity, and therefore as evidence of the kind of self-love capital will value and reward. This is why to resist this – to not participate, to refuse to buy or own beyond one's immediate needs, to work less, to ignore the overtures of network life, to take your pleasure outside of mass culture, to cultivate non-capitalist affects and practices and knowledges – is to appear to shrivel subjectively and render yourself as opaque to your (loving) creative self and others.[76] In fact it is to fall into the greatest of sins of contemporary capitalist life: self-abnegation (and now parlously) social invisibility. As such, it is important to recognize that the demonic-infinity of the commodity form is in these terms a fetishized form of neotony; the perpetual taking of pleasure in the excess of need is a process that always returns the taking of pleasure *to the beginning*. Indeed, neotony and uxoriousness combine as the affective substrate of surplus *jouissance*. And this, in turn, reveals the specific form of sexuation characteristic of surplus *jouissance* and libidinal economy today: its explicit feminization.

The sexuation of neotony is not to identify women's anxiety in the face of the desire for desire, as the feminization of the libidinal economy. Women are neither the pliant victims nor primary producers of the *jouissance* of libidinal economy. Such reification of gender leads to an identitarian-sadism of the critique of femininity and feminization, that is, leads to the assumption that women are not just complicit with capitalism's libidinal economy, but largely define its pleasurable dysfunctionality and success. This misplaced critique is particularly evident in Tiqqun's critical reflections on femininity and desire in their *Preliminary Materials for a Theory of the Young-Girl* (1999).

> There is nothing in the Young-Girl's life, even in the deepest zones of her intimacy, that escapes alienated reflexivity, that escapes the codification of the gaze of the Spectacle. This intimacy strewn with commodities yields entirely to advertising, and is entirely socialized *as intimacy*, which is to say that she is part-for-part subject to a fallacious commonality that does not allow her to express herself ... Nothing in the identity of the Young-Girl truly belongs to her, even less her "youth"' than her "femininity." She does not possess attributes, instead her attributes possess her, those THEY have so generously loaned her ... *The Young-Girl is like capitalism, domestic servants, and protozoa: She knows how to adapt and what's more*, she's proud of it.[77]

This is deeply problematic, ugly and highly revealing of the sexist admonishments of the neo-Romantic insurrectionary milieu of Tiqqun. However, there is a problem that does need to be addressed and that at some point Tiqqun no doubt hoped productively to work through: that is, how well and how easily the neotonic form of the commodity captures feminine desire for surplus *jouissance*. If the love of the love of self is overdetermined by youth and feminization, this is increasingly so in the digital sphere of the libidinal economy, where the feminization of male, female and transgender desire is key to the ductility and anxiety of consumer self-identity and self-realization as the adaptive pleasures of economic reason. Thus, if we are compelled to talk about 'young girls' here, such talk should be unswervingly separated from young girls themselves: the love of the love of self is not grounded in the lives and experience of biological *women* as such, young or old, but, rather, by the construction of feminization as a non-shaming, masochistic openness to pleasure, in which young women have a *disproportionate* say over the general uxorious form of surplus *jouissance*, insofar as young women are overwhelmingly encouraged to find pleasure in these forms of self-scrutiny.

Distribution of pleasure

Capitalism, then, is extraordinarily accomplished and efficient now at distributing pleasure as enlightened reason, particularly to the young and female. It therefore is also highly successful and efficient at naming that which *promises* pleasure as the love of self-love as enlightened reason. So, pleasure is something people now expect as a given, in some form, no matter how small or temporary, as a consistent fact (and reward) of living, dreaming and working under capitalism; indeed, for all of the problems 'out there' that appear to threaten the consistency of these pleasures, capitalism never seems to fail to allocate pleasures – lots of them, no matter how small – to all classes, but particularly workers and young workers. It is clear, then, that pleasure is not confined (as it mostly was) to the rich and powerful; pleasure works for capital and workers alike, indeed works in the interests of both capital and workers alike in a common *endeavour*. In fact, it is precisely because the pleasure industries are always in business – are always creating jobs and new consumers and new horizons – that there is more pleasure and better and more various pleasures to go around. Pleasures never seem to stop and are relatively cheap, and even 'free' on occasions; thus, if there is always more pleasure to be had, and sometimes better pleasures to be had, this cannot but be comforting and reassuring, for if capitalism was so bad and balefully destructive, there would be no pleasure at all, or it would be rationed like it was under state socialism, as if it was deleterious for you. But pleasure can't be bad for you – alienating as clever people call it – because everything points to how pleasure and capitalism need each other, and, in turn, how capitalism, for all its shortcomings, helps to get you through the working day; work may be hard and tedious, but pleasure is always there to get you back on your feet. At my desk I hold out my hand, and pleasure is there at my fingertips; I walk down the street in my lunch break, and feel I know pleasure better than anything else; it is there everywhere, plentiful and inviting; it never lets me down. Well perhaps sometimes it does let me down, I know that, I'm not stupid, and I know that there are those who have less pleasures than I do – many people – and pleasures that lie out of my reach, but there are always other pleasures that soon take the place of those unsatisfactory pleasures, without discomfort, as if the loss of pleasure never happened, and I move on, without worry; and this is the beauty of pleasure: I maybe tired and inconsolable, but pleasure is always there to repair and reinvigorate me and at some point divert me, in a wholly uplifting way, from thinking why I need pleasure in the first place.

So, if *Capitalism and the Limits of Desire* comes on the tail of a growing literature on libidinal economy, affect, *jouissance*, network culture and social reproduction, surplus populations and the crisis of living labour, it makes no concession to the idea that some version of a more equitable 'creative' capitalism is the answer to a 'post-work' post-capitalism. This is a fantasy, for there are no market socialisms, no 'communist capitalisms' no 'frictionless communication capitalisms' lying in wait that will relieve us of neotony and the uxoriousness of the commodity under the value form. In this sense, we need to be clear about what are the possibilities and limits that individuation brings to emancipatory struggle, in the period of the deepening crisis of the labour–capital relation. Indeed, if individuation under capitalism is in fundamental cultural crisis, as Honneth and Stiegler stress in their very different ways, it, nonetheless, will be the processes of individuation that will define the break of the capitalist control of *jouissance*, and as such shape the unmet needs of all. In the next chapter, then, before I embark on my discussion of self-love and perfectionism, I want to give some further and extended thought to the issue of individuation and to de-individuation.

Chapter 2
Individuation, egoism and social reproduction

Individuation and de-individuation

It would appear in the light of the last chapter that the present crisis represents a perfect storm of subjectivation (subjective ruination, repetitive compulsion, ductility, intensity, demonic-infinitude, de-individuation, autolatry, neotony), disaggregation (the expulsion of living labour, the crisis of exteriority, loss of relation and 'insignificance') and libidinal capture ('joyful alienation', 'happy slavery', anxiety, masochistic pleasure, ataraxy, surplus jouissance, uxoriousness). From this perspective, indeed, it would seem to confirm, at a high level of micro-analysis, the wider assumptions of Adorno and Horkheimer's *Dialectic of Enlightenment*: the structural integration and production of subjectivity into the instrumental processes of capitalist valorization. In fact, in the same way Lacan talked about critical thought always ending up back with Hegel, despite all critiques of and exits from Hegel's metaphysics, we always are compelled to return in this epoch, to the *Dialectic of Enlightenment* as a source of realism on the operative functions of capitalism as engaged in a war against autonomy and subjectivity; it remains a kind of incomparable study text, the thing that we continually have to navigate our way through in order to avoid the identitarian pitfalls of thinking too highly of emancipatory reason as an unfolding, linear narrative. Much of the critical thought we have already discussed is indirectly indebted, in a broad sense, to Adorno and Horkheimer's diagnostics.

But, nevertheless, there are four major things that have radically changed since Adorno and Horkheimer's book was published, that alter its structural assumptions about capitalist totality and emancipatory thought, subjectivity and agency: the growing global expulsion of living labour from production that threatens capital accumulation; the chronic ecological crisis that threatens the actual metabolic reproduction of capitalist growth; the increasing dissociation of workers from the workers' movement, 'freeing' workers from the corporatist logic of social democracy and trade union 'consciousness' and the old industrial, ethnographic identities and the extraordinary efflorescence of new forms of 'individuation' as a consequence of real subsumption – the expansion of new forms of self-differentiation. The combination of these forces provides, therefore, a set of objective and subjective coordinates for emancipatory thought and practice, that, through their interconnection and aporetic challenges, radically expose the contingency of the old assumptions and unities regarding capitalism's progress and systemic stability. In other words, they provide a set of points of breakdown, dissociation and self-negation that immanently offset the vast heteronomous forces of reaction and disaggregation that these conditions have put in motion, and that we have discussed in detail.

These transformations, consequently, offer a methodological and dialectic lesson on how we might think, imagine and strategize – *work through* – the extended crisis, that at an important level removes us from the conspectus of *Dialectic of Enlightenment*, and thereby, establishes a new range of questions to old problems: how might we rethink those repressive unities that have held reason in its allotted place since the Second World War, and, as such, in what ways does reason operate in the interests of pleasure under libidinal economy as a conflictual problem of real subsumption (reflected in the conditions above), as opposed simply to evidence of 'alienation' and 'reification'? That is, the current crisis of the Enlightenment legacy and universal emancipatory thought calls for a model of reason that grasps those tendencies simultaneously: the repressive tightening of the link between economic reason and pleasure under the name of freedom, and the desire for other affects and pleasures, new forms of individuation, not assimilable to market rationalization. In this sense, methodologically, the struggle over individuation has to find its agonistic form immanent to the libidinal forces of real subsumption, and not in some internal exile, in which individuation in its isolation is assumed to be free from alienated pleasure. For to fail to do this is to miss how the struggle over individuation and subjectivation is now a political and emancipatory struggle *over* pleasure itself and not the call for an exit from alienated pleasure as the primary condition of 'true' individuation. Thus, there is no 'crisis of reason', as such here, but rather evidence of how the struggle for reason and forms individuation that are not determined by capital is set by capital's unfailing identification of reason with pleasure and therefore overwhelmingly by the transparent and powerful functions of pleasure-as-reason under real subsumption. This is why emancipatory struggles are predetermined by the immediate wage-labour interests of workers and the financial state of non-workers, who are – first and foremost – reliant on capital for the means of their survival and reproduction.

Breaking with the acceptance of these immediate interests has been, accordingly, one of the key intellectual and cultural struggles of both the old workers' movement and late Western Marxism and post-war critical theory (Guy Debord and Theodor Adorno passim): *the universal content of unmet needs cannot be mediated by narrow capitalist notions of pleasure and self-autonomy*. This led, of course, certainly in the official workers' movement and the old social democratic parties, to the rationalist inflation of those cultural and intellectual practices, interests and activities, that were assumed to secure some relief or freedom from the alienations of labour and bourgeois cultural authority (i.e. that could act as a defence of those humanist habits of learning and modes of attention, that privileged, reflective judgement, study and empathetic engagement, over and above, that of immediate pleasure and distraction in the pursuit of appetitive relief from the exertions of factory and office).[1] As such, mass culture was seen as the great demiurge of alienated pleasure, the industrial behemoth that misdirected the capacities, energies and interests of workers, and, ultimately, removed them from the intellectual influence of trade union and political party alike. That this virtuous humanist model and critique never worked, or only worked for a relatively few, represents the crisis of a reflective culture that has long accompanied the crisis of the workers' movement. We can see clearly now how deeply entwined is the demise of this ideal of humanist self-education and radical auto-didacticism with the loss of class identity and what once represented workers' independent culture. Stiegler's cultural proletarianization thesis does not hold back on the depth of this retreat and crisis, for this crisis is real and painful enough.

But, nevertheless, this loss is not the result of a failed application of a workable model, and, therefore, another indication of the unfolding crisis or destruction of reason; on the contrary, the humanist model was from the very beginning the result of an implausible set of aims and expectations, given the workers' movement's fundamental misrecognition of the real content of real subsumption after the 1950s: with the fully achieved incorporation of workers' subjectivity into production as the basis for a new regime of consumption, there could never be, realistically, an independent and heterogeneous culture in which workers 'flourished' outside of the workplace, according to their own dictates.[2] There could only be a culture of consumption, in which workers' habits, interests, desires, were shaped by the cultural interests of capital, insofar as industrial capital was now in a position through the vast growth in the powers of technological reproducibility to structurally impose its sense of what is (profitably) pleasurable on workers' free time and on their purchasing power. But if mass culture has shaped the cultural interests and desires of workers in the modern period, workers have also been able to reshape the boundaries and content of what is assumed to be pleasurable and popular, according, that is, to the cynical lights of those who design and run the communication and pleasure industries. Since the 1950s this has been accomplished mostly through the increased involvement of (ex) workers in cultural production (specifically music), who have been able to establish new audiences and new values that opened up or challenged prevailing and would-be agreed notions of the popular. It is workers' resistance to the status and authority of inherited forms of the popular (specifically those that reinforce class conformism and populist sentiment), that has formed the basis of what we might call the vital, if uneven, production, since the 1950s, of a popular *counterculture*.

This remaking of the popular has been at the centre of those processes of individuation that have defined the dissociation of working-class identity from ethnographic class belonging since the Second World War, and can be traced back to the beginning of the workers' movement in the 1830s[3] and, therefore, represents those points where the negation of subjectivation produces new forms of individuation which detach themselves from class subjection (something that Horkheimer and Adorno were not prepared to acknowledge, or to be honest, couldn't see). This is why the countercultural production of individuation underwrites the extraordinary achievements of this popular, musical counterculture, for example, between 1965 and 1975 in Europe and North America, a truly astonishing upsurge of youthful working class and lower-middle-class cross-class creativity.[4] And, in turn, this is why an imposed model of high cultural authority never worked as a counter-hegemonic strategy for the workers' movement, because it bypassed

– even ignored – the active capacity of workers as producers and consumers to both transform the heteronomous conditions of those cultural forms and traditions notionally available to them (such as popular music), and, as such, challenge the mass culture that presumed to speak in their name. But since the 1970s the remaking of the popular as a marker of working class autonomy and creativity has been radically eroded, given the increased contraction on the part of the centripetal rationalizations of the culture industry, of the spaces of independent cultural activity that are involved in the re-channelling and revocation of dominant cultural values, rather than the pursuit simply of the marketization of the 'new' (namely, today, the serried and disaggregated addition of 'content' to an online depository).

Under real subsumption, then, the question of individuation is a process that is fundamentally fraught for capital. On the one hand, the production of new forms of individuation is crucial to the capacity of the system to reproduce itself through consensual and inclusive forms of pleasure and enjoyment and difference; the production of desire for desire through new forms of consumer discrimination produces those libidinal attachments that define individuation as self-realization. In this respect, individuation is attached to the use of cultural and 'lifestyle' products and services that define and secure the subject's consumer choices as freely determined and 'creative'. On the other hand, these forms of individuation and powers of judgement have to be 'held in' and channelled into a narrow range of activities, pastimes and cultural interests, values and ambitions that are compatible with the economies of scale of mass culture and the mass synchronization of public and individual memory – as the basis for the future capitalization of the memorialization of history as a market opportunity for the commodification of 'times past'[5]; individuation and desire, then, cannot swerve collectively too far from this path in order to invest libidinally in non-capitalizable or marginal activities, pastimes and critical practices (when, that is, these collectively threaten consumption), for this would disrupt the transition from work into commodified leisure and diminish the exercise of forms of profitable subjectivation. Thus, this is where individuation threatens the *de-individuating* functions of individuation under capitalist social reproduction as the production of enjoyment. Individuation, in other words, *serves* de-individuation as master, and therefore when individuation escapes this process, capital and the cultural industries development of individuation seek to capture, where possible, these attachments and affects for a re-stabilization of de-individuated desire. Capital, accordingly, is quick to adapt to non-market contingencies and see their commercial possibilities, and, as such, where possible, appropriates these novel and heterodox attachments and affects into an expanded process of de-individuated individuation; sometimes, though, it cannot and will not do this on the grounds that the stabilization of reproduction and the protection of various market sectors is the priority. And this is the point where de-individuation as an ideology is most exposed.

In those instances where capital is unwillingly to monetize and marketize it simply excludes such attachments and affects from public visibility, withdrawing credit culturally, so to speak, turning such attachments (and their ideological threat) into a desert of desire. This is where actual financial credit achieves its other and complementary ideological function: by withholding financial support (public or private funding) it withdraws legitimacy. But for the majority this withdrawal of legitimacy is not a problem, when it is noticed, that is, for what is not visible is not worth attention and *jouissance*. We might say, then, that capitalism produces individuation as a condition of its successful 'joyful' reproduction. And by definition this includes forms of individuation that resist capitalist processes of individuation itself, given the liberal refusal to discriminate hierarchically between individuations as the basis for market pluralism and freedom. But ultimately capital is only interested in stabilizing those forms of individuation that are able to secure the heteronomous forces of accumulation, and coterminously, a de-individuated desire for desire; desire, therefore, cannot escape the commodity form and de-individuation without censure; that is, if it does so, it has to be made incompatible with reason and pleasure, or more precisely reason as pleasure.

This struggle between individuation and de-individuation in the realms of cultural production and consumption has been central to individuation theory (or autonomy theory) since Adorno and Horkheimer's *Dialectic of Enlightenment*. In Axel Honneth, for instance, in his extensive philosophical genealogy of individuation and individualization, individuation represents the transformative and emancipatory destabilization of monological self-relation, identifiable with the emergence of the 'self' and bourgeois 'interiority' and individual prestige and personal validation, from the vestiges of feudalism and fealty to crown and alter.[6] Under the emerging capitalist division of labour and the development of a class of owners and managers of capitalist enterprises, the emergent bourgeoisie identifies its new class identity and interests and aspirations with classical precedent: the powers of discrimination, discernment and refined accumulation of property and goods of the landed aristocracy. But these forms of individuation were underwritten by, and even compromised by, the attachment of individuation to enlightened reason. The bourgeoisie didn't simply 'ape' the manners and cultural prerogatives of the aristocracy but, on the contrary, saw their role and historical mission as involved in the production of new and radical forms of individuation – new forms of secular self-realization and individual attainment – across all disciplines and practices, from horticulture to cosmology. This, in short, is the *raison d'etre* of the radical Enlightenment at the height of bourgeois self-acclaim (and its radical differentiation from aristocratic reaction): the rational production, creative application and philosophical justification of individuation as the incremental development of human powers. That this view of individuation and progress came under attack, even before the Enlightenment was able to state its case in full, is an indication, that bourgeois individuation, like aristocratic claims to individuation, confused, self-realization, self-acclaim and prestige with bourgeois civilization and progress. Hence, the singular importance of Jean-Jacques Rousseau to the individuation debate in the 1750s and 1760s, who held out little hope for universal, emancipated individuation under bourgeois society.

In the following, therefore, I want to look at the formation of the individuation problem in the bourgeois period (specifically in Rousseau and Marx), in the period, that is, before real subsumption and the structural convergence of individuation with de-individuation under the industrial production of subjectivity, and the formal crisis of the notion of the bourgeois self. This will allow us to prepare the critical ground for our later discussion of self-love and perfectionism. It will also establish a number of points of reference for our discussion of self-love, I-cracy and subjectivation today.

Rousseau's individuation

Rousseau's attack on bourgeois individuation occurs most famously in the Discourses (particularly 'A Discourse on the Arts and Sciences'),[7] and is defined, by what we might call its recognition of the *oppressive mimetic forces* of individuation as de-individuation: that is, by the tendency on the part of those with cultural power to secure their individuation through the reinforcement of tradition and the display of class power, as things to admire and aspire to in themselves. Admittedly Rousseau tends to focus on those visibly corrupt forms of public ritual and forms of self-display and self-validation attached to the arts – rituals and pursuits that inflate class authority on cultural matters over actual individual achievement – but overall, he has little sympathy for the idea that the bourgeoisie, and the bourgeoisie alone, is where individuation might be defined and secured. Indeed, he sees the intellectual elevation of certain forms of individuation in bourgeois society as actually in direct contravention of the spirit of universal human self-realization. Far from the attachment of individuation to enlightened reason increasing the powers of self-realization, they produce, rather, 'indolence and vanity'.[8]

> So long as government and law provide for the security and well-being of men in their common life, the arts, literature, and the sciences, less despotic though perhaps more powerful, fling garlands of flowers over the chains which weigh them down. They stifle in men's breasts that sense of original liberty, for which they seem to have been born; cause them to love their own slavery, and so make of them what is called a civilized people.[9]

As such, bourgeois individuation for Rousseau threatens the production, judgement and discernment of real individuation, those forms of individuation that he sees as attached to the hard-won labours and skills of those who are not tainted by indolence and vanity: principally peasants and artisans: 'It is under the homespun of the labourer, and not beneath the gilt and tinsel of the courtier, that we should look for strength and vigour of body.'[10] In this regard, Rousseau is the first philosopher to examine the content and value of individuation in relation to the social division of labour. Philosophers before, of course, had attacked the vanity and presumption of aristocratic claims to virtue and cultivation, but Rousseau is the first philosopher to systematically attack the pursuit of individuation on the part of the powerful as a critique of the hierarchical attachment of individuation to the higher achievements of the arts and sciences, the pursuit of which, by definition, excludes peasants and artisans – or the great majority of humanity. For Rousseau, the bourgeoise's pursuit of artistic and scientific distinction – as a struggle for individual prestige – opens up individuation to the corruptions of self-regard, the misrepresentations of intelligence as 'intellection' and a disdain for civic virtues. Rousseau's challenge is an extraordinary one then: far from welcoming and celebrating the Enlightenment's defence of education and the universal pursuit of individuation, he attacks the nascent Enlightenment from within, prefiguring Horkheimer and Adorno's own immanent critique of bourgeois progress.

Amour-Propre and *Amour de Soi*

In this light, Rousseau is a very particular kind of Enlightenment philosopher. He disparages abstract thought and bourgeois claims on the universal (which underwrite his perverse indifference to slave exploitation) and elevates 'feeling' above 'reason', yet at the same time is critically attuned to how government in the hands of the bourgeoise and aristocracy weakens and oppresses the self-interests of those without cultural and intellectual power. This is why his version of Enlightenment begins and ends in a concept of public virtue, given that virtue for Rousseau is that which separates the 'distinterestedly' true from the presumptions of privilege – that is, from those who assume to know and act on the basis of status alone. Given his antipathy to metropolitan intellectual self-regard and abstract thought, and his defence of peasant and artisanal common sense and stoutness of heart – for Rousseau it is natural feeling and natural affection that gives rise to wisdom – his thinking is crossed and shaped by a certain *völkisch* sentiment, making him less of a heterodox Enlightenment philosopher, than an Enlightenment *anti-philosopher*. In *A Discourse on Inequality* (1755), for instance, he attacks the would-be modern crisis of virtue as the excess and intrusive reach of what he calls the 'artificial in man's present nature'.[11] But artificiality has a precise meaning here in its 'anti-philosophic' articulation of the virtues of the 'natural'. This artificiality is not to be confused with the pleasures of distraction and the moneyed entitlements of privilege, but, rather, with that which underscores presumption and self-regard, *reason itself*, insofar as reason (judgement and reflection), is, for Rousseau, the fundamental creator of division and invidious comparison.

> It is reason which breeds pride and reflection which fortifies it; reason which turns man inward into himself; reason which separates him from everything which troubles or affects him. It is philosophy which isolates a man, and prompts him to say in secret at the sight of another suffering: 'Perish if you will; I am safe'.[12]

Hence intellectual presumption, coupled with the pleasures of social and cultural entitlement that are pursued specifically by the aristocracy and bourgeoisie, produces for Rousseau a pride that inflates individual self-worth and the pursuit of individuation, in fact, creates self-love or *amour-propre*. If all Rousseau's mature philosophy is taken up with the question of public virtue as a popular antipode to bourgeois and aristocratic power, it is also taken up with this notion of *amour-propre* as the very antipathy of virtue and natural feeling. For Rousseau, *amour-propre* represents the greatest constraint on the cultivation of virtue in the modern period, the thing, in turn, that threatens the very integrity of 'the people'. In this respect, in *A Discourse on Inequality* he constructs a genealogy of the rise of cultured artificiality and self-love in order to show how reason and civilization are accompanied by an increase in inequality derived from pride and self-regard.

> People grew used to gathering together in front of their huts or around a large tree; singing and dancing, true progeny of love and leisure, became the amusement, or rather the occupation, of idle men and women thus assembled. Each began to look at the others and to want to be looked at himself; and public esteem came to be prized. He who sang or danced the best; he who was the most handsome, the strongest, the most adroit or the most eloquent became the most highly regarded, and this was the first step towards inequality and the same towards vice.[13]

This history, admittedly, draws on a strange and obtusely idealized anthropology, but, it shows nonetheless, how sociability and culture – contrary to the claims of the Enlightenment *philosophes* – provide the conditions for the growth of *amour-propre* as comparative judgement and the erosion of natural affection. In other words, the greater claims that the *philosophes* make for the advance of bourgeois reason and individuation, the more reason distances itself from a natural equanimity. As Rousseau says, notoriously:

> So many authors have hastened to conclude that man is naturally cruel and needs civil institutions to make him peaceable, whereas in truth nothing is more peaceable than man in his primitive state; placed by nature at an equal distance from the stupidity of brutes and the fatal enlightenment of civilized man ... this state [this primitive state] was the true youth of

the world, and that all subsequent progress has been so many steps in appearance towards the improvement of the individual, but so many steps in reality towards the decrepitude of the species.[14]

So, we can discern here a clear critical lineage, even the feint outlines of a dialectic of enlightenment. As individuation, self-discernment, self-regard and self-realization grow – as the outcome of the bourgeois social division of labour and the expansion of sociability and social discourse – social division and a chronic pride in status and self-evaluation attach themselves to the ideal of self-realization as a form of explicit class entitlement. In fact, chronic pride as the carapace of class privilege takes over the very ideal of self-realization and individuation, overwhelmingly capturing *amour de soi* – a practical concern for one's own well-being – for *amour-propre* and the inflated concern for an evaluation of oneself in comparison to others and, therefore, in turn, supporting the domination of one's own self-regard – through the advance of reputation and status – over the presumed successes and failures of others. In these terms we can see in Rousseau the beginnings of a secular critique of semblance and modernity. As a society based on the subjugation of the subject to alienated images of self emerges, images based on false or irreal assumptions about true self-worth begin to flourish.

Rousseau's concern with *amour-propre*, then, in his struggle to construct a virtuous and martially vigilant civic-minded subject and concept of the 'people' defines those desires and impulses that threaten, from within, the ability of the 'people' to defend its liberty. On this score *amour-propre* comes to be identified by the philosopher, above all else, with what he perceives to be the greatest of all institutional threats to Republican virtue: the self-corrupting drive for hierarchical comparison in the *world of culture and the arts*. For it is in the advanced and sophisticated world of the arts and culture where individuation turns easily into competitive evaluation and narcissistic judgement and, therefore, represents the institutional formation of those values that directly threaten civic virtue. Indeed, for Rousseau *amour-propre* is predominantly a *cultural category*, given that the arts and culture are the places where 'looks' and 'public esteem' seek social advantage for the individual not only over other individuals competing for the same rewards, but over the common will and the 'people' as such. The arts and culture, accordingly, represents the space where the comparative self-evaluations of *amour-propre* are most inflamed. For *virtu publique* cannot function in a society where the dominant values of the society are *solely* cultural, that is, based on bourgeois and aristocratic 'taste' and discrimination as the exercise of exclusion and hierarchy. As Honneth argues in his discussion of Rousseau in *Disrespect*:

> The all-sided struggle for prestige ensuing from the rupture in our monological self-relation necessarily results in social inequality, since the artificial need for increased prestige – *amour propre* – is accompanied by the compulsion to acquire private property, which in turn paves the way for social classes.[15]

So, Rousseau sees government divorced from martial virtue, the 'general will' subordinate to self-interest, culture divorced from popular participation, knowledge divorced from 'natural affect' and *amour de soi* subordinate to *amour-propre*, as being a disaster for humanity. His anti-philosophic defence of individuation, in this respect, is not exactly consistent; he is far from being the unswerving critic of the Enlightenment; indeed, in contrarie fashion, he is no less a social 'constructionist' than other leading *philosophes* when it comes to education and human self-development. 'To form citizens is not the work of the day; and in order to have men it is necessary to educate them when they are children.'[16] 'From the first moment of life, men ought to begin learning to deserve to live.'[17] But, nevertheless, unlike his peers, he is sensitive to those points in Enlightenment thought where learning, education and cultural accomplishment are *corrupted by entitlement and presumption*, that is, where they are subject to arbitrary authority and unexamined tradition. As such, his infamous, *völkisch* defence of primitive 'pre-socialized' man is less fantastical and reactionary than we first might assume. Contrary to received opinion Rousseau does not argue that modern societies should return wholesale to premodern conditions of production and 'ignorance' and the unadorned and balanced virtues of pre-individuation. But, rather, he insists that what appears to be underdevelopment is, in fact, evidence of 'self-control'. In primitive communities – in societies not subject to an extended division of labour – humans live *within* themselves, whereas under bourgeois society men and women willingly and disastrously take their self-identity from the opinions and achievements of others. As Rousseau says in the *Discourse on Inequality*:

> The Savage lives within himself; sociable man, always outside himself, is capable of living only in the opinion of others and so to speak, derives

the *sentiment of his own existence* solely from their judgement ... in a word, forever asking of others *what we are*, without ever daring to ask it of ourselves.[18]

This is a singularly important argument in the development of emancipatory thought in the Western tradition, and as such has had a profound impact, in various ways, on Marx, Benjamin, Lacan and Adorno's respective treatment of the question of autonomy, experience and self-realization, and the development of their own anti-philosophic critiques of bourgeois individuation – that is, their respective critiques of the self-aggrandizing, professional and idealist identification in bourgeois society between the progress of scientific knowledge and freedom.[19] In this sense, for Rousseau the social as the production of meaning is as much the domain of alienation, misrecognition and pathological reproduction, as it is a space for communication, reason and sharing. And, therefore, in failing to acknowledge this split it is very easy to confuse the cultivation of one's own self-worth and powers of individuation with the flattering or persuasive and rational interests of others. This is Rousseau's key point: emancipation is not the critique of individuation as a realm of false prestige as such, but, rather the cultivation of an individuation that is free of the heteronomous power of de-individuation and therefore worthy of the hopes of self-realization for all. And fundamentally, this is what Marx inherits from Rousseau: a normative account of individuation, based significantly on the *relativization* of skills and creative attributes across the intellectual and practical; like Rousseau Marx disdains the notion that individuation and freedom are only matters of intellectual achievement and moral worth. But, nonetheless, Marx is also the indefatigable heir of the classical perfectionist tradition through Kant and Hegel, and as such, attaches singular importance to the universal achievements of the sciences and the arts, in which all humanity shares, and, hence, all are able to contribute intellectually at some level.

Marx's individuation

Perfectionism – as the philosophical tradition derived from Aristotle[20] – is that form of 'maximalizing morality' which obligates each person to develop, in the best way he or she can, his or her capacity for rationality, and has been central in various ways to the claims of all three 'modern' emancipatory traditions of engagement with the self and human capacity and flourishing: late medieval Thomism (Thomas Aquinas),[21] largely derived from St. Augustine, the radical Enlightenment (Rousseau, Friedrich Schiller, Denis Diderot, Immanuel Kant) and the post-Enlightenment (G.W.F. Hegel and Marx).[22] The first tradition focuses on the development of rationality and moral perfection in the light of the knowledge of the love of God and 'good works', the second on the development of rationality and moral perfection and the development of intellectual and artistic skills – the aesthetic life – as the basis for human 'wholeness' and the third on the development of rationality as a form of non-moral perfectionism (although, Hegel and Marx differ on this issue). That is, in this tradition, perfectionism is not solely, or predominantly, a question of moral virtue; rather, human development and flourishing covers all aspects of human capacity or 'essence': the practical, physical, intellectual and artistic – the non-moral perfectionist tradition emphasizing, consequently, a wider range of perfectionist goods.[23] The crucial distinction, however, between the latter version of perfectionism and the moral perfectionism of the first two traditions – expressly in Marx – is that the achievements of 'one' is of necessity inseparable from the achievement of 'all', and therefore, perfectionism as an act of purposeful and self-transformative individuation is only truly achievable as a transindividual process; to 'perfect' oneself, in whatever capacity, is to be part of a collective process of shared 'perfectionism' that calls forth the integral transformation of all (a transindividuality that, in fact, is not alien to Kant's post-Christian and anti-ecclesiastical moral perfectionism; Kant, contrary to conventional opinion, is not a moral *individualist,* but rather, a *moral existentialist*).[24] Hence if in Kant and Marx perfectionism is highly attenuated, if it is not experienced by all under shared conditions, nevertheless it is the *self and the self alone* that pursues the social 'ends' of perfectionism, insofar as no one else can achieve these ends in the name of 'perfectionism for all' for oneself; no one person or external agency can 'award' perfectionism to another. (The failure of Stalinism, and Maoism post-1949, to act on Marx's perfectionist legacy, is fundamental to the constitutive nihilism of Stalinism's and Maoism's abstract collectivism, and its functionalist attachment to Party and State.) But, if Marx's perfectionism is an open and maximizing model of self-transformation that importantly disconnects human flourishing and development from purely moral perfection as an abstract ideal alone, his idea of 'all roundedness' is militated by the contingencies and variability of human ability and needs. If Marx distinguishes his version of perfectionism from the too close association of perfection with the mastery of an abstract ideal, by maximalizing human perfectionism beyond the narrow development of the higher faculties – moral and intellectual – into a broad range of practical, intellectual, cognitive and creative skills and accomplishments, he also recognizes that such 'all roundedness' is the outcome of a process of unconditioned individuation; 'all roundedness' can take many forms.

For Marx, then, contra Rousseau, the bourgeoise's pursuit of 'higher' forms of individuation does not imperil individuation but, in a sense, 'steals' and reconfigures it in the interests of bourgeois power. *That the arts and sciences produce and reproduce forms of class domination does not diminish what exceeds their class function.* This is where Marx implicitly attacks the 'classist' leftist critiques of perfectionism that draw on Rousseau and its legacy in Jacobin 'levelling', in the *Grundrisse*, and, as such, those who would dismiss all learned culture and achievement as elitist. Rousseau's critique of bourgeois *amour-propre*, consequently, for Marx, is touched too much by *völkisch ressentiment*; Rousseau blocks off both a recognition of the achievements of individuation under early bourgeois culture and the possibilities of the non-bourgeois classes refunctioning of the higher processes of individuation. Hence for Marx the powers of human individuation have to expand and find new resources, and, therefore, need to be grounded in the most advanced conditions of knowledge and technique; otherwise, they fall into regression and the opposite prevails – the hypostatization of individuation as the development of craft-based knowledges and skills and a return to a condescending vision of the majority as the passive and adaptive cultivators of mere 'practical reason'. Such *ressentiment*, then, only leads in one direction only: to a populist identity with the provincial and perspectival. In a rejection of this *ressentiment*, Marx defines his own anti-philosophic position. Following Rousseau, he defends non-bourgeois claims on individuation as an attack on a spurious and narrow professional identification between the intellect and self-realization, but in the spirit of Kant and Hegel, he also clears out all the *völkisch* anti-intellectual tendencies and attributes attached to this position in Rousseau's thinking, as ultimately regressive.

Rousseau and Marx's conceptions of individuation, then, offer quite different, even conflicting, versions of self and autonomy. One seeks a limit to intellectual individuation through the cultivation of civic virtue and artisanal crafts; the other sees no reason to put any limits on intellectual and practical individuation at all; indeed, he encourages its Promethean possibilities. In this respect, there is no stable solution to this conflict, no harmonious point of resolution, between these positions. But importantly Marx recognizes that, in defending an unbounded individuation, there is in principle no conflict between Rousseau's delimited individuation and the *ideal* of self-realization as such. That is, the higher reaches of individuation are not incompatible with a Rousseauvian investment in artisanal skills, as long as both are free of the coercions and hierarchies of the capitalist social division of labour. There is no greater virtue to excellence in higher mathematics, than there is in being a skilful barrel maker, painter of watercolour landscapes or teller of jokes.

Nevertheless, if Marx relativizes human perfection, he nonetheless does not tie the equalization of human capacity and individuation solely to the forms of workplace labour. The dissolution of the capitalist division of labour is not simply a means of 'balancing' intellectual work with manual work, but of challenging the class-based attachment of individuation to occupation as such. This is why, irrespective of what (limited) kinds of necessary labour one might perform under a system free of the social division of labour (whether for a few hours a week one is clearing away garbage or working as a dental assistant); for Marx, there should be no occupational and artificial boundaries placed on individuation. Hence, the crucial importance of Marx's famous encomium in *The German Ideology* about the value of 'all round' development of skills and capacities:

> In communist society, where nobody has one exclusive sphere of activity but each can become accomplished in any branch he wishes, society regulates the general production and thus makes it possible for me to do one thing today and another tomorrow, to hunt in the morning, fish in the afternoon, rear cattle in the evening, criticise after dinner, just as I have a mind, without ever becoming hunter, fisherman, shepherd or critic.[25]

Under a system in which freely determined labour shapes individuation, the attachment of status to specialist knowledge and practices will no longer prevail, allowing all to find some proficiency – even expertise – in both intellectual and manual skills. Rousseau's critique of the division of labour then ties individuation too closely to a naturalized anthropology; for Marx individuation is not occupation based and class specific, but the domain of universal accomplishment.

Individuation and egoism

In this light, we can see how much of the individuation question is prefigured by the issue of the 'ego', as the source of individuation and difference in Marx's thought. Marx's early writing is principally concerned with the relationship between individuation and self-realization and the philosophical status of the 'self' and egoism, at a time when questions of the aesthetic self, self-realization and human flourishing (derived from a critical reading of Friedrich Schiller's *On the Aesthetic Education of Man* (1795)[26] and Rousseau's defence of *perfectibilité* and enlightened *amour-propre*[27]) were still uppermost in his interests, having just given up his self-identity as a poet. In the *Economic and Philosophic Manuscripts* and *The German Ideology*, for instance, Marx sets out to settle scores with the pure subjectivism or bourgeois interiority of German idealism and German Romanticism. In a critique of Johann Fichte and Friedrich Schelling's absolute interiorization of thought Marx argues that the form of individual consciousness and what appears to be the individual attributes and achievements of human activity are *constitutively* social. 'Not only is the material of my activity given to me as a social product (as is even the language in which the thinker is active); my *own* existence *is* social activity … '[28] The individual is 'the social being.'[29] This, of course, is the founding programme of Marx's materialism and the basis for his socialization of individuation; self-realization *is* the transindividual work of collective thought and community; the transindividual is the means by which self-realization is accomplished. 'I make of myself for society and with the consciousness of myself as a social being.'[30] But running through this early materialist programme – as a supplementary force – is the critique of the critique of the 'ego', in the late Romanticism of Schelling and Schiller. In their writing the 'ego' is the uncontrollable excess of the social as an extraneous destabilization of subjectivity; this is because as a consequence of the French Revolution the 'ego' has lost its spirit and brought about the terrifying release of uncontrollable passion and the would-be loss of reason. As such, 'ego' becomes a threat to selfhood and a threat to community, or more precisely, to 'good order', 'good practice' and social stability. In contrast, however, the early Marx sees the supplementary excess of the 'ego' as the *living substance* of community, the means by which individuation as social practice is given form and agency and, consequently, the passion of the 'ego' is not just the invasive and regressive agent of disharmony and ultimately unreason, but the means by which the realization of the powers of the subject displaces or challenges the given form of a community and the processes of socialization; the singularities of 'ego' negate the assumed transparency of community and tradition, and defy their assumed and given needs and interests. As Marx says in *The Holy Family*:

> Communists do not put egoism against self-sacrifice or self-sacrifice against egoism ... Communist theoreticians ... are distinguished precisely because they alone have discovered throughout history the 'general will' is created by individuals who are defined as 'private persons'.[31]

This is why in the *Economic and Philosophical Manuscripts*, community and the realization of 'individuality'[32] don't seem to quite cohere. 'Social activity and social enjoyment exist by no means *only* in the form of some *directly* communal activity and *directly* communal enjoyment.'[33] But more pertinently, it is in Marx's very earliest known writings, his doctoral thesis on Democritus and Epicurus, where the problem of the 'ego' is radically exposed, for we can see more clearly in this writing how the 'ego' for Marx is not the enemy of emancipation but paradoxically that which shapes and drives it.

'What is possible may also be otherwise'

In his dissertation *Difference Between the Democritean and Epicurean Philosophy of Nature* (1841),[34] Marx distinguishes between Democritus and Epicurus on the grounds that despite Democritus's demonstrably more distinguished claims to scientific reason, Epicurus (the sensualist) is the greater scientific thinker. Discussing these two philosophers' respective theories of the atom and the void, Marx asserts that for Democritus 'the atom means only *stoicheion*, a material substrate,'[35] and 'blind necessity',[36] whereas for Epicurus the form determination of the atom is subject to declination, insofar as the atom's shape and arrangement, and as such position, are differences the 'atom possesses in relation to something else'.[37] Far from the atom functioning as the passive determinate of appearances, it is the active 'repulsion and the ensuing conglomerations of the qualified atoms' from which the 'world of appearances now emerges'.[38]

Hence, as soon as [Epicurus] posits a property and thus draws the consequence of the material nature of the atom, he counter-posits at the same time determinations which again destroy this property in its own sphere and validate instead the concept of the atom. *He therefore determines all properties in such a way that they contradict themselves.* Democritus, on the other hand, nowhere considers the properties in relation to the atom itself, nor does he objectify the contradiction between concept and existence which is inherent in them. His whole interest lies rather in representing the qualities in relation to concrete nature, which is to be formed out of them. To him they are merely hypotheses to explain the plurality which makes its appearance.[39]

For Epicurus it is the particular qualities that atoms possess that determine their patterns of repulsion. Consequently, for Marx, the crucial distinction between Democritus and Epicurus lies in the fact that Epicurus is the first philosopher-scientist to separate the abstract form of the atom from its material side. Thus, for Epicurus the concept of the atom is realized in the differential negative force of its repulsion and therefore its *abstraction* from its essence. Democritus, in contrast, 'sees in the repulsion only the material side, the fragmentation, the change, and not the ideal side, according to which all relation to something else is negated and motion established as self-determination'.[40] But, overall, what interests Marx here is not Epicurus's specific contribution to ancient physics, but, rather, how Epicurus's concept of abstract individuality expresses itself 'through the whole of [his] philosophy',[41] as a critique of the idea of a static and independent nature, and therefore, a rejection of the notion of nature as simply possessing the individuality of things, as opposed to individuality shaping and determining the nature of things themselves. For Marx, Epicurus's principle of abstract individuation may push atomistics ultimately into dissolution and opposition to the universal, thereby weakening the real investigation of nature, but his notion of the atom as an active principle of indetermination provides the philosophical ground for the critique of Sufficient Reason, and as such, the notion that 'what is possible may also be otherwise'.[42] Consequently, Epicurus's application of concrete forms of repulsion in his physics in his social thought attests to his atomistic theory of repulsion as being the 'first form of self-consciousness'.[43] That is, repulsion corresponds in Epicurus's philosophy to abstract individuality as a form of egoism that swerves or declines from received unities.

Marx has an oblique, 'secondary' aim in defending Epicurus as a critic of positivism and as a sensualist: a critique of the reactionary account of egoism that had gained ground since Thermidor and the French Revolution, and in a highly aestheticist fashion, in the qualified notion of the 'ego' in Romanticism. This qualified understanding of 'ego' is evident in both Schiller and Hegel's response to the French revolution. Hegel, alone amongst his contemporaries was the unbowed defender of the Revolution, and as such held the egoism of unmet needs to be indivisible from freedom. But, nevertheless, the rise of modern forms of individuation for Hegel had also destroyed the glorious 'unities' of ancient civilization, and this loss profoundly shaped his understanding of modernity[44]; in Schiller, an early defender of the revolution and then later its rebarbative critic, egoism is given far less dialectical space. Far from being the negative motor of history it confirms the rise of a new barbarity that the progress of the French Revolution was unable to correct:

> Reason has cleansed itself from the deceptions of the senses and delusions of sophistry, and philosophy itself, which first made us disloyal to nature, now loudly and insistently calls us back into its arms – why, then, are we still barbarians? ... A complacent egoism seizes the heart of the man of the world.[45]

We see the beginnings here, accordingly, of the first shoots of a non-identitary dialectic in Marx in which the triad of 'ego', repulsion, and self-consciousness is defended against the bourgeois reduction of individuation – that is when individuation threatens bourgeois order – to *mere* measureless passion and appetite and loss of harmony. In the early writings, 'egoism' and 'atomism' figure not as evidence of the decline or loss of reason, or evidence of the misty effusions of bourgeois interiority, but rather as agents of the opposite: as a non-identitary incursion into illusory unities. As Mikhail Lifshitz was to argue perceptibly in 1933, Marx in his dissertation:

> Restored Epicurus as an enlightened thinker who discovered in egoism the foundation of human society. In deviating in its descent, the atom manifests self-love, personal interests, but it is only through this deviation that it can meet other atoms in space and form various contributions with them. Mutual repulsion creates the sociality of atoms.[46]

As such Marx's critique of bourgeois egoism covers two principles:

The egoism of 'private interest', seeking exclusive domination and oligarchy, such as Robespierre and his government fought against. [And] on the other hand ... the egoism of revolutionary toilers opposing unsocial acts on the part of citizens: the mass egoism of peasants wishing to divide landowners' estates or that of industrial workers demanding better conditions of work and freedom from employers' whims. Such is the revolutionary dialectic of the 'principle of atomism', its self-negation and transition to a higher level.[47]

Effectively, the collision of atomistic egos is the conflicted agency by which dead unities are dismantled and new unities – through deviation – are created; the point being that new unities cannot be modelled simply on the transcription or modification of old unities. The declination of the atom brought to self-consciousness as a living abstraction, is both *arche* and *stoicheion*; both revolutionary principle of disconnection, connection and reconnection and a state of inertia. In this sense 'ego' takes on a mass (conflicted) Hegelian role in these early writings of Marx: change is produced through the diremption of the singular as a claim for individuation on the collective, as opposed to change occurring organically through the measured calculations of a collective identical to itself. In other words, if the transindividual produces the conditions for socialized individuation, individuation is the diremptive force that challenges the given forms of socialization.

Individuation and transindividuation

There is an important issue at stake here that has significant implications in thinking through disaggregation and the contemporary forces of individuation–de-individuation today. That is, the struggle for, and realization of, unmet needs of humanity lies in a perpetual conflict under the capitalist division of labour, between individuation and the collective. Indeed, this is the great theme that critical theory, Western Marxism and psychoanalysis inherit from the early Marx. As such, it defines the very terrain of class identity–disidentification, self-realization and community, the *jouissance* of self-love and the necessities of *amour de soi*, in the modern period; *individuation is the thing that emancipation promises and workers desire, but it is also the thing that escapes the collective agency of its realization.* This is why in the twentieth century, after the destruction of revolutionary forms of individuation under Stalinism into a reified (and anti-Marxist) concept of anthropological class belonging, so much theoretical and critical energy has been spent on thinking through and diagnosing how what escapes working class identity can be re-incorporated into a worker's programme and an emancipatory politics. That is, the unifying problem of agency and class identity, certainly from Lukács' *History and Class Consciousness*, in twentieth-century Marxist theory, is how the supplementarity and indisciplinarity and promise of individuation can be 'stabilized' within the formation of a collective working-class identity, particularly in the wake of the demise of the classical workers' movement, when today skilled industrial workers only comprise a minority of the working population. In this sense, the extensive reflection in this period on class composition, de-composition and re-composition is precisely a response to this problem: how is the promise and demand for individuation to be actively sustained within a unifiable class politics and unified workers' movement? All the conceptual and strategic refashioning of agency and class, identity and class, identity and the 'collective', the political and the party or political and non-party organization, from the 1960s, then, falls under these considerations. That is, the multiplicitous conceptual reinventions and reordering of the limits and vicissitudes of class identity and agency in the second half of the twentieth century and in the beginning of the twenty-first century (the 'marginal', 'new subjects', the 'post-industrial' subject, the 'multitude', the 'counter-hegemonic' front, 'movementism', 'universal proletarianization', the popular 'consciousness of capital', the networked communist 'party of the multiple') all address the same problem: how can the actuality and promise of individuation that escapes working-class identity, serve some notion of unity that incorporates both the immediate needs and unmet needs of workers and non-workers alike. In this sense these radical and revolutionary re-conceptualizations seek to resolve – or least work through – despite their very different political allegiances, the flagrant and persistent contradiction of bourgeois politics – the fact that capitalist subjectivation encourages a core incompatibility with respect to social identity, revealed extensively in the parliamentary programmes of all conservative and centrist social democratic parties around the globe: namely, the ongoing conflict between the promise of an unfettered individuation, defined, shaped and supported by the market, and, conversely, a commitment to, and belief in, the continuity of stable cross-class community (invariably these days mediated through national self-identity) as relief from the relentlessness of this process of market individuation. Bourgeois politics, in a sense, functions and reproduces its pleasures of expectation and self-realization and disappointment through this dysfunctional opposition.

Marx's great insight in the early writings lies in the fact that individuation is not a problem which class agency can simply subsume and assimilate as part of unified working class self-identity and 'collective class consciousness'. But, rather, it is that which determines and shapes the efficacy and possibility of class identity and agency itself. In other words, Marx recognizes that the promise and actuality of individuation makes class a fundamentally unstable category of subjectivation, particularly when the labour process consistently expels living labour, dissolves the integrity of the collective worker and detaches the worker in the place of work from any active knowledge of the production process; 'class belonging', as a result, becoming a mere formal belonging, as Marx noticed in the 1860s.

There are two important methodological issues here given that we live an extended period in which working-class identity as formal class belonging has deepened (as an express manifestation of surplus *jouissance*) under the integrative forces of real subsumption. Firstly, Marx's early work on individuation and egoism gives us a far more long-range view of social disaggregation – or unity-in-separation – than recent accounts of 'control society', neoliberal governmentality and 'joyful alienation' would suggest; questions around disaggregation are far from being a 'post-workers movement' issue alone; individuation and subjectivation are there from *the very beginning* of industrial modernity and the division of labour; and secondly, that hidden inside the subjective instability of class as a category and, therefore, as an immanent factor in the realities of social disaggregation are a range of theoretical assumptions that present a quite different Marx than is defined by the conventional chronology of early (ethical-critical), mid (mature-systemic) and late ('eccentric'-heterogeneous) Marx. Indeed, the Marx that emerges – without sounding flippant – is one that we might say has been topped and tailed: that is, the beginning and end of Marx's career as a revolutionary form the core continuity of his life's work, and the massive, research-heavy writing on political economy forms the interregnum. This provides a very different 'epistemological break' between the ethical-humanist and the 'scientific' that Althusser once proposed. That is, the early ethical-critical work and late 'post-political economy' work provide across the decades a link between the early pre-figurative critique of capitalism as a systematic and oppressive engine of de-individuation, and a late retroactive *re-assimilation* of this early critique as a revaluation of the *social form* under which individuation might best flourish. In this respect, in retrospect, there is way of seeing the mid-period interregnum as an extensive prelude to a disconfirmation of its findings in practice, as if Marx had to find out theoretically what he had intuited all along: that the forms of capitalist socialization that workers produce and reproduce defensively under capitalism, cannot provide an affirmative basis, intellectually, culturally – in the name of progress and individuation – of a post-capitalist society of free producers, given that capitalism destroys the identity of the worker as worker, indeed, produces, as I have outlined, the very conditions of the worker's subjective ruination as worker as the constitutive subjective form of this struggle. This is why class struggle is caught up in a paradox vis-à-vis individuation: workers need to organize *as* workers, despite the disidentification that workers feel between their unstable identity as workers and workers' collective identity in the abstract, and despite the conflict between the need to organize as workers as a class and the wider emancipatory requirement of class struggle as the means by which workers fulfil their exit from class itself.

Consequently, worker's dissociation from their identity as workers (as an expression of the form that capitalist growth and labour power takes) is the very condition *of* workers' identity as workers; there are no workers that are identical to their role as workers, no stable workers-as-workers. This is why workers' consciousness is split between their identity as workers (the fictive unity) and their constant struggle for autonomy beyond their given class identity; dissociation between occupation and class identity, therefore, is the very basis under which workers *do* organize. Workers organize, *in spite* of this subjective ruination. Two subjective positions present themselves in the wake of this.

Workers either adapt themselves to this ruination consistent with capitalist reason, what we might call the basis for the *jouissance* of capitalist individuation; or this ruination opens up a space for the 'consciousness of capital' and unmet needs beyond waged labour, and repressive forms of individuation. The latter option, of course, is profoundly unstable, as we have seen in detail, given the power of the pleasure industries attached to the first position; immiseration is accompanied, and thrives on, a range of passive pleasures and adaptive actions. Yet, the subjective ruination of workers as workers does present a serious cultural and social problem for capital: that is, as the gap by which an emancipatory non-identitary class politics is opened up beyond the immediate needs of workers, the subjective ruination of workers as workers reveals how capitalism is unable to reproduce and sustain the very thing that secures its profits and growth: labour power; particularly so now, given the mass exclusions of living labour from the global economy. Thus, paradoxically, the subjective ruination of workers as workers is the subjective space through which the historical contingency of labour power is in fact exposed and, as such, the political space through which the uncoupling of individuation from political economy, and the exit of producers from the social division of labour, will emerge.

In this light, in the very late writings Marx draws a line under the link between workers' collective power, industrial progress and modernity, insofar as he distances himself from the notion that socialized individuation (or communist individuated community) can only realistically be generated and sustained by workers through the slow and conflicted passage of humanity through the brutal conglomerate forces of industrialized capitalist development. In this Marx reformulates his early disparate and heterogenous thoughts on the disaggregative forces of capitalism and the crisis of class belonging into a range of mature reflections on the critique of industrial progress, in his innovative writing on the popular Russian commune. Indeed, at the end of his life rather than writing the anticipated next volumes of *Capital*, Marx (much to Engels's chagrin; he wanted to destroy Marx's voluminous last notes) learned Russian and began researching the history of the peasant commune form as an alternate path to large-scale capitalist industrialization and to workers' emancipatory passage through the de-individuated hell of real subsumption. The late-nineteenth-century Russian commune for Marx represents those aspects and immanent (non-capitalist) forms of a 'higher culture' already at work in capitalism. In this he challenges his own (occasional) earlier historicist assumptions about the modern and modernization: 'the form of communist property in Russia is the most modern form of the archaic type which has itself gone through a whole series of evolutionary changes.'[48] This is because once the state and industrialized capital steps in to destroy the would-be premodern form of the rural commune, 'the economic superiority of communal property – as the basis of co-operative and combined labour – is lost',[49] revealing how the modern and modernization might find an alternative path through the 'archaic',[50] rather than at its expense or destruction. This anti-historicism is neither a fit of premodern nostalgia on Marx's part in his old age – confronted by the ravages of European industrialization – nor is it a betrayal of his critique of Rousseau's *völkischism*. On the contrary, the advanced rural commune acts as a historical flash point for the idea that the modern can be incubated in the premodern:

> Precisely because it is contemporaneous with capitalist production, the rural commune may appropriate all its positive achievements without undergoing its [terrible] frightful vicissitudes ... Did Russia have to undergo a long Western-style incubation of mechanical industry, steamships, railways, etc.? ... Everyone would see the commune as the element in the regeneration of Russian society, an element of superiority over countries still enslaved by the capitalist regime ... In short, the rural commune finds it in a state of crisis that will end only when the social system is eliminated through the return of modern societies to the 'archaic' type of communal property.[51]

Marx's anti-historicism here, then, acts as a radical form of atemporal retrodiction, in which 'archaic' social forms potentially represent a higher form of collective ownership and production, given their absence from processes of industrial-scale de-individuation. As Marx was to say, drawing on this work, in his introduction to the Second Russian edition of the *Communist Manifesto* (1882): 'Can the Russian *obschchina*, a form of primeval common ownership of land, even if greatly undermined, pass directly to the higher form of communist ownership?'[52]

It is perfectly understandable, then, how Marx's late writing has come to form a new corpus of anti-historicist Marxism. Marx's writing on the Russian peasant commune synthesizes the anti-progresssivist-progressive tendencies of the early writing (particularly the work on machines and the expulsion of living labour in the *Grundrisse*), in order to de-temporalize the intellectual and imaginary assumptions of the evolutionary development of the productive forces. It therefore repositions Marx's thought at the very centre of the crisis of metabolic reproduction, living labour and unilinear growth–non-growth today. Across the work of Daniel Bensaïd, Jarius Banaji, Massimiliano Tomba and Goldner,[53] for example, there is an assimilation of late Marx's reflections on the Russian commune into the concept, broadly, of a *post-continuitist* modernity. As Tomba argues:

> The non-capitalist forms of 'precapitalism' functions as indicators for possible postcapitalist forms. The issue is not a vague romantic longing after premodern forms of civilization … The unwritten history of the oppressed cannot be grasped with the tools of historicist historiography, but only with a sensitivity toward the different temporal rhythms of histories that are simultaneously present. From this perspective, non-capitalist forms should not be regarded as stages towards the capitalist mode of production and as the individual's liberation from the communal bonds, but as contemporary alternatives.[54]

Indeed, as Goldner declares, this is the post-historicist Marx, 'first suppressed by Engels, and lost for more than a century in the Second, Third and Fourth Internationals' confusion of the developmental tasks of the bourgeois revolution and those of the proletarian revolution'.[55]

In this body of anti-historicist writing, there is a systematic attempt to reorder Marx's priorities, indeed to re-temporalize the concerns of the writing on the basis of linking the late explicit critique of historicism to the interim critique of the value form and thoughts on the limits of collective labour power. But little of this new writing on anti-linearity and historical multi-temporality touches, specifically, on the question of individuation and the re-temporalization of desire and unmet needs, and, as such, generally on the contribution of the debate on individuation as part of the conceptual reflection on the transition problem today (and this is where Marx's work on egoism and declination is crucial) – that is, beyond a gestural inflection towards re-temporalization and autonomy. Certainly, in Tomba and Banaji, there is a residual reliance on an orthodox Marxist anthropology, in their respective notions that the release of Marxism and emancipatory politics from the prison house of unilinearity and historicism will release class struggle from the burden of cultural de-individuation. Thus, on one level when Tomba talks about the successful bourgeois 'struggle against class struggle'[56] in this epoch, he rightly recognizes how the suppression of Marx as an anti-historicist and anti-teleological thinker is part of the general regressive, anti-Enlightenment climate and war on living labour. But on another level, there seems to be little reflection on how the freeing up workers' identities from the old unities intersects with those powerful libidinal forces of disaggregation and de-individuation that rush in to fill the void. Hence, it is not adequate enough to talk about the 'struggle against class struggle' as evidence of the war against labour alone, as if the massive forces of these processes of disaggregation were solely a consequence of *ideological enforcement*, or conversely the martial *ineffectualness* of the contemporary workers' movement to protect jobs and wages. As we have discussed, this disaggregation is the living and entangled space of labour and *jouissance* and the 'joyful' production and reproduction of economic reason; the living space, indeed, in which the terrain of libidinal economy intersects with class relations and the subjective ruination of workers as workers.

After subjective ruination and the transition problem

Questions of individuation–de-individuation and perfectionism, and self-love, consequently, require a greater integration and theoretical reflection into the framework of the new anti-historicism and anti-progressivist progress. For, if model three commits theory and practice to a working through of the libidinal subject and subjective ruination, it also requires a thorough analysis of how individuation and self-love are challenged and changed by the new (four-fold) transformation of political economy, I outlined earlier. How, that is, these possibilities reconnect to a radical rethinking of the transition problem: what subjective and objective resources are available, immanent and extant, that are able to break with de-individuation and the neotonic/demonic-infinite structure of the commodity form? What social and cultural resources from below can capture and sustain a range of anti-capitalist practices, affects and forms of individuation as a transitional set of techniques? This is why Marx's early writing on declination comes into its own within this framework: there is a way of seeing Marx's theory of egoism and concept of socialized individuation as a critique of 'dead unities', as part of the historical transformation of the workers' movement itself. In other words, hidden in the long-term realities of disaggregation and de-individuation is the promise of a non-dominative and 'post-work' individuation and perfectionism.

Individuation and Class Reproduction

So, in this respect, we might say the workers' liberation from the old Party-state and ethnographic class identities represents the promise of new affects; new forms of individuation. For, paradoxically, the split between class consciousness and the reproduction of the class relation may weaken the possibility of worker solidarity, but it also distances workers from their capture by the workerist machinery of the old workers' movement. Indeed, its release from these relations and expectations actually draws attention to what class subjectivation actually meant under the old reformist and statist workers' attachments. Class subjectivation was predominantly a defensive mode of class attachment to workers' rights and welfarism. If, this provided the symbolic strength and practical resources for reformism, once reformism went as a living ideology in the late 1970s, so did the sense of unity and a shared history; hence the increasing sense of the workers' movement under post-war capitalism as a disaggregative unity; this is the reality of collective class consciousness today.

Yet, this separation of the working class from anything resembling a workers' movement, and from collective class consciousness, thus, importantly, has an upside, and as such represents the immanent negative function of labour power in the present period. In the release of the worker from collective class consciousness as a workerist fictive-unity, the issue of subjective individuation becomes properly a political and cultural matter, that is, it reattaches the separation of the worker from the ethnographic hold of class identity and its old identitary machinery as a newly emancipatory question. In other words, if workers are indifferent or antagonistic to being workers, or unable even to be workers, what might replace the old processes of workers' movement/party/trade union subjectivation?[57] The further extension of workers' identity (specular relation) into that of the petty bourgeoisie, as we see today on a global scale? The nostalgic attachment to non-class-based collective substitutes for class consciousness as in the rise of nationalist driven forms of authoritarian populism? Or, more productively, *the reconfiguration of the processes of capitalist individuation as an emancipatory and transindividual political horizon beyond workerist-class identity*? Thus, if we are prepared to accept the validity of the latter, the present period is actually more interesting than we might dare assume for revolutionary thought; insofar as workerism and the old workers' movement fast disappear into the past, it opens the door to a new discussion of emancipation and the relationship between class reproduction, and crucially, *post-capitalist* individuation, or what I call here the tradition of radical perfectionism.

In this respect, Endnotes are correct: that the communist horizon of the present can no longer be based on the hoped-for arrival of a new unity, based as the old unity was on an inert and fetishized notion of collective class consciousness, that never in fact arrives. Today when workers come together, 'they no longer do so as a class, for their class belonging is precisely what divides them. Instead they come together under the name of some other unity ... which appears to widen their capacity to struggle.'[58] As such, the diversification of struggles announces itself today more concretely 'in a growing consciousness of capital'.[59] Endnotes, however, do not explain what this concreteness might mean in any enforceable sense, or indeed, how 'class consciousness' might mediate a consciousness of capital, and conversely, how a consciousness of capital might generate new forms of individuation and class struggle. Or, indeed, how a consciousness of capital might distinguish itself from the sanguine and commonplace inclusivities of Toni Negri and Paulo Virno's industrial working class substitute, the 'multitude' – or even worse, how it might distinguish itself from a renewed identity politics.

In this respect the group's announcement of a new horizon possesses a kind of enigmatic brevity, particularly given the severe, but invigorating qualities of their history of the workers' movement. Yet, the construction of a new politics and new unities out of the disaggregative experience of capital nevertheless provides a new, if fragile, space of subjectivity, insofar as the conflictual emergence of new 'atomistic energies' touches again on foundational questions of the relationship between *amour-propre* (comparative self-regard) and *amour de soi* (individual survival) in this epoch of capitalistic individuation and love of the love of self.

That is, the question of atomism, as in Marx's day, recalls us to the profound historical stakes of perfectionism as human flourishing and self-realization, given that the conflation of *amour de soi* and 'soft' perfectionism ('self-development') is the terrain upon which capital is now pursuing its 'friendly' and 'joyful' work, indeed, is now pursuing its interests in heightened comparative pleasure and status in ways that would be unrecognizable for the majority of workers who laboured and desired under the old workers' movement. If the management and valorization of a narrow kind of perfectionism is the means by which capitalism now seeks to maintain its regime of 'joyful alienation' and its identification of the love of the love of self with autolatry and the uxorious love of capitalism, it is also the terrain from out of which self-love will find the resources to critique and exit capital's 'friendly' and 'joyful' work. The *jouissance* that drives the love of the love of self prepares the ground for the subject's recognition that the love of the love of self and capitalism are not compatible. Indeed, the 'growing consciousness of capital' is the means by which new forms of individuation, affect and self-love will produce new forms of unity and reason in the emancipatory struggle against the production of value, or more generally 'capitalist life': a new *amour-propre*. The strategic and political point here, though for any communist practice, is not to assume some miraculous meeting of 'atomistic energies' and creative individuation released from the dead unities and attachments of the old workers' movement, but a recognition that new forms of political subjectivity will be increasingly tied to the increasing and oppressive gap between capital's capture of the love of the love of self and *amour-propre* as a non-comparative and non-competitive ideal as a transformative horizon.[60]

Yet, we should not confuse this move with a standard form of the negation of the negation. My recovery of Marx's account of Epicurean egoism is not an affirmation of the 'secret' emancipatory work of history. The conditions we live under – proletarian deskilling and the destruction of knowledge and individuation for many – are as grim as we might imagine.[61] We cannot simply reframe Marx's Epicurean 'atomism' as a new *amour-propre* affirmatively, to make the loss of the old workers' movement more palatable. Cognitively reframing the love of the love of self is no magic bullet for the libidinal investments in 'joyful alienation' and the pain involved in acting on 'truth' under neoliberalism. Yet, in noting that Marx's account of egoism is a *transindividual* move – a move for new unities – we can nevertheless avoid – as an emancipatory claim on the future – the chronic dualisms, that beset current accounts of individuation and de-individuation, the self and the collective, under neoliberal control societies, and as such recognize that new progressive unities will be produced from out of the dismantling of the old unities and the reorganization of those unassimilated forces that can no longer be named or contained by them, indeed, derive their energy from the four substantive conditions of the current crisis I outline above. As such, in these terms, at least historically, armed with a popular 'consciousness of capital', it is perhaps now a little less easy to imagine the end of the world and a little easier to imagine the end of capitalism. For, in the short term, the growing ecological crisis and the mass expulsion of living labour from the system will, of necessity, make manifest the transindividual possibilities of other, non-comparative forms of *amour-propre* – new individuations, new affects, new desires, new pleasures – a pressing, even revolutionary matter.[62] My concern, in the next chapter, then, is to explore, in more diagnostic detail the promise and conflicts of individuation and the contemporary dynamics of *jouissance*, desire and self-love.

Chapter 3
Self-Love, *jouissance* and desire

Pleasure contra desire

In the film *Good Bye, Lenin!* (2003), directed by Wolfgang Becker, which is set in East Berlin just before the Berlin Wall comes down, the young hero Alex Karner (Daniel Brühl) travels from the German Democratic Republic (GDR) across the border to explore new cultural vistas and visits a porn store. He stands agog, along with a motley audience of men and women, young, middle-aged and old (as if they were all on a day excursion to the West), watching on monitor high up in the shop, a young woman rubbing cream from an aerosol can over her large breasts. There is a mixture of fascination and anxiety and yet deep pleasure on the faces of the audience, as if they are all secretly thinking: 'This is great: we just want to watch this without being disturbed, leave us alone.' This is, no doubt, a crude approximation of the director's intentions here, an idle extrapolation on my part from the particular to the general. But the intense pleasure and fascination on display on the faces of the spectators, nevertheless, captures an important truth about the current epoch and the weakening of the power of dianoetic action under advanced libidinal economy. Intensive and adaptive pleasures appear to have a greater efficacy – that is attachment to well-being and to self-identity – and thus a greater sense of biopolitical realism, than those long-term pleasures associated with the postponement of pleasure or suspension of immediate pleasure, because of the way they appear to transparently discard the cognitive labour associated with conflictual judgement and value formation. Late Freud and Lacan, of course, disavowed the idea of the function of pleasure in this straightforward utilitarian fashion, and argued that immanent to such pleasures were other mechanisms at work, defensive mechanisms, that suggested humans were not unproblematically adaptive pleasure seekers at all, but, rather, willing agents of a fundamental desire to withhold or postpone pleasure as a condition *of* pursuing it; the possible continuation of pleasure is formed by the pleasure taken from its failed or unrealizable realization (as in political struggle, for example). Lacan, in this sense, refuses to accept that this logic of unfulfilled pleasure is anything other than the indivisibility of pleasures and unpleasure; pleasure and unpleasure are mutually defining or, more precisely, pleasure finds its drive in the pleasure–unpleasure of its postponement, for otherwise, pleasure denies desire its due.

But, even so, this scene in *Good Bye, Lenin!* – given its conspicuous role in the film as a transitional moment from East to West – functions as evidence that a massive release of affirmative libidinal energy is now underway as a consequence of the impending collapse of the GDR (an energy that has until now been blocked or forestalled in a weakly libidinous East Germany) and, therefore, points, in a simple symbolic fashion, to not only how political economy produces a vast engine for the postponement of pleasure as pleasure, of surplus *jouissance*, but also how pleasure operates as a powerful autolatory release from the pain and unpleasure of the consistent realization of critical and normative values, indeed, of desire. There may be pleasure in the repeated failure to find and sustain pleasure, but pleasure also takes its 'orders' from the *resistance* to unpleasure: 'pleasure ... is the law of least effort,' as Lacan says.[1] As such, in this very short scene we are presented with a sharp reminder, in the raw, of how capitalism pathologizes desire (the desire for desire) in the name of a pleasure freed from value formation, the most obvious manifestation of this being the antipode between pleasure and politics; that is, political struggle being something that is invariably seen as happening under duress (as we noted with Castoriadis), and as such represses or delimits pleasure is, in fact, the enemy of pleasure. And this is why as the film unfolds the porn store scene takes on an increasing importance to the diegetic structure and libidinal polarities of the film. Principally, its function is to show up this dissociation between pleasure and desire as a *crisis* of the political, insofar, as it points to how workers desire appears to have disappeared from the historical stage, to be replaced, more concretely, by the greater practical reason of workers' immediate needs, workers' *pleasure*. This is 'real democracy': as they surge across the Wall, workers from the East are now the rightful libidinal equals and partners of workers from the West;

indeed, they are now the *bona fide* new comrades of pleasure and *jouissance*. And, to recap briefly, this precisely is how Bernard Stiegler understands the 'pleasure principle', under what he calls hyper-capitalism, from the perspective of the crisis of primary narcissism. In terms very similar to that of Lacan he sees pleasure – or more specifically pleasure as disengagement – as that which *destroys* the autonomy of desire.

The faces lined up in the porn store scene, therefore, provide an interesting semiotic displacement of the recent political past. In condensed form, the scene presents a subtle inversion of the famous proletarian painting from 1928, *The Internationale*, by the German artist Otto Griebel, in which receding lines of immiserated and bolt-upright workers stand starkly and defiantly gazing at the spectator; here though in the porn store, the group of faces miss our returning gaze, and stare so to speak, over our shoulder at the monitor in a kind of rapt avoidance of our presence; they are not waiting, as in the painting, for our recognition or advocacy but for the image on the screen to maintain its intense hold over their attentions. This removal of advocacy from the desire of the spectator is crucial, consequently, to the organization of the libidinal polarities of the film and its general reflections of the crisis of the political. If the film's hero sets out to explore new 'cultural interests' across the border, his mother, an ardent defender of the GDR and an active citizen, is for a large part of the film unconscious in hospital having collapsed in shock after seeing her son violently arrested during his participation in a 'new democracy' demonstration, as the final crisis of the regime approaches. The mother, who is portrayed sympathetically before her loss of consciousness, as a sensuous, sensitive and trusting figure, spends a good part of the film cut off from her desire as an engaged citizen as the GDR state comes to its final close; in this sense she is truly the fairy-tale sleeping princess. But rather than waiting to be awoken from her 'dream-state', she awakens into a 'State-dream'. When she regains consciousness in the new Germany, her friends, disarmed by her continuing cheerfulness and good faith, are pleased to see her passion for the GDR has not suffered and are happy to go along with her son's desire to maintain the illusion until she is fully recovered. The conceit and the humour of the film lies, therefore, in the son's filial commitment to maintain this illusion through a range of fanciful deceits to protect her from the new reality and the impending arrival of a new united Germany, including buying all the old GDR products he can find, and collaborating with a friend to produce fictional videos of state news (purloined from old archive footage) that they pass off as state broadcasts. The film's diegesis, accordingly, is framed by the deep crisis of the desire–pleasure axis: the mother invokes desire without substance and pleasure (her pleasure may be heartfelt but it is routine and non-reflexive); and the captivated citizens of the 'new Germany' in the porn store invoke pleasure without desire; an immobile and identitarian passion for intensity. Thus, in this split between desire and pleasure is demonstrated all we need to know about why the end of the GDR Stalinist state ended so benignly, that is without violent struggle: the historically invested desire to be a worker under the name of a would-be workers' state appears to have been even more of an illusion for workers than the resistance of workers to their identity as workers in their pursuit of pleasure. The rush to libidinal immersion in capitalism feels, then, less like a loss of identity – imposed by the West – than an act of rational self-interest. And because it seems like an act of rational self-interest, it is hard to shift, even when experience and knowledge contradict it.

This libidinal construction of rational self-interest is the fundamental means by which capitalism defines its future and accommodates workers' desire for self-realization under the forces of de-individuation. Indeed, as we have stressed, this is how capitalism reproduces itself through the production of enjoyment, as opposed to the idea that it reproduces itself – with any degree of efficiency that is – through a moral investment in the necessity of labour; and this, precisely, is what this short scene from *Good Bye, Lenin!* encapsulates and is worth acknowledging briefly here, at least, for its realism and pathos, despite its fictional form. *'Empty' desire or desire at a standstill is worth less than the restless pursuit of pleasure.* Thus, in this chapter, I want to focus in these terms, in greater micro-analytic detail on *jouissance,* pleasure and self-love, the destruction of desire, rational self-interest and self-realization as interconnected aspects of this new stage of libidinal economy – before we begin to look at self-love, perfectionism and the political and cultural *reconstruction* of desire in Chapter 4.

The production of I-cracy and capitalist reason

One of the governing tacit assumptions of contemporary conservative political journalism and bourgeois social science that has rushed into the vacant space produced by the libidinal crisis of the political – with overwhelming echoes of the neo-conservative Leo Strauss's elitist nihilism[2] – is that we live in a time where people want reassurance and consolation above all else. People want 'good stories', hopeful stories, not 'facts' that talk of ecological catastrophe and the fatal expulsion of living labour from the system; they want reassuring stories far more than they want political strategies. There is nothing new in this mobilization of 'benign' fictions by the powerful, of course. In ancient, medieval and modern bourgeois politics, ruling classes have sought recourse to the power of consoling illusions; Niccolò Machiavelli was the great diagnostician of the consensual and coercive force of these illusions, particularly in relation to those rulers with the most to lose.[3] But in the neoliberal period, the recourse to consoling illusions such as material progress, the increase in welfare for all or creativity under capitalism, needs little consensual encouragement from civil institutions and the negotiated consent of workers (through wage bargaining) for it to function. Indeed, civil institutions no longer play the same role in the negotiation of consent that they once did, given the weakening of the links between trade unions, non-market ideologies and public culture. This is why one of the operations of 'friendly power' today in the libidinal 'struggle against class struggle' is to actually dissolve the very notion of consent – insofar as it implies irreconcilable differences and therefore submission to power. In other words, consent is the language of division, as if workers and managers did not share certain interests and were not faced with the same kinds of problems – indeed existential problems – in the workplace: that is, the overwhelming need to retain their jobs in the face of external global forces that 'threaten us all'.

Bourgeois representation is, of course, defined by this convergence of interests as a condition of capitalism's claims to the greater rationality of class compromise and liberal universality. This is how bourgeois inclusion thinks its relationship to democracy and inclusion, pragmatically changing the terms of this inclusive form and powers of advocacy all the time. Today, though, because the exercise of this convergence is no longer compromised by the threat of excessive collective working class demands, the power to act as a class of owners independently of what the working class might do is greatly enhanced by the representatives of capital – hence the antagonism on the part of conservative governments globally to worker–government dialogue, notions of bi-partisan 'good governmentality' or any pretence that capital and public culture represents the same values. This is why the power of the representatives of big capital (financial and productive), and non-state technocrats, has grown enormously, in the desire and capacity of these representatives to adjust, obviate or ignore national-state constraints on capital mobility and market penetration.[4] Representatives of big capital and the non-state technocrats of the bourgeois political process feel now that they can run the show without the inconvenience of having to negotiate politically with the representatives of national constituencies, that is, precisely, negotiate with workers and those non-workers who suffer disproportionately from the system's inequalities and exclusions; but also, those who want to see fundamental democratic change in the face of corporate malfeasance. Conservative national governments rarely see the freedom of these non-state actors to act unilaterally without constraints, and the economic concessions they seek, as being in conflict with the interests of the national state. Indeed, if some governments (of the left) do hold out – as they have done in South America in the millennium – they are eventually worn down externally and from within.

Hence the image of 'unconstrained' pleasure on offer to the workers in *Good Bye, Lenin!* may well provide a realist insight into contemporary libidinal economy, but today over thirty years since the fall of the Berlin Wall it also appears wholly recherché when attached, by its defenders, to democracy and freedom. Immersion in mass cultural pleasure today no longer has that utopian attachment to libidinal freedom and creativity as an 'escape' from routine, religious constraint and virtuous humanist uplift, as perhaps it last did in the late 1980s, when postmodernism was at its height. Indeed, the notion that pleasure is a constitutive category of capitalist freedom breaks down once the libidinal economy on offer in the West presented to the people in the porn store is attached to those (hidden) macro-decisions of non-state actors that determine what counts. For the scene to work for sceptical viewers today, therefore, it is imperative for viewers to assume that the workers in the store believe that there *are* no such things as malfeasant non-state actors; non-state actors – the doyens of the culture industry – appear here, rather, as the very agents of individuation and freedom. Today, however, the deepening conflict between democracy and freedom fatefully undermines this assumption even more starkly. The alliance between creativity and democracy is unambiguously one in which the opportunities and actions of individuals, organizations and groups are predetermined by the strict subordination of what is *allowed* to be creative or stand for creativity (and give pleasure) in the light of the absolute control of capital over the products of the culture industry and pursuit of market share. This is why there is currently no intellectual investment or systematic interest by governments and CEOs, in trying to match their promoted ideal image of the 'creativity' of capitalism with the *would-be life and creativity of democracy itself*, when 'creativity' has so little meaning outside of the monetization of individuation and financial dependency. There are no longer any convincing bourgeois humanist defences of culture's civilizing mission; no celebrations of the literary and artistic canon as a measure of critical public values, no pedagogic exhortations to cultural uplift, not even a pluralist advocacy of the respective qualities of the 'popular' and the 'avant-garde'; 'creativity' is simply formally capitalized as entrepreneurialism, and as such, cultural success is always mediated by the notion of new – and accessible – 'product'.

Consequently, bourgeois public culture today is unable to securely represent its own constitutive interests as a public realm of freedom and individuation, given that to do so is to expose its own cultural and political limits; freedom and individuation are revealed to be privatized matters alone. Thus, the broader civic aspirations of the public sphere as a place where different classes interrogate each other's interests in the broader interests of democratic accountability – even in this anodyne social democratic sense – becomes an inhospitable, uncomfortable and 'inefficient' drag on the entrepreneurial spirit and the monetized rationalization of pleasure. The result, therefore, is a mature capitalist symbolic regime in which the greater accountability across cultural forms and practices is always attached to affect, as opposed to critical knowledge, for critical knowledge always *slows things down*, that is, it blocks, delays or prevents pleasure from securing its emotive 'truth' (its stabilizing, repetitive and consolatory power; its line of least resistance). Capitalism, then, cannot allow pleasure any *determinate* epistemological role other than as a negation of value formation, for value formation is a process that is radically unstable and therefore subject to conflict and the possible withdrawal of judgement from consent. In this sense dominant ideology acts in the interests of the widest expression and pursuit of pleasure, thereby, removing from public culture any explicit attachment of coercive and disciplinary power with moral order. As William Davies has noted, in neo-Adornian mode, under late neoliberalism this process takes on a kind of punitive 'avoidance of critique', and 'circumvention of crisis', politically and culturally:

In place of critical forms of knowledge [that one would associate with capitalism's technical creativity], which necessarily represent the deficiencies of the present, forms of empty affirmation are offered, to be repeatedly ritualistically. These, lack any epistemological or semiotic ambition to represent reality, but are instead ways of reinforcing it. When political leaders say that austerity will result in economic growth, the purpose of such speech acts is to repeat, not to represent. Likewise when benefit claimants are compelled to recite slogans such as 'My only limits are the ones I set myself', these are plainly not statements of truth or fact. They are what Luc Boltanski has termed 'systems of confirmation', performative utterances which seek to preserve the status quo and to occupy the discursive spaces that that might otherwise be filled by empirical or critical questions about the nature of reality.[5]

In this sense, to reinforce my comments above: 'power now seeks to circumvent the public sphere, in order to avoid the constraints of critical reason.'[6] This is why the repeated attack on expert knowledge, and the validation of populist 'feeling' and 'intuition' – in Edmund Burke's sense[7] – that underlies this culture, is presently a crucial move for neoliberal power, for it allows claims to truth and common sense to circulate free, not just from the exercise of critical reason quite obviously, but from those offices of public report and cultural and political institutions that hold to some notion of civic accountability. In fact, when these attacks on expert knowledge are made accountable it dismisses criticism as partisan interference, and as such relativizes those aspects it doesn't like. And this is why at the political level, the fictive and the aesthetic powers of the 'strong illusion' are fundamental to capitalist reproduction and 'empty affirmation' (and 'empty desire'), underlining how willing capitalism is to draw, even today, on a counter-Enlightenment religio-mythic structure of control in the interests of continuity. This is why Slavoj Žižek is right and wrong on this score. When he argues ideology 'does not reside primarily in stories invented (by those in power) to deceive others, it resides in stories invented by subjects to deceive themselves',[8] he fails to recognize how the stories invented by those in government, actually give the space and permission for people to invent stories to 'deceive themselves', or more precisely, to invest in the pleasure of self-deception. Indeed, the religio-mythic structure of the 'strong illusion' is a kind fictional metanarrative that people redefine or re-inflect in order to discover their own voice. Hence, these self-made stories may converge with the interests of power and deception –

stories that are self-consoling and adaptive – but, nevertheless, they refuse the notion that what I share as a speaker with the story being told to me by the powerful is the same as *my* story, as if my opinion doesn't matter: 'I hear what you're saying, it makes sense, but this is my decision alone, my judgement'. The upshot is that ideological interpellation is always expressly the *détourned* borrowed voice of power in liberal democracies. The reception of its alien form is re-shaped by personal advocacy, and, therefore, by the notion that a judgement has been arrived at autonomously. This is why the 'strong illusion' of government narratives gains greater credence through the 'Bonapartist' use of 'direct speech', and consequently, through the dismissal of those who would use abstract 'ideas' to undermine what, 'we all', rational and reasonable people – the government and 'you the responsible citizen' – already intuitively know. This form of populist address provides a pleasurable and Burkean reinforcement of the idea that critical knowledge and debate is fundamentally compromised and suspect; and, perhaps more decisively, *inefficient* – hence the widespread cynical indifference on the part of CEOs, technocrats and bankers today about what politicians tell their electorates about the nature of the ongoing social and ecological crisis. Blatantly false or misleading narratives provided by the advisors and think tanks of the centre-right and right – even by liberals, intent on winning the centrist vote – are all to the good for CEOs, banks, hedge fund managers and the captains of industry. Indeed, if hundreds of millions of people believe that populist leaders are independent anti-elitist candidates, compelled by a righteous commitment to democracy and a better deal for workers, then so be it, their success electorally is no less our success. Furthermore the injection of a little more authoritarianism into the political system by conservative or centrist politicians is also good for us and for the 'struggle against class struggle' and the economic life of the system as a whole, because it 'gets things moving'; as leaders of commerce and industry, we, therefore, do not fear so-called 'post-truth' (sic) politics – indeed we willingly invite it into our calculations; it is a necessary part of 'good' governance – for it acts as a creative buffer against all the enemies of capital, the free market, difference and progress.

Thus, the vast shift (again) globally to the populist right and far right, is an indication, therefore, that where the recent economic crisis has been confronted on a popular left basis (Greece, Spain, Venezuela, Brazil in the early millennium), capitalism will do its best to close down alternate narratives, with the help of whatever conservative, nationalist-populist, ethno-nationalist and neo-fascist forces available to channel the popular will, particularly when the left achieves power or is on the verge of achieving power. If the left does reach power – constrained albeit by the capital markets, recalcitrant bureaucracies and mass media attacks – relentless accusations of financial incompetence and attacks on a disproportionate commitment to public spending define the constant firefighting these governments have to face, in defence of the mildest social democratic reforms. Under the sway of this narrative by the right and liberals it is easy, then, for electorates to be 'frightened off' by systemic change, given the relentless association of non-market change with destabilization, mismanagement and even the threat of criminality; and this, as such, increasingly enforces the sense for those many millions who don't vote, the feeling that their vote is worthless whether the left is in power or not. This powerful counter-narrative of leftist 'incompetence' and 'ineffectualness', however, is never gainsaid by the greater incompetence and venality of the right in government. This is because the gap between action and outcome on the right rarely weakens the captive power of capital – even if incompetence might eventually result in the removal of a conservative administration. Given, that the right in power has no commitment to change beyond allying all economic and social interests with those 'freedoms' that meet the needs of the market, change is merely the reinforcement of 'freedoms' that are deeply entrenched already. Consequently, the neoliberal right's repeated failure to achieve the absolute domination of free market ideology when in government (faced with worker resistance, residual attachment to social democratic rule of law, an independent judiciary, local custom), is, thus, rarely undermined by the betrayal of its promises to do so, because there are no ideals attached to these ends and therefore nothing to betray in any substantive sense; there are only (state) enemies and real or imaginary naysayers to defeat. The loss or betrayal of ideals repeatedly haunts the left as the 'mortal' form of its horizons, making any new collective project after the failure of a previous radical project and sequence of struggles within the span of a generation, incredibly hard, given that politics and practice are attached to the uneven and contingent outcomes of extended time cycles.

This gap between pleasure and knowledge is where I-cracy and capitalist individuation does its contemporary libidinal work as the constitutive form of this constantly delimited space for action (the crisis of the dianoetic). It is no surprise, accordingly, that there is a tendency for the individual to remove himself or herself under these constraints – in the interests of self-protection – from this uncertain space. As a result, workers' sceptical assessment of collective action, and consequently the valorization of self-possessive notions of socialization (in Marx's sense), repeatedly compress belief formation in one habituated, pragmatic and self-ratifying direction: that is, *to an attachment to capital and the love of the love of self as the best, the least deleterious, ways of becoming a self-regulating and efficient capitalist subject*. As Lacan says in this respect: '*I-cracy* emerges irreducibly,'[9] as the master's common-sense discourse. I-cracy is 'the essence of every affirmation in culture that has seen [the] master's discourse [the autonomous, sovereign self] flourish over all others.'[10] In this sense, this is what we have prefigured so far in our discussion of social reproduction, individuation and libidinal economy, and what is briefly on display in *Goodbye to Lenin!*: namely, the prospect of internal *stability* that the continuities of pleasure brings – in Freud's sense – as opposed to the instability that desire brings; *desire brings disorder, pleasure brings continuity*.

But of course, the pleasure–desire axis is never in itself stable. Firstly, because the self-possessive 'I', is illusory, and as such is subject to fracture; and, secondly, because of the aporetic condition of pleasure itself: as the logic of repetition pleasure as a source of continuity, 'properly speaking is what goes against life' (against desire, that is, for Lacan).[11] This is why the breakdown of the assumed rationality of this adaptive belief formation and narrative is, of course, what defines the declination of the 'ego' in Marx, and the constitutive subjective force of any progressive or revolutionary politics; the 'ego' as desire produces a *cut* in this continuity, leading to the reassembly of a given state of affairs or unity.

To recall our earlier point then: pleasure cannot fully stabilize the diremptive and negative force of desire (resistance being in these terms always the beginning of a possible new account of pleasure–desire), because, although pleasure is interstitially powerful and the very ground of human metabolic reproduction, it is in the final analysis, a *principle of least resistance*, and therefore subject to destabilization in its own right when faced with interests and forces that question or reject the comforts of stability and continuity. Indeed, the resistance to this 'least resistance' is always ready to come to life when the stability of pleasure is no longer able to contain the desires of unmet needs, particularly under conditions of extreme repression, or when governments drive down wages and destroy social services (today's austerity policies) or when governments lead countries into unnecessary wars. This erosion of living conditions and the threat to peace produce great waves of scepticism and doubt, and, as such, a desire that escapes pleasure's finitude. But, this emancipatory desire, in turn, is itself unstable, wholly contingent upon resistance turning into systemic negation, as we see in the aftermath of the collapse of Stalinism, the war in the Middle East and today's ecological crisis. As in the exit from Stalinism, disappointment and anger today – the loss in faith in politicians and governments and the 'crisis of the political' – is invariably re-assimilated as part of capitalism's destructive creativity, and, therefore, subsumed under the pragmatic and adaptable ductile signs of this creativity, what we have called the 'making of tolerable of that which is intolerable'. Thus, for example, in the wake of the recent banking crisis the collapse of the banking system in the United States in 2008 seemed like a tipping point for a new politics and a new democracy, in which the self-correction of the banking system and predatory finance capital would allow the ironing out of fiscal anomalies and egregious banking practices. That this didn't happen has not altered the received view that this is what appeared to happen or something like it. Moreover, the failure of a collective fight back by workers in order to diminish the impact of the crisis on lives after the collapse of the banks (the failure of the working class to protect wage levels and social services), in the end, appeared, as if the crisis was no crisis at all, and simply, an administrative blip, reinforcing the efficacy of the pleasure principle and the would-be illusions of emancipatory desire. At the point of its own self-destruction and incoherence, the system seemed to confirm that the greater rationality of pleasure and possessive individualism is the best and only way of regulating the vicissitudes of social and economic life; the socialized 'ego's' cut is soon healed.

All roads, then, tend to lead back to I-cracy because I-cracy – certainly in periods of defeat or political withdrawal for workers – restores the equilibrium of capitalist order as a continuum of pleasure or, more precisely, the *non-conflictual* pleasures of *amour-propre* and eudaimonist self-realization. And this is why as we have noted, this disaggregative process is not diminished by the continuous social realities of the workplace either. Thus, it matters little to workers under these conditions that they produce collectively, that they share skills at the expense of individuated expertise, insofar as the easily graspable and 'common sense' actuality of possessive individualism – through consumption and pleasurable forms of social privation outside the workplace – restores a degree of comfort and rationality via non-work experience and everyday habits. Hence, in turn, the gap between these individuated pleasures and the workplace reinforces the alienated and unpleasurable character of collective experience and struggle itself, as if struggle was the very essence of a reason stripped of pleasure. This is why resistance rarely becomes revolution. As such, possessive individualism never 'fails', so to speak, because it always rewards *consistently*, even if the rewards in actuality are thin and uncertain. And this is why, following Tomšič, we affirm here that the forces of repression and pleasure ('friendly power') are indivisible under conditions where the organization of pleasure and the threat of the absence of pleasure are fundamental to real subsumption: to repeat: 'the production of the relations of domination [are secured] by means of the production of enjoyment.'[12]

Capitalist I-cracy, therefore, continually protects and re-charges the subjective link between self-love and 'love' (adaptation) for capitalist reason, against its weakening and erosion through collective reason. And, it achieves this through the demonstration of the greater rationality of self-possession and self-preservation – *amour de soi* – within the formally guaranteed freedoms of the market. Workers' failure to act consistently on the reason of their own vested interests or unmet needs – or 'ego' – is precisely a claim on reason, and not a loss of reason as such, that is, a reason without reason passively adapted to circumstances. Putatively non-rational beliefs or 'weakened' reason are limited attempts, consequently, at making the world intelligible.

As Michael Rosen argues, the challenge of any psychoanalytically grounded anti-akratic model of reason and action (akraticism being the idea that reason has to *overcome* the 'instabilities' desire and pleasure in order to realize itself), therefore, is the notion that reason and desire are indivisible; the privileges of reason alone defines a very narrow (Aristotelian) model of rationality, in which pleasure follows the stable, teleological realization of a given purpose or action.[13] For Aristotle all pleasure that doesn't fall under this rational teleological purposiveness is superfluous and essentially beneath serious attention.[14] This is why Aristotle, for Lacan, under capitalism's libidinal economy of reason, is the very philosophical *persona non grata* and the great betrayer of desire as reason.

In Aristotle's work it is very clear, things are very pure: pleasure and the good can only be equated in what I will call the master's ethics [the ethics of the expert]. The flattering ideal awards itself the term 'temperance,' as opposed to 'intemperance,' suggesting as it does the subject's mastery over his own habits ... Desires are exiled from the field proper to man, assuming man identifies with the master's reality.[15]

This neatly sets up a vital conflict between the Aristotelian grounds of the perfectionist tradition and the vicissitudes of desire in anti-akratic thought (which we will discuss in Chapter 4).

Thus, if reason establishes the norms which tell us what desires we should have, desire breaks this virtuous circuit by telling us what forms of reason are worthy of our desire. As such, it is no surprise that under mature capitalism, in which adaptation to least resistance is a model of 'good reason', that the reason of pleasure is more persuasive than the reason of desire. Hence anti-akraticism has to be at the centre of the critique of libidinal economy. For it offers a critique of capitalist reason without falling into unreason. The challenge is to pursue, as Rosen says, the 'construction of a genuinely anti-rationalist understanding of the self that will not simply capitulate to unreason'.[16]

This is why 'joyful alienation' is so telling as a notion. In its present neoliberal stage possessive individualism is connected to forms of agency in which individual choice offers a reasonable return on autonomy and pleasure and, therefore, crucially provides a *protection* against a greater uncertainty and loss that is attached to desire (intellectual abstraction; underdetermined political outcomes; 'unachievable' ideals). This is why, in turn, self-love and the love of the love of self provide a pragmatic defence of the pleasure principle as individuation *against* de-individuation, even if this process of individuation leads the subject deeper into the hell of de-individuation. But, for our purposes, this does not mean the insurmountable corruption of individuation under capitalism, as we have noted, and will discuss in detail in Chapter 4. To recognize these libidinal processes as being attached to the compensations of self-love is not to assume, thereby, that self-love is fundamentally antithetical to the influence of wider social identities or collective processes, that is, that the notion that self-possession and self-love are processes subservient to 'private' experience alone. On the contrary, the promise of individuation is always determined by the collective limits and possibilities of the experience attached to these processes of self-realization, as the early Marx recognized. And this is why capitalist processes of inclusion and identification (ataraxy, autolatry, uxoriousness, ductility, neotony etc.) remain so effective, insofar as they produce and shape this link between self-love and reason as a constant *default position*, insofar as individuation always compensates for or overrides collective loss and disappointment as a range of supplementary pleasures, as opposed to being the drivers – in periods of collective struggle – of new unities and new collectivities.

So, how precisely do self-love and I-cracy operate in these terms under mature capitalism? In what ways is the subject of self-love attached to pleasure as a mode of psychic self-protection? How does the power of affect work here? What precisely are the means by which enjoyment secures domination? Firstly, then, we need to return to Lacan's writing on desire and *jouissance,* for there we will find some preliminary guidance on the questions of self-love and pleasure.

Jouissance, desire and self-love

Lacan's writing on *jouissance* covers a large number of the Seminars in the 1960s and early 1970s, pointing to a striking consistency on his part about its centrality to the psychoanalytic project and as such to the analysis of desire and pleasure, subjectivity and subjectivation. In the following, I want to focus on those Seminars, where desire and *jouissance,* are most discussed in particular *Seminars V, VI, X, XVII, XIX* and *XX.*

Lacan's thought, essentially, establishes the conflict and intersection between desire, pleasure and subjectivation; the subject is, thus, 'formed' and 'deformed' by this conjunction and conflict of forces. Thus, in his well-known account of this process of subjectivization in *Seminar X,* he identifies the mismatch between desire and pleasure as a kind of repetitive misalignment. This lies in the fact that the object *a,* the signifier which desire attaches itself to in order for desire to do its psychic work, is fundamentally unstable (there is no subject without the passage through the signifier). Indeed, the object *a* is not the actual object of desire at all, but rather, that which always, necessarily escapes desire, its non-equivalent, that is, the thing that 'lies *behind* desire',[17] as desire moves elsewhere. In this respect, the object of desire is a kind of 'waste product' of desire.

> The *a* is precisely what resists any assimilation to the function of a signifier and this indeed is why it symbolizes that which, in the sphere of the signifier, always presents itself as lost, as what gets lost is signifierization. Now, it is precisely this waste product, this scrap, which resists signifierization, that comes to find itself constituting the foundation of the desiring subject as such.[18]

So, desire 'misses' its object and feeds on scraps, not because it is careless or aimlessly voracious, but because desire always exceeds the object *a*. It refuses to settle for the object that it settles on, for to settle on it, is to let desire wither or die. Hence, for Lacan the function of object *a*, therefore, is to keep open the pathways of desire via a detour through and around the object, living and inanimate. Crucially, in this sense, the object *a* acts as a support for the subject's imaginary relation to the object, in as much as it is constitutive of the fantasmatical structure of desire-*as*-detour. The more the subject attaches himself or herself to what he or she believes to be the object of desire, 'the more he is in fact diverted and distracted from it. Everything he does on this path to move closer to it gives evermore body to what, in the object of this desire, represents the specular image.'[19] In this light, the subject knows 'nothing', so to speak, of what they desire, that is, they know nothing of why they desire this particular object they have settled on, why *it* appears at this moment rather than others: 'desire cannot be articulable even though it is articulated.'[20] That is, the subject misrecognizes what the object *a* actually stands for in the economy of his or her own desire. So, the object *a* is not to be confused with a propositional claim on what is desired and therefore with the transparent intentions of the subject. On the contrary, the object *a* is the constantly expendable signifier of the subject's desire: it goes 'off to hook on whatever it can'.[21] This is why this 'going off' or 'detouring' is for Lacan, the process which establishes the relation between the object *a* and the subject's anxiety, what we called earlier the *truth* of desire, that moment of recognition by the subject of its inescapable encounter with its endless seeking out of the object. So, here, we are confronted by what this endless seeking out of the object, of detouring, is predicated upon: the desire *for* desire, or *jouissance*.

Desire under these conditions for Lacan presents itself precisely as a 'will to jouissance',[22] insofar as *jouissance* is the state of pleasure–displeasure that results from this process of desire's detouring and its endless postponement. *Jouissance* is the pay-off for blocked desire. The object *a* is not just the signifier through which desire detours itself, but the support mechanism by which the subject structures its pursuit of pleasure. The detouring of desire is the means by which pleasure, or the *jouissance* of desire, is maintained. Consequently, if desire is a lack, it is a lack for good reasons: it sustains the metabolic continuity of pleasure that the subject seeks; the object *a* is the facilitator of this continuity. Thus, if *jouissance* and desire are indivisible, they are not the same thing, and therefore, as such, want different things, even if desire, in the end, covets the *jouissance* that failed desire secures. So, desire *for* desire *is* the pleasure of the detour, irrespective of the displeasure and 'waste' it carries with it.

The fundamental issue in relation to libidinal economy is that Lacan's negative dialectic of pleasure and desire, following Freud, achieves a conceptual clarity that splits open the interiority of the reasoning subject. Given that desire is grounded in relation to the signifier, the analysis of pleasure and desire is no longer tied to an idealist account of consciousness, in which desire is from the very outset the thing to be 'reduced' or 'traduced' ('controlled'), and pleasure the thing to be expelled as the *ex-timate* of reason.

> Over the centuries, philosophers never formulated a single moral theory in which the pleasure principle, whatever it may be, was not immediately defined as hedonistic. This means that that man, whether he knows it or not, fundamentally seeks his own good, such that errors and aberrations of his desire in practice can only be viewed as accidents.[23]

Thus, the crucial point for Lacan in relation to psychoanalysis's relationship to agency and ideology is that the unconscious is 'already dominated by the state of the signifiers'.[24] In this sense to be taken up by signifiers means two interrelated things. It means first of all, most obviously, to be taken up into a system of signifiers that pre-exist the subject as the socialization and acculturation of the individual, in Marx's sense; and secondly, to be 'taken up' into the Other, as the place where the answering call to the subject's desire is produced as the ground of the object *a*. And, this of course, is sexuated: men and women are not *jouissance* compatible. 'Between what symbolically grounds the argumental function of the terms *man* and *woman*, there remains the wide gap of an indeterminacy in their common relation to jouissance. They are not defined in relation to [the same] jouissance by the same order,'[25] insofar as they separated by access to different signifiers. Consequently, the restless detouring of the object *a*, is not the result of the subject's 'executive' choice, in any abstract sense, but, rather, the unconscious rendezvous between the subject's desire and the desire of the other, or more accurately, the demand on the part of the subject to elicit love (attention) from the other. So, the detouring of desire is always conditioned by the fantasy of what it hopes to receive from the object *a*; and this is why desire is not attached to the objective and calculable value of *objects* per se, but, rather, to the structuring force of this fantasy. The outcome is that the subject's desire is always marked by the imagined demands of the answering call of the other. 'What do you want from me, that will make my desire acceptable or worthwhile?' Yet, the call is thwarted or miscued. This is because the subject is unable to freely answer the question, insofar, as given the fact that the fantasized character of the exchange, the subject is not in a place *to* know exactly what is being asked of him or her, and, conversely what he or she is actually themselves. Thus what is being exchanged is not mutual recognition but one signifier with another. But if desire and communication are constitutive of the 'unsaid', nevertheless, thought is not the thought of the 'unsaid' alone, as if there is no access to the real, only mutual illusion. In order for the 'unsaid' to act as the 'unsaid' the subject must speak, qua, the Other's discourse, *as if there is a possibility of understanding and truth*. To speak is to speak the 'truth', even if the truth is the outcome of misrecognition and detouring. The subject reveals 'truth' even if he or she directly avoids speaking the truth, or, indeed, conversely, tries *to* speak the truth. By not saying something one 'says it', that is one speaks the truth of what is *not* said; and it is this truth-of-untruth, evasion and silence, of course, that constitutes the working-through of psychoanalysis.

Lacan's psychoanalysis, then, follows a particular 'anti-philosophic' path in relation to the status of the subject and reason and desire. If there are neither subjects *and* society, neither is there any distinction between the libidinal economy of the subject and the libidinal economy of capitalist society; fantasy and libidinality are the shared substance of socialization (and its unconscious and conscious resistances). Human reality is constructed 'against a backdrop of prior hallucination, which is the universe of pleasure in its illusory essence'.[26] This is why Lacan in his later writing is emphatic about how the subject's entanglement with the object *a* – as a condition of subjecthood – finds a ready place in the circuits of capitalist accumulation and exchange. If subjecthood and desire are constructed through the passage from signifier to signifier, the subject is exposed to, and shaped by, an unprecedented range of 'hallucinatory' significations that vastly expand the detouring of desire; indeed, this is the epochal dimension of real subsumption in the period of expanded individuation. Thus, it is no surprise to see Lacan in the later Seminars tying *jouissance* to this process of accumulation and expansion through his insistence on the structural intersection of surplus value and *surplus jouissance*. As he argues, expressly, in *The Other Side of Psychoanalysis* (2007):

Of course, it wasn't Marx who invented surplus-value. It's just that prior to him nobody knew what its place was. It was the same ambiguous place as the one I have just mentioned, that of excess work, of surplus work. "What does it pay in?" he says. "It pays in *jouissance*, precisely, and this has to go somewhere." What's disturbing is if one pays in *jouissance*, then one has got it, and then, once one has got it it is very urgent that one squander it. If one does not squander it, there will be all sorts of consequences.[27]

The point, consequently, is that there is an intersection between the subject's desire and the producer's desire: the subject's desire must squander itself in order to maintain the good order of pleasure – its continuity – in the same way that, in addition, workers must squander their energy as producers in order to squander their desire in consumption as the means of maintaining their metabolic connection to pleasure and the capitalist life cycle; the investment in the *jouissance* of repetition and continuity in one follows the *jouissance* of repetition and continuity of the other. So surplus *jouissance* follows surplus value in finding continuity in pleasure as least resistance; there is a search for *jouissance* in repetition. As such, for Lacan – following Freud – the squandering of desire has a deeper cost here: *entropy*. Through supporting the principle of least resistance or tension, the *jouissance* of repetition for Lacan is not a steady state of continuity in pleasure but, on the contrary, a limit with respect to *jouissance* that 'is a function of a cycle that embraces the disappearance of this life as such, which is the return to the inanimate'[28] – in other words the death drive. When the object *a* produces its detouring of desire through lack, it also produces entropy and the loss of *jouissance* through *jouissance*-as-repetition. And this is where surplus *jouissance* derives its 'death drive' or 'deathliness': pleasure is repeatedly produced out of loss; that is, 'deathliness' is derived from the repetition of loss. However, the 'deathliness' of *jouissance*'s entropy is not a 'death *wish*' as such or evidence of libidinal self-destruction. The subject does not seek death through *jouissance* or symbolic exhaustion. Rather, the death drive is the name given to the attachment of surplus *jouissance* to the compulsive production of '*more life*' from the endless detouring of desire through the signifier. The 'death-drive' is the compulsive re-signification of libidinal self-investment.

The squandering of desire for Lacan, therefore, has a normative, social dimension: surplus *jouissance* has a genealogy that is attachable to the growth of the 'calculable'[29] (i.e. something that adapts and changes) and therefore to the plasticity of the commodity form:

> Surplus value is a memorial to surplus *jouissance*, its equivalent of surplus *jouissance*, its equivalent of surplus *jouissance*. "Consumer society" derives its meaning from the fact that what makes it the "element," in inverted commas, described as human is made the homogeneous equivalent of whatever surplus *jouissance* is produced by our industry – an imitation surplus *jouissance*, in a word.[30]

For Lacan surplus *jouissance* and 'industry' are indivisible and psychoanalysis finds itself, thereby, working through desire as the very valency of capitalism (surplus value), and not just in relation to the logic of consumption, where it usually sits in orthodox Marxism and critical theory. This is why in the later writings Lacan widens his focus on surplus *jouissance*. The logics of repetition and least resistance also operate where they seem least likely to: the production of knowledge. The commodification of knowledge for the intellectual worker is no different to the factory and office worker: they all have to 'produce something',[31] and having produced something they need to consume something or somethings in order to produce something else, echoing Marx's production–consumption dialectic in the *Grundrisse*. But, in addition, for Lacan the production of knowledge defines the 'calculable' logic of value, especially in the area of science and technology. In this, the production of knowledge in science and technology complies extremely efficiently with the positivistic norms of I-cracy and what Lacan calls the 'master's discourse' of knowledge production, namely the 'curious copulation'[32] between capitalism and science produced by the university. The 'master discourse' of knowledge for Lacan, accordingly, falls under the broader 'master discourse' of value: they both serve surplus *jouissance* as the calculable form of repetition, insofar as they find a common ground in the production of the pleasures of neotony, that is, the detoured return to the 'beginning-as-the-same' – the relentless production of a new forms of knowledge, new of objects of detoured desire, that support the phantasm of objectifiable self-control, 'personal development', scientific progress and unimpeded economic growth. Interestingly, this is where Lacan's theory of surplus *jouissance* and the 'master's desire' to enforce the pleasure of repetition through loss enters, in a small way, into the debate on capitalism as religion: the 'master's' power to control repetition as the pleasure of least resistance encourages the love of the supplicant. This is why the emancipatory drive of psychoanalysis for Lacan 'is well and truly atheism, provided one gives this term another, sense than that of "God is dead" ... '[33] Truth occurs when knowledge and belief fall into the category of failure, that is, when the speaking subject moves, as a condition of non-repetition, from the sovereign, 'I think therefore I am' (identity) to the non-sovereign, 'I am he who is thinking' (non-identity).[34]

Lacan's critique of repetition and surplus *jouissance*, then, offers a significant point of entry into the analysis of those forms of self-love and pleasure that secure social reproduction, least resistance and the production of subjectivity. The libidinal economy of the subject and the libidinal economy of capitalist society are effectively the same – even if the subject is irreducible to the libidinal structures that define it. Hence the subject who fails or refuses the repetitive demands of the desire *for* desire and surplus *jouissance*, for Lacan, like the force of negative labour power for Marx, represent similar kinds of 'cuts' into the logic of repetition and continuity. Indeed, the break with repetition in the analytic session for Lacan represents locally, a prefigurative break in the chain of subjectivity identifiable with the value form and real subsumption. For Lacan there is strictly no distinction between politics and this localized critique of identity; the exit from 'capitalist discourse'[35] can only realistically occur once the work of detaching the subject from the fetishized processes of self-objectification are put in place. What is at stake, therefore, across Lacan's psychoanalysis and Marx's critique of political economy is the production of a *new subjectivity*, what we have been calling so far, the production of new forms of individuation, insofar as the 'old' forms of individuation – individuation–de-individuation – *block desire as non-repetition*. So, in a way to recap: the libidinal function of capitalism is not to veil the realities of capitalism, even if the veiling of the true nature of capitalism is the outcome, but to establish a pleasurable continuum in which surplus *jouissance* is the stable agency of economic reason and the de-rationalization of these realities. This is a far more effective as form of ideological interpellation, given the fact that it produces a pleasurable investment on the part of the subject as producer and consumer in the reproduction of their own subjectivation, that is, in their own ethical rationalization of what is tolerable and intolerable, pleasurable and unpleasurable. Therefore, the critique of this subjectivation cannot be conducted on terms that would detach subjectivity from these processes of socialization. This is the meaning of 'working through' for emancipatory politics. The subject is not an 'effect', anthropological given, or undivided ego, but a structured ensemble of bio-cognitive processes that are subjectively incomplete and unstable as a result of the subject's conflictual entry into the symbolic (into the realm of the signifier), and the subject's drive for self-preservation (*amour de soi*). This is why, as Tomšič says: 'There is no non-alienated and non-divided ego preceding libidinal self-investment.'[36] The subject is the constitutively alienated substance of this drive to self-preservation and libidinal investment. In other words: subjectivity *is* the labour of surplus *jouissance* under these conditions, not the preformed rational core of self-identity that adjusts or limits its exposure to desire and the passions, according to some autonomous notion of 'pure reason'. The making of the capitalist subject finds its orientation through its attachment to, and dis-attachment from, the object *a*, the love object.

Self-love, the love of the love of self and its vicissitudes

Consequently, we come to one of the most troubling and vexed areas of libidinal economy: what kind of love objects does capitalism actually produce, and what is the nature of the attachments/dis-attachments of the subject to these objects? This returns us, by definition, to our earlier brief discussion on self-love and the *love of the love of self*. For self-love would appear to be the very thing that links surplus *jouissance*, social reproduction, the 'ego', autolatory attachments and the process of neotony together, the very motor of individuation–de-individuation, the very ground of capitalist subjectivation.

Crucially, in what sense is the subject of surplus *jouissance* the subject of self-love? What form does self-love play in the production of subjectivity and subjectivation and how does this shape the subject's attachment to the love object, living or inanimate? In this we will need to return our concept of the love of the love of self to the notions of the 'happily dominated', 'voluntary servitude' and 'adaptive preference'. This is because we need to answer one substantive question at least before we address the reconstruction of desire and the perfectionist tradition: what actually is 'loved', and as such what encompasses the experience of love, when we talk of the love of the love of self? If the desiring subjects of capitalism don't truly love capitalism, nevertheless, in what ways does the love of the love of self, determine surplus *jouissance* and the economy of desire? How do desire and the love of the love of self, intersect? Or rather, how does the love of the love of self, shape the detouring of the object *a* of desire?

In *Willing Slaves of Capital: Spinoza & Marx on Desire* (2014), Frédéric Lordon broadly follows politically and philosophically the libidinal model of social reproduction and desire we have been working through in relation to the Lacanian and (non-orthodox) Marxist and critical theoretical traditions: *the need for a new account of subjectivation, beyond the old antinomies of 'reason' and 'desire' 'self' and the 'social'*. In this he correctly argues that we need to 'rethink the concepts of exploitation and alienation from the ground up'.[37] In this respect, he follows the key precept of any materialist account of alienation and reification today: that capitalism draws out a supplementary pleasure from the presumed continuity of social reproduction: 'desiring predominantly conforms to the capitalist order of things'.[38] However, Lordon develops this on a non-psychoanalytic basis, although he occasionally adopts psychoanalytic terms and assumptions. His model of desire and subjectivation, rather, is derived from Baruch Spinoza's concept of desire: *conatus* or the energy of desire. That is, to be and act is to be and act as a being *of* desire; being and desire are indivisible.[39] Of course, Lacan recognizes Spinoza as one of his significant philosophical precursors and mentors on desire and being, indeed, one of the major philosophers of anti-Aristotelian anti-akraticism, but Lordon offers no reflection on this link. Indeed, there is no reference to Lacan or *jouissance* in the book. Similarly, in his use of Marx, he is less interested in the struggle for individuation internal to and 'beyond' class identity and the social division of labour than in the role of the money form in the control and shaping of desire generally. In this sense, strangely, his book is an extensive discursus on credit and desire without him actually discussing the intersection between credit and subjectivity or, in fact, credit at all. This is because, for Lordon it is the money form alone – as an abstract concept of financial bondage – which does all the necessary mediatory work on the production of desire and subjectivity, given that for the majority, all desires – all detoured desires, to put it in the Lacanian language we have been using so far – must pass through the dependent relation between labour power and capital. That is, all desires are constrained by the primary fact that 'individual labour-power must reproduce itself daily'.[40] Meaning that the majority of producers and consumers are overwhelmingly 'held down by the gravitational pull of their mere reproduction',[41] as opposed to the owners of capital who are not beholden to these relations of dependence. Thus, for Lordon, it is the dull compulsion of the economic, in this conventional sense, that, in the final analysis, shapes for the majority the vicissitudes of desire. But if this dependency in reality for Lordon delimits the capacity to desire, here, it nevertheless shapes an abundant joy when wages and salaries are paid, or about to be paid, opening up the *jouissance* of expectation: 'getting paid is the employment relation's joyful moment.'[42] Indeed, 'securing the money that allows satisfaction of the basal desire causes joy.'[43]

Adaptive preference

Lordon, in this respect, seeks to account here for what we called earlier, the intense identity between desire and the *ideal expectations* of capitalism; pleasure lies repeatedly in the endlessly postponed realization of these expectations, tightening the link between adaptation and hope. In this there is an echo of Jon Elster's work on reason and ideological adaptation in *Sour Grapes: Studies in the Subversion of Rationality* (1983) in *Willing Slaves of Capitalism*. Elster's work from the early 1980s offers one of the first incursions of anti-akratic thinking into analytic philosophy, or, more precisely, into analytic Marxism, providing a notional investigate link between reason and desire and a post-Adornian critical theory. Thus, for Elster, as for Lordon, acting rationally involves more 'than acting consistently on consistent beliefs and desires'.[44] That is, 'irrational' belief can be 'rationally' sustained and, indeed, bring real or imagined benefits to the subject. From this perspective Elster's key point is that actions are not always explainable in the classic akratic sense in terms of utility maximization. Subjects may pursue actions – indeed invariably will pursue actions – in which utility maximization is a marginal or limited consideration, given the long-standing beliefs of the subject or contingent desires, desires that appear to offer the 'best reason' available at a given time. Consequently, following Marx, Elster rejects the orthodox methodological individualism of the analytic tradition, accounting for action and belief (specifically working class action and belief for Elster), not in terms of reflective rational self-interest (the exercise of rational principle) but in terms of adaptive preference, the adaptation of belief and action to reality criteria and context.[45] In this respect he dismisses the notion that there are rational preferences that meet a given situation, based on the 'fair' and 'reasonable' gathering of evidence and information. Rather, 'rational action' and its optimalization can only be assessed on prior commitments of agents that are socially preformed, if irreducible to ideological consent alone. The adaptation of action and belief to circumstance invariably operate either on the basis of socially preformed desires, or on the development of new desires that break with old preformed desires to fit in with prevailing reality criteria, what Elster calls 'dissonance reduction'.[46] Indeed, 'dissonance reduction' is closely related to the way in which desires act as a form of rational *self-ascription*: 'this is true because, I believe this to be true': 'the well-grounded belief is also the one that the believer wants to be true and indeed believes because he wants it to be true.'[47] Hence, as we have noted in lieu of this: under post–Second World War social democracy there has been a widespread identification on the part of workers with prudential reason: the adaptation to restricted and stable norms of action as a means of class 'self-defence'. Following Elster, in 1985 Adam Przeworski explored in extensive detail how post–Second World War social democracy produces this prudential working class subject as a condition of, and the means by which, 'class compromise' is organized. 'Neither "ideological domination" nor repression is sufficient to account for the manner in which workers organize and act under capitalism. The working class has neither been a perpetual dupe nor a passive victim ... '[48] Rather, workers' consent and adapt to domination, on the basis of a voluntary, if ultimately unstable, investment in capitalist reason.

> Social actors, individual and collective, do not march around with "predispositions" which they simple execute. Social relations constitute structures of choices within which people perceive, evaluate, and act. *They consent when they choose particular courses of action and when they follow these choices in their practice.* Wage-earners consent to capitalist organization of society when they act as if they could improve their material conditions within the confines of capitalism. More specifically, they consent when they act collectively as if capitalism were a positive-sum game, that is, when they cooperate with capitalists as they choose their strategies.[49]

Thus, would the majority give up what they've come to expect and enjoy under parliamentary democracy in the name of a whole roster of emancipatory intangibles? The answer, as we have stressed, is not as simple as we would assume, particularly in the light of psychoanalysis's critique of pleasure: in some instances people would be willing to do this, would be prepared to risk a loss of pleasure as a rational expression of their passions, particular when those passions cut across social and cultural divisions to form a progressive alliance of interests with others, in the belief that the successful outcome of this alliance will offer greater rewards for the majority; and of course, historical experience tells us why this is so in various revolutionary or proto-revolutionary situations and, therefore, why expressions of resistance defy all utilitarian considerations.

But the counter to this has equal and even greater weight in the modern period: workers and non-workers would defiantly not risk loss of pleasure at any cost, on the basis that their present interests are greater and more secure than any imaginable future interests, and as such, are a more realistic expression of their passions: that is, to maintain a level of pleasure and enjoyment secured by their labours and pragmatic self-interest. Questions of class interest for workers may shape 'self-interest', but ultimately class interests cannot expose self-interests to existential jeopardy, particularly violent jeopardy. What the modern debates on 'self-interest' and 'collective interest', as in Przeworski flag up, therefore, and what defied the comprehension of some of the first modern enlightened philosophers of power who noticed this conflict, such as Étienne de la Boétie, and Niccolò Machiavelli is: even if 'self-interest' challenges 'collective interest' why don't the majority of people simply walk away from exploitation and oppression? When the interests of the majority prevail, self-interest would appear to lose its efficacy, indeed self-interest and majority interest would appear to coalesce in these circumstances, so there seems to be an obvious argument for the interests of the majority prevailing. Yet 'walking away' has seemed the least feasible of options, historically; even when the mass or general strike in the early twentieth century was a viable form of mass action, and carried with it, it was assumed, the interests of the greater majority. As de la Boétie argues in *Slaves by Choice* (1552–3): 'Freedom is the one thing which men have no desire for.'[50] This needs unpacking, for de la Boétie is a philosopher of some subtlety.

De la Boétie is not saying that, in the end, freedom from exploitation is unassailable – of course, freedom from exploitation is indeed desired by men and women, passionately so. But, rather, the issue for de la Boétie is that freedom as the freedom of the majority is not exercisable as a *unifiable* passion. Although the governed may exist as a larger cohort than the few who govern, and thereby stand in position of numerical superiority over the few who govern, there is no stable and collective set of interests that match the interests of this majority. This is because many of the majority stand in relations of *dependency* to the few, and therefore benefit from these relations, in fact, seek to strengthen these relations in their own interests and persuade others of the greater rationality and rewards of these relations; in fact, they are willing to stand with the few to defend these relations and, more contentiously, defend the system of power that secures these relations. In this sense de la Boétie is the first philosopher to note how 'contradictory class locations'[51] tend to push agency mostly in one direction: what we have been calling 'least resistance'. And de la Boétie backs this up with various arguments to the effect that people are more willing to trust those who secure their interests through the immediate promise of pleasure and relief from misery, than those who have their long-term 'welfare at heart'. This is why de la Boétie is considered an important philosophical precursor to the modern 'self-interest' debate, particularly as it has come to be defined in psychoanalysis. However, if Przeworski doesn't discuss de la Boétie, Michael Rosen and Slavoj Žižek certainly do. Here I want to talk briefly about Žižek's de la Boétie.[52]

'Walking away'

Žižek reconfigures de la Boétie's argument in order to put it on a modern psychoanalytic footing. The failure or unwillingness of the majority to walk away from exploitation and capitalism is not simply a matter of internal division, as if it was just a case of competing interests and perspectives failing to find the means to pursue a common goal. Division is also impacted by the *anxiety* of freedom itself. What I do with freedom once it is realizable? What happens to my desire for freedom, if freedom is little more than a gift? Thus, the perfectly rational voluntarism of the majority – we have the capacity, here and now, to change the world and release ourselves from privation – is not just threatened by internal division and relations of dependency with those who govern, but by the crisis of desire at the point of its realization. That is, the possibility of 'walking away' from capitalism is an interesting thought experiment precisely because it generates a 'risk-paradox': on the one hand it provides comfort knowing that the majority can prevail over the few through sheer weight of numbers and, therefore, lessen the threat of possible failure; but, on the other hand, as a collective act of withdrawal it is devoid of transformative risk and therefore threatens to dissolve what attaches me to my position as a desiring subject. If we can simply walk to freedom what is the value of a freedom achieved without conflict over interests and ideas? It is a freedom that is inconsequential; without self-transformation. It, thereby, weakens my individuation as someone who is defined by the *struggle* for freedom, and all that this means in relation to my passionate self-identity as part of the majority. The walk to freedom, as such, is – in its abstract finality and absoluteness – an act that threatens a pure 'saturation' of pleasure in freedom and, thereby, 'completely blocks the space of desire.'[53] The fulfilment of the idea of freedom through 'walking away' dissolves the desire for desire, for future desire; disables it. But what Žižek doesn't mention is that this feared loss of desire is also accompanied, conversely, by an increase in the threat of displeasure through the pure saturation of desire. The voluntarist realization of freedom exposes me to 'duties' and 'responsibilities' far beyond my initial pleasure in the dream of freedom. To walk to freedom is not just to be confronted by the 'crisis of desire', the emptiness that comes with saturation, it is to be released into a world that requires me to act on things that are the very antithesis of freedom; freedom may release me from the old bonds and oppressions, but it also means recreating myself as part of a process outside my control, indeed that threatens my autonomy and pleasure; and this creates dread and fear, as much as expectation and joy. This, essentially, is what de la Boétie means by men and women having no *desire* for (universal) freedom: even if the thought of freedom compels and organizes the passions, the realization of it is onerous and difficult; and this is why such desires for freedom from exploitation are invariably accompanied by a countervailing desire that is invariably stronger or more persuasive than the primary desire. And this is where the loss of desire and the recompense of pleasure combine, in two powerful counter-rationalizing forces.

Following de la Boétie there are good reasons why the majority don't do the most obvious and direct thing: 'walk away' from capitalism: firstly, nothing can be done without the calculations of rational self-interest, that shape desire and belief and, therefore, make the numerical advantage of the majority fragile; and secondly, to achieve freedom without its realization in struggle (in practice) is to empty freedom of content when it is won. This is why the Marxist revolutionary tradition has taken a dim view of the rational voluntarism of the majority: there is never a good time to 'walk to freedom', because to arrive is to arrive in the same state that one started. But the majority know their self-interest well and need little guidance on this, given the high risks of practical failure and the risk of a spiritually empty desire. Hence, the increasing recourse on the part of workers in the second half of the twentieth century to come to an accommodation with capitalism as the guarantor of a certain continuum of pleasure. In not risking the pursuit of a maximalist concept of freedom men and women find good (or equally bad) reasons to deny this kind of freedom as practicable, for fear that the bitter struggles to achieve and realize it in action might in the end offer less than the limited freedoms they already enjoy. This is what we have called evidence of adaptive preference and as such represents the conditional form of relations of dependency between the governed and those who govern. Collective interests shape self-interests across class lines, but self-interests are not isomorphic with class interests. In this sense class interests as self-interests and self-interests in conflict with class interests are unstable. As a result, we cannot calculate the impact of class interests and the cost of freedom from exploitation by utilitarianism alone – as if the self-interest of the majority were fixed in the image of those self-interests and not dependent on changing circumstances and consciousness. Hence the unwillingness to 'walk to freedom' by the majority does not thereby mean that the majority are indifferent to the wider demands of freedom from exploitation, as a possible exit from capitalism. For the costs involved in the pursuit of a maximalist concept of freedom are also measured by the *limitations* of existing freedoms; the freedoms that are already enjoyed are never as secure or generous as their legislators and advocates assume. Thus, a maximalist conception of freedom acts as a means by which the success of these freedoms and the success or failure of the struggle for new freedoms are measured. But this measure is not active; it is latent, so to speak; it accommodates itself as part of this process of rational calculation. And this is where self-interests re-define themselves, certainly in the post-war period, as a rational exercise in delimitation.

In these terms, Elster's notion of adaptive preference aligns itself broadly with the re-building of the concept of 'collective reason' in 1970s' free-rider theory's engagement with post-1960s' electoral politics: that is, the notorious notion that emancipatory agency in politics is always determined by the agent's radical assessment of the costs of participation: in what ways might participation in a collective action diminish or threaten my autonomy, even though I agree and support the action?; and secondly, is the support of the collective action large enough for my contribution not to be missed, and so large enough to not necessitate my involvement, thereby diminishing any threat to my would-be autonomy? My willingness or unwillingness to participate in an action is based on whether or not I consider my contribution to be superfluous.[54] Of course, free-rider exclusion is not generalizable;

otherwise everyone would exercise the reason of their non-participation. But the point of free-rider theory is not to expose its logical incoherence and vacuity as a moral imperative, but to recognize that under modern social democratic conditions a large number of people are freely willingly able to exercise their reason in order to participate (to vote, for example), enabling a large minority to exercise their reason in order not to participate, producing a (floating) constituency that sees prudential non-participation as the 'best' exercise of reason: it is best not 'to participate' because, all things considered, this is a more secure way of securing my autonomy and pleasure, even though I willingly support the action in question. Free-riding, therefore, is an extreme instance of adaptive preference. Yet, nevertheless, it provides a crucial insight into how the sovereign self in the libidinal economy builds a defence of least resistance for itself from the idea that, under democracy there will always be those who are in positions of power and influence, with the requisite training and knowledge, who 'know better' than I do and that have passion on their side and, therefore, are better placed to do what I might do or should do. Hence, Elster's notion of adaptive preference, despite its hazy distance from actual politics and the libidinal economy, does make a particular kind of normative claim on free-riding: free-riding is precisely what happens in mature democracies when avoidance is a condition *of* adaptive self-rationalization and 'best reason'. Castoriadis's reflections on the crisis of dianoetic action infer this.

But Elster has little to say on this self-rational prudential subject and *pleasure*, as his work sits like Lordon – methodologically, if not provocatively, despite his critique of the rational analytic philosophical subject – outside of the psychoanalytic tradition. Thus, his vivid notion of 'dissonance reduction' is set adrift from the continuity of pleasure and its cognate 'least resistance', resulting in a kind of awkward *fait accompli* about the conservatism of the prudential subject, as if this subject had no conflictual relationship to 'master's desire' at all, and simply constructed its desire for 'dissonance reduction' mechanically from the interests of the dominant. This is because for Elster the question of autonomy or the struggle for individuation free from domination is merely 'residual', not *constitutively* residual; that is, it is simply what is left 'after we have eliminated the desires that have been shaped by'[55] preference adaptation. Indeed, this prudential subject leads directly in Elster to an inelastic 'voluntary servitude' in which the oppressed openly identify with their oppressors in 'good order', and the submission to pleasure as least resistance becomes expressly non-autonomous: historically, the oppressed have spontaneously invented ideologies that are sympathetic to their rulers. 'I am strongly in sympathy [with the] view that the oppressed believe in the superiority … of the ruler because it is good *for them* … legitimation was spontaneously invented by the oppressed.'[56] And this can be explained, Elster argues, by the dominated rationalizing this imputed superiority through 'dissonance reduction'. This dead *amour-propre* (the passively mimicking of one's 'betters') is poor critical recompense, therefore, for a break with an akratic conception of reason; indeed, it lurches straight into to an anti-dialectical, even reactionary, account of adaptation preference.

Self-love and the workplace

Lordon's revival of the debate on adaptation and desire from the 1980s rightly rejects the univocity of Elster's position: it is one thing to say that we need a model of reason and desire in which adaptation and resignation require thoughtful analysis as forms of reasoning-in-the-interests of domination, and it is another to say that the capitalist subject's picture of the world is univocally the one he or she constructs from the image of his or her rulers. Hence the principal merit of Lordon's version of the adaptive preference model, despite his own distance from the psychoanalytic tradition (which I will explore below), is that his entry point into the debate on reason and desire is through the division of labour and the conflicts and contradictions of the labour process, crucially, as a result, reconnecting action and desire to *pleasure* as the *conflicted* site of social reproduction. In this respect he links the question of adaptation preference and domination to the continuity-of-pleasure question, not as the outcome of passive mimicry, but, rather, as the basis for the more rewarding notion that workers produce a reason of pleasure from their adaptation and dis-adaptation to 'master's desire'. From this perspective Lordon describes the contemporary workplace as a place in which workers and 'master's desire' engage in a 'new passionate situation of employment',[57] in which employees find an *active* position in their submission to 'master's desire'. Following the writing of Eve Chiapello and Luc Bolstanski[58] – as well Paulo Virno, Toni Negri and many other writers in the post-operarist tradition – Lordon argues that the new workplace provides unprecedented opportunities for 'creative' worker–employer exchange.

On this basis Lordon makes a kind of unacknowledged Lacanian move in accounting for the new neoliberal conditions of real subsumption. Under the increasing intersection of desire and the money form the employer and capitalist take on the unconscious function of 'master-desire' and, therefore, provide a heightened focus for 'joyful alienation' and *jouissance*. If money guarantees pleasure for the worker, then, investment in the work process in the workplace and identification with the 'life of work', in order to please or appease the 'master-desire' of the employer and his or her access to the monetary means by which future pleasure is to be secured, provides the necessary means for accessing pleasure. In a way there is nothing new in this: if workers have to work in order to reproduce themselves, they accept that they have to offer a modicum of deference to their employer in order to make their lives easier and remain in work. But, more precisely, the assumption here is that this process of submission under neoliberalism has lost its instrumental functionality in the workplace. Lordon's argues (following Chiapello and Boltanski), that capitalism in its neoliberal form has, in sense, learned as a condition of the demands of the libidinal economy and its drive to offset consent and conflict through pleasure, how to bring the need on the part of the worker to access pleasure through the realities of the wage form into closer *alignment* with the desire of the employer. The desire of the worker to secure pleasure through the wage form is transformed in the place of work into a desire to *please* the 'master-desire' of the employer, the figure who, in the end, determines the worker's continued access to pleasure. In other words, the employer not only provides access to future pleasure but provides a range of conditions and opportunities that pleasurably reinforce this access to pleasure. Thus, the new work place creates a situation in which the worker works for the employer – despite all possible conflicts and disagreements with his or her boss – as a joint enterprise in 'master-desire', encouraging the worker unconsciously to find ways of pleasing the employer as the provider of future pleasure. Lordon calls this the 'co-linearization' of desire under the pull of the 'master-desire' of the employer and the enterprise (or the production of value).

> The strength of the neoliberal form of the employment relation lies precisely in the re-internalization of the objects of desire, not merely as desire for money but as a desire for other things, for new, intransitive satisfactions, satisfactions inherent in the work activities themselves Put otherwise, neoliberal employment aims at enchantment and rejoicing: it sets out to enrich the relation with joyful affects.[59]

The neoliberal enterprise, in this sense, replicates what we have outlined above in relation to neoliberal governmentality and the 'strong illusion'. Co-linearization at the workplace aims to produce 'obedience without burden'.[60] Or rather, more accurately, it mobilizes obedience as a perceived act of autonomy, given that the actions and judgements of the subject are solicited in the spirit of shared respect and joint enterprise.

As such, self-love is key to this process, for co-linearization in the workplace requires that the worker learns to love himself or herself as both a condition of giving pleasure to the employer, and in relation to the facilitation of workers' continuing access to their own future pleasure. The subject acts to make the best of its capacities in order to receive the master's approval. The subject learns to do this, therefore, by developing a capacity to know and bring about what gives the 'master' (employer) joy: 'I do what allows me to please the master, and therefore to be identified by the master as the cause of his or her joy, so that the master will love me and I will take pleasure in having brought joy to the master.'[61] So, the cultivation of interests and capacities that bring joy to power are attached to the support of desires that are *not the subject's own* but, nevertheless, serve both the subject's pursuit of present and future pleasure and the process of co-linearization. In this way, the effect of this co-linearization is to produce a subject in the workplace whose desire is split; that is, both aligned with the 'master's desire' and with the subject's own imagined sense of autonomy released by the attention he or she receives from the employer. This is how 'friendly power' works: the worker makes himself or herself available to power in the passionate cultivation of his or her subordination to the 'master's desire'. But it is unclear in Lordon what kind of interpellation is at work under these conditions; what kind of libidinal pay-off is being produced for the worker. For, despite the critique of Elster-type passive mimicry and 'voluntary servitude' the assumption in *Willing Slaves of Capital* is that neoliberalism's efforts to establish a regime of 'happy labour' is largely successful, and that the new employee is engaged through the cultivation of self-love in a shared love between themselves and their employer and the capitalist enterprise. This is highly contentious, in the same way that free-riding is contentious – for two reasons. The new capitalism certainly draws on the strategies of 'friendly power' in the workplace to bring about an alignment of 'worker's desire' (for future pleasure) with 'master's desire' (to subordinate the worker's struggle for autonomy to the interests of value production); but this co-linearization is by no means secure, given the widespread antipathy to 'work' itself, and as such the presence of fault lines between employer and employee that remain as a condition of exploitation, and cannot be dissolved into a stable set of 'inclusive' or 'harmonious' work practices. As such the identification between 'worker's desire' and 'master's desire' is continuously being fractured by the betrayal of 'worker's desire' by the 'master's desire' ('tough love') and, therefore, by the resistance on the part of workers to the overtures of the 'master's desire', irrespective of workers' unavoidable desire to please and maintain their job and secure their access to future pleasures. As Peter Fleming argues in his commentary on Lordon in *The Mythology of Work* (2015):

> If the contemporary capitalist enterprise is anything remotely like a love affair (a particularly dreadful metaphor no doubt) then it would be one with a partner that gains pleasure from persistently announcing that he or she plans to leave you, and sooner rather than later ... Management today has no interest in whether you like or love it (although it would like you to think it does). And it certainly *does not* like itself. General happiness is not its concern; nor are lasting social bonds.[62]

And this takes me to my second reason: the dominant libidinal relationship in the workplace is based not upon the cultivated love of the enterprise as an expression of the free exchange between 'master's desire' and 'worker's desire' but, rather, the relentless instability of 'master's desire' as the determining force behind the request of the employee from the employer to be flexible and, as such, do the 'best they can do' under all circumstances. Fleming calls this the 'abandonment' ideology of neoliberalism, and, in these terms, it foregrounds those forces that have shaped what we have been calling the subjective ruination of the worker. Far from building stable bonds of inclusion and the cultivation of self-love in the workplace, neoliberalism aligns 'creativity', in fact, with a punitive regime of destabilization, demobilization and divestment. Neoliberalism does not want a workforce to be attentive at all costs to the actions and initiatives of management, a workforce who, in fact, identifies with the problems of management and trusts in it (for all this, in a way, is far too intrusive and time consuming). On the contrary, in the big enterprises certainly, it wants a workforce that is continuously off-balance and whose interests and problems are 'not really welcome'[63] beyond the ratification of management decisions. Hence the current widespread reliance on a culture of subcontracting and outsourcing in both big and small enterprises, that enables companies to not hire anyone or very few people directly. And, of course, this is the general direction in which management practice and 'master's desire' in the workplace is heading under the new Third generation of robotics: a workplace in which few people are employed on the enterprise's actual premises and, therefore, opening up a gap between control and face-to-face engagement, enabling capital to construct a workplace where the workforce is not required to be managed, regulated or negotiated with at all at the point of production or distribution. In this sense neoliberalism is increasingly concerned with securing enterprise–workforce *detachment* as a condition of increased cost-efficiency, as opposed to cultivating new bonds of worker–management collaboration. And this is why Lordon fails in any systematic way to account for the disaggregative political and social costs of the expulsion of living labour from the enterprise. Under the global regime of the expanding expulsion of labour power there is a deepening of the fragmentation of the bonds of worker solidarity, as we have noted.

But if Fleming is correct to question the bonds of love and the cultivation of self-love in the workplace, it would be wrong to assume that self-love as self-reliance in the workplace does not play a part in the ratification of neoliberalism and the 'love of capitalism'. There maybe not much love lost between 'worker's desire' and 'master's desire' in the workplace, but, the increasing cultivation of self-reliance across many new enterprises provides a working continuity between 'creativity' in the place of work and the massive cultivation of the love of the love of self, outside of production in the domains of consumption. Indeed, 'the love of capitalism' for the majority of producers and consumers is not achieved solely through what happens 'creatively' at work at all, but what happens in those domains where the possibility and fluidity of individuation re-enchant the notions of the autonomous will and sovereign self-control. If to labour for a wage is to gain access to the resources for future pleasure (or increased amounts of pleasure), it is also, by extension, to regain a sense of sovereign self-control through the active pursuit of this access to future pleasure. Pleasure and acceptance of sovereign self-control coalesce.

Self-love and voluntary servitude

Lordon's alignment of 'worker's desire' with 'master desire' in the workplace, then, offers little sense of the crisis of work itself, and the reality of capitalism's antagonism to real collaboration and the bonds of shared enterprise, given capital's overwhelming imperative to abandon labour to an atomized domain of 'outsourcing' and unstable self-employment outside of the enterprise. Capitalism certainly has an interest in workers' self-reproduction being attached to the reproduction of the desire of the 'master' as condition of labour–capital continuity. But capitalism is certainly not interested in this as the basis for workplace democracy, particularly when the job of delimiting and constraining workers' autonomy is more efficiently achieved through greater levels of atomization outside of the enterprise. Capital realizes 'inclusivity' in the workplace is a losing game, faced with the high levels of antagonism and apathy to the new ductile work regime on the part of workers, based on the constant threat of management's destabilization of work norms on workers' morale and, ultimately, the fear of the abandonment of the workforce by management in part or as a whole. The limitation of London's position, accordingly, is that 'happy domination', or workers' adaptive desire is not secured solely through the persuasive powers of management to encourage the worker to invest in the reason of the 'master' and, indeed, ultimately the shared reason of worker and employer. This is because the vicissitudes of 'happy domination' are not a condition simply of the worker adapting to and finding pleasure in the alienated relations under which they labour. Rather, the new 'passionate conditions' of workplace collaboration and sharing produce consent through self-love or *self-reliance*. The contemporary worker is not looking to please their employer in order to achieve recognition and approbation from the employer, but to find the resources that will allow them to survive in the workplace with the minimum of disruption – and if this grants the worker a little recognition from management and pleasure in the process, then fine. And, in a sense, this is what the 'master's desire' truly encourages, because, it means, that, for management the worker seeks their *own sense of worth*; and as a result the employee is equally focused on working for themselves as much as working for the enterprise; and, therefore, from the employer's perspective this weakens any potential conflict between workers and management, as an employee is less concerned with seeing themselves as part of a recalcitrant workforce and, therefore – which is particularly threateningly for management – as a possible 'class bloc' of disgruntled employees. Capital doesn't want workers to 'love' capital or the enterprise but to *love the nature of what they do or achieve at work, and as such what they might aspire to as sovereign workers through their exertions*. In this respect, the dynamic of 'master's desire' is more purposely concerned with management winning workers over to the *pleasures of self-reliance*, for this, increasingly, is assumed generally to be an indisputable fact of contemporary economic life, the agential form under which the disaggregative force of labour power in the age of surplus populations functions. And, of course, workers know this well themselves, not as a threat but as a daily reality, relieving millions of workers of any illusions about finding stable full-time, long-term work. Hence the only way for workers to survive the instability and flux of the labour process as a living reality is to strengthen their powers of self-reliance and self-love as a means of achieving a notional sense of self-worth.

Thus, this is where self-love finds its libidinal character under neoliberalism: not in the worker's 'voluntary servitude' in the workplace but in the *active production* of self-love as a general form of psychic defence, that is precariously caught between the worker's residual desire for autonomy and the pleasurable cathecting of the worker's belief in the sovereign subject to I-cracy and the 'love of capitalism'. So, yes, the production of I-cracy is formed in the workplace under the exigencies of real subsumption, but it is the result of a defensive move on the part of workers in relation to the wider conflict between capital's need to destroy or weaken the autonomy of workers, and, conversely, the basic need for workers to retrieve or recover a sense of individuation from this struggle. This split therefore is continuous with the broader pressures – not just on workers but on all producers and consumers – to find in self-love a means of both securing the access to necessary levels of pleasure in order to function under the demands of the market, and, at the same time, the resources to resist these expectations in the hope of something else, something not attached to these pressures. The problem, however, as we have analysed in detail above, is that self-love's pursuit of autonomy under these conditions invariably returns the subject to the pleasures of de-individuation, for these are the pleasures, as Lacan insists, that are not simply the most easily available – offering the least resistance – but that appear to be in closest alignment with reason as such.

The production of self-love, then, finds its wider orientation in mature capitalism through its subjective attachment to the love of the love of self. But as, I have hinted, self-love and the love of the love of self are not the same thing. Self-love (*amour-propre*) is the means by which at work and in consumption the subject finds the resources and capacities in order to properly function as a capitalist citizen. The *love of the love of self*, in contrast, is that ensemble of subjective and libidinal attachments and investments that enable the subject to be *worthy* of the wider libidinal demands of capitalist desire – capitalism's invitation to pleasure and the 'master's desire' – that is, the demand it makes of the subject to be a 'good' sovereign consumer of individuated-de-individuated pleasure. The question of *jouissance*, in its expanded form of surplus *jouissance*, therefore, obviously comes to the fore in the latter, as opposed to its subsidiary function in the former, given the needs of I-cracy to channel self-reliance into self-realization and personal development more efficiently. We might say the love of the love of self is how self-love operates in the domain of consumption and self-realization.

The love of the love of self

The substantive question, here, nevertheless, is what exactly *is* the 'love of capitalism', under these subjective determinations and objective conditions? If capitalists don't exactly want workers to love capital in the workplace (given that this means the development of reciprocal attachments), and workers don't straightforwardly love capitalism as the basis of their struggle for survival and access to future pleasure in the workplace (given that they are mostly concerned with securing their reproduction), how does the love of capitalism reveal itself amongst workers? Solely in consumption? This is hard to credit, given, the libidinal continuity between the workplace and the domains of consumption, despite workers' defiance of the 'master's desire'. Indeed, workers take pleasure from their successful survival and adaptation in the workplace and the securing of their access to the continuity of pleasure. As we noted in our brief discussion of worker masochism in Lyotard and Tomšič, the libidinal attachment to this displeasure is not to be underestimated, even if the notion of a fully constituted masochism is implausible. But is this actually a love of capitalism, as opposed to love of the pleasure–unpleasure that the struggle with the 'master's desire' inevitably brings? The issue of the love object, then, is vague here. Or it appears to be vague. For if there is no love of capitalism as a *definable object of desire* in the workplace, there is certainly an attachment by workers to the *jouissance* of struggle that the 'master's desire' provides. In this respect, the struggle for survival supports a libidinal continuum between the worker's sovereign sense of themselves as engaged in an individual struggle and the sovereign self of detoured desire: both operate according to the principle of the love of the love of self as a form of adaptive and defensive reason. But how exactly does this adaptive reason produce the 'love of capitalism', given the defensive (and unconscious) formation of these attachments? In what sense is the love of the love of self a love of capitalism at all in these terms? In fact, in the realm of consumption doesn't the love of the love of self, seek out attachments that breach the continuum of pleasure as least resistance, given the ambiguous and conflictual relationship of the subject to individuation-de-individuation? Let us start by recalling what we discussed briefly earlier.

The love of the love of self is a self-rationalizing commitment to the 'master's desire', in order to be equal to the fundamental demand of capitalism outside of production: the demand for the subject to match the endlessly giving individuation of capitalist life – or more precisely its immersion in the pleasure of individuation-as-deindividuation. Thus, in matching the production of this individuation the subject has to be ductile and open enough to recognize its desires in those of the master. The 'master's desire' operates here, therefore, according to all power relations based upon perceived 'shared interests' as opposed to those based explicitly on coercion or moral persuasion: the subject freely recognizes its own desires in those of the master, even if these desires appear to be external to the subject's control. In this they are grounded in the pleasure of *confirmation*, insofar as they appear to uphold the interests of both subject and master. But if this is an illusion of fair exchange on the part of the subject this is not an illusion without real rewards. Hence, this does not mean that the subject's libidinal investments in this exchange are false or are psychologically insubstantial. On the contrary, the pleasure generated through the exercise of a detoured desire not of the subject's own making is powerful enough to resist any talk of the disappointments of surplus *jouissance* as being fundamentally alienating or, indeed, as evidence of capitalist manipulation. This is because surplus *jouissance* continually corrects and adapts feelings of loss and unmet needs as the unfolding, expectant work of pleasure, and as such, is connected to the ideal expectations of capitalism that we have talked about. And this is how *jouissance* supports capitalism's ideal version of itself. It enables pleasure to defy the anxiety of a desire that is not confined to least resistance. So, the love of the love of self is the form that subjectivation takes faced with the subject's exposure to the maintenance of pleasure as continuity. And consequently this represents the form that subjectivation takes in order for the subject to be in alignment with 'master's desire' and capitalist demands.

But, of course, this love of the love of self is not a labour attached to a sovereign self in control of its libidinal attachments. It has to be produced *out of* the divisions of subjectivity itself; indeed, it has to be produced out of the very wretchedness of subjectivity and the failure of the subject to maintain its imputed sovereignty. The love of the love of self is the work, therefore, of a self that is desperate to organize its pleasures in defiance of its feelings of lack of self-worth and division. How then is it possible to talk of the 'love of capitalism' *at all*? In what sense is the defensive production of *jouissance*, out of loss and division – as a protection against, individuation-as-de-individuation – actually a love of *capitalism*? Are we confusing 'love' with the pleasures of adaptation?

The love of the love of self under capitalist libidinal economy is the labour of pleasure pursued by the subject in order to secure a degree of defence from the effects of de-individuation and loss of autonomy. In this regard it finds both pleasure in de-individuation and the need to adapt to circumstances that it is unable to influence or control, in order to prevent further loss of autonomy and pleasure. But, this limited support of autonomy as a defence against de-individuation is conducted on the terrain of de-individuation itself, that is, through the detoured object *a* of desire and surplus *jouissance*. The libidinal investment in this process is active and productive and, consequently, unselfconscious. Indeed, it is indivisible from the life processes of capitalist reproduction. Accordingly, the *love* of the love of self is the means by which the subject adjusts its self-interests and hope for self-realization to the sovereign demands of economic reason, irrespective of the discomfort that this causes, given the constraints imposed by de-individuation. As we have also noted, this process is, of course, not stable given its derivation from subjective division. Hence the love of the love of self is governed strictly by the anxiety of the subject that we have identified with detoured desire and surplus *jouissance*. This is why, if detoured desire seeks to offset or suppress anxiety, the experience of anxiety creates the relentless need for pleasure to (temporarily) quell this anxiety. The subject's pursuit of a continuity of pleasure is generated by both the experience of, and repression of, anxiety. The love of the love of the self is both pleasure-giving *and* painful; or more, accurately, the pleasure given and the pain received are indivisible.

The idealized internal self and the love of capitalism

But, in what ways does the love of the love of self find its identity expressly in the ideal expectations of the demands of capitalism and 'master's desire'? In what sense is the love of the love of self a version of an ideal self, that is, identifiable with the idealized other of the 'master's desire'? This is difficult to answer, because there is no idealized other of the 'master's desire', no idealized capitalist figure that is perfect in its non-sexuated invitation. Indeed, the 'master's desire' of the capitalist fails to take on a singular, figural character at all. In fact, when such images of the 'ideal capitalist' do appear, they appear gross, even barbaric and hence destroy the fantasy of free exchange between subject and power (even, if this appears less of a dilemma and is defensively negated by those who see in the successful and rebarbative capitalist life the prospect of the deepest kind of pleasure and attainment). Nevertheless, even for these ardent defenders of capitalism, the ideal image of capitalism is one built, not from the reality and exacting demands of the competitive successful capitalist life alone but, rather, from the enchanted semblable of this life: the phantasmagoria of the continuum of pleasure and success that it invokes and invites us to participate in as consumers and beneficiaries of the rewards of *amour-propre*. Yet, this does not mean, thereby, that to be worthy of the 'master's desire' is not to be worthy of an *image* at all. But this is an image that is constructed by the subject as an internalized ideal self from the flux of the demands of the 'master's desire'. In other words, to be worthy of the 'master's desire' is to be worthy of this constructed internalized image of an ideal self composed from this congeries of signifiers. So, to talk of the love of the love of self is to talk not in the conventional psychoanalytic sense of identification with an idealized *other* (of putting the idealized other in the place of one's ego-ideal) but, rather, of the self's identification with this composite image of the 'master's desire'. This is another way of saying, consequently, that the idealization of the representatives of capitalism is not part of the fantasy here, that is, they are not part of any transfer of love to capitalism. Rather, what is being idealized is the subject's narcissistic identification with its sovereign capacity *to* desire, the sense that to love the love of self is to do *justice to oneself* as a desiring subject that is equal to the demands of the 'master's desire'. That is equal to the painful question: am I worthy of the master's 'love'?

Meeting the demands of this 'master's desire', accordingly, is grounded not in the love of capitalism per se (although, to reiterate, this may be the outcome for its most ardent ideologues), but the conflicted libidinal work of making oneself available to pleasure as a condition of living as well and as purposively as is possible under capitalism. This is why the love of capitalism is not the same as the ideal image of capitalism. The love of capitalism has little or minimal hold on the libidinal investment of workers and non-workers, indeed, such a notion appears bathetic, even for bankers and CEOs, who themselves do not necessarily love capitalism at all, but see it cynically, as the only workable bulwark against an 'unrealisable' and 'chaotic' non-formal equality; in this way capitalists first and foremost exercise a love of power as an expression of their greater sovereignty (and self-worth), as opposed to a commitment to the love of capitalism in any foundational, ontological sense. What does have a broad hold on people, however, is the semblable image of an ideal capitalism that enables large numbers of people to invest in pleasure as the rational and attainable basis of their self-realization. Thus, the unalloyed love of capitalism, strangely, cannot in fact secure the 'hallucination' of expectation and self-transformation so efficiently, insofar as the identification with capitalism's powers and rewards in the abstract, invites *submission* to the love object, as opposed to an invitation to shared creativity; and, of course, love produced as idealization-as-image in this manner, easily sours; the rush to identification and idealization turns to pain and disappointment once knowledge dissolves the image. This touches crucially on what I mentioned earlier: the love of the love of self is not an ideology of religious submission to the realities of capitalism, but an attachment to the ideal of self-realization inscribed in the flux of signifiers of surplus *jouissance*. This is why, precisely, the love of the love self is based on this semblable image of capitalism: its pursuit of sovereign creativity and pleasure is constitutive of the repetitive desire to meet the fantasy of the multiplicitousness of capitalist reason and the relentless demand 'to enjoy'.

How then is self-idealization operating here exactly? How are the subjects' feelings of being worthy or unworthy of capitalist multiplicitousness and 'master's desire' – as external to production – formed by the subject's self-conceptions of sovereignty? The important issue, consequently, is not that the love of the love of self constitutes the defensive-active form that the drive takes, confronted with lack. The love of the love of self is not about how capitalism encourages and teaches us how to love ourselves, in the language of cognitive therapy, and, therefore, how happy we are doing what we do when we love the love of self; the love of the love of the self is not the successful ideological outcome of some kind of affirmative capitalist 'makeover'; on the contrary, the love of the love of the self is fragilely interposed between the subject's being worthy of the 'master's desire' and the constant feelings of unworthiness and rejection – hence, the centrality of the drive to maintain the self's defence *against* the anxiety of desire. Only new forms of *jouissance* can hold the anxiety at bay or render it malleable; only consistently maintaining the sense of being worthy of the 'master's desire' can overcome the wretched feelings of loss produced by *jouissance*. Thus, the self-idealization demanded of the love of the love of self and the maintenance of detoured desire is one familiar from the analysis of narcissism: *the self refuses to give up its sense of omnipotence, for it is this that guarantees pleasure and the relief from anxiety.* As Jessica Benjamin argues: the powerful defensive force of narcissism derives from 'the insistence on being one (everyone is identical to me) and all alone (there is nothing outside of me that I do not control)'.[64]

In these terms the love of the love of self is an extreme form of the ideal self or ideal ego, which for Lacan is at the very core of narcissistic investment. Lacan makes a distinction between the ego-ideal (symbolic integration into a world of values larger than the self) and the ideal ego (the imaginary projection of the self as a totalizable whole).[65] In this sense whereas the ego-ideal involves a limited identification with a particular trait or form of behaviour (for example, to be a 'good friend' or a 'political activist'), the ideal ego involves a fundamental identification with the sovereign or omnipotent self, which has its 'representational' and integrative origins in the child's recognition of himself or herself as a 'whole' in the mirror during the self's 'mirror phase'. The image the child sees in the mirror is something stable and co-ordinated. For Lacan this imaginary construction of sovereign integration is fundamental to the formation of psychic self-possession; otherwise the subject would be prey to, and overwhelmed by, a continuous flux of competing identifications that would render speech and action as incomprehensible and therefore subject to psychotic dissociation. In other words, the ideal ego is at the heart of the imaginary production of the 'self' as self. Indeed, the precipitation of the ego in the mirror stage, clearly seems, as Bruce Fink puts it: 'to have a quantum of love or libido attached to it, which Lacan refers to as narcissistic libido: love of libido attached to the self ... to cathect our*selves*, we require a totalizing image of ourselves as in some way positive and worthwhile.'[66]

The force of the ideal ego is compelled to assert its privileges as a condition of maintaining the self's intelligibility as a subject of desire. This is why the love of the love of self finds its rationality as an ideal ego in its intense identification with the multiplicitousness of libidinous capitalist reason; ideal ego and ego-ideal intersect and *converge* as the 'stable' substance of selfhood and self-realization. But, as I have stressed, the ego-ideal under the passionate attachments of the ideal ego to sovereignty is not attached to an image in the singular; this is because the ideal ego's is subordinate to detoured desire and the relentless passage through the signifiers and symbols of surplus *jouissance*. Detoured desire cannot afford singular attachments and passions or finds them difficult to sustain. This is also why it is hard for the ideal ego to consistently assert its non-passive and de-subjectivized demands (such as those attached to politics); such demands are always threatened by the reason of pleasure, which consistently and successfully relieves the ego-ideal of its desire and commitments and, crucially, relieves the pain of the negation involved in its lived exposure of the ideal ego's sovereignty. The ideal ego possesses all the 'answers', or, rather, those answers that seem most reasonable. Consequently, mature capitalist I-cracy is a space where the ideal ego is not simply 'captured' by real subsumption but, on the contrary, operates as the gravitational and granular force of subjectivation; the tightly determined means by which capitalism repeatedly returns itself to the same as the condition of the new and therefore to the expectation of the dissolution of anxiety through the pursuit of sovereign pleasures.

Chapter 4
Perfectionism, individuation and self-realization

'We laugh at critique'

As is clear from the last three chapters, the processes of subjectivation constitutive of the libidinal economy of capitalism have radically shifted under neoliberalism. The capitalist subject is no longer encouraged to masochistically find pleasure-as-compensation in de-individuation alone – that is, to endure the repeated struggle to access pleasure through the wage form – but, rather, to take an active pleasure in the struggle for self-reliance and self-realization, in which the love of the love of self takes on the key determinate function in mature capitalism's expansion of the desire for desire and capture of surplus *jouissance*. This is why the post-1968 counter-libidinal 'anti-repressive' subject of Lyotard seems today so recherché as the driver of an emancipatory politics, given that the 'voyage of [libidinality's] search'[1] in defiance of the inertia and 'stupid[ity]' of 'structure'[2] is the very language of capital itself; indeed, Lyotard is unabashed about what is at stake for this new libidinal subject: the 'well-prepared flight' of this new searcher is the 'avant-garde of capital'.[3] This rhetoric, consequently, makes painfully ironic reading in its over-compensatory critique of the 'sterility' of the libidinal stasis of post–Second World War social democracy and state socialism. The capitalist libidinal economy is to be permanently 'set in motion' in order to libidinize the 'repressive'[4] function of the concept; only the continuous and unfolding intensity of the 'circulation of *jouissances*'[5] can secure the intensity of freedom, displacing the deductive machinery and tedious analytics of mere 'critique'. 'We laugh at critique;'[6] 'We have no plan to be true.'[7] This paean to the Nietzschean adventure of 'punctual incandescences'[8] is, in fact, mildly hysterical (and funny of course; one can almost hear Lyotard cackling) conditioned as it is by a mad, intoxicating transcendentalism, that is full of mourning for the lost revolutionary object of May 1968. Lyotard and his generation were deeply affected by Herbert Marcuse's notion of an emancipatory politics as a liberation of the instincts and the 'release' of pleasure from reality, as if the 'pleasure principle' lagged behind the 'reality principle'.[9] But, of course, this combination of punctual incandescence and anti-epistemology is the working ideology of a mature libidinal capitalism that unambiguously and happily 'laughs at critique' and plans 'not to be true' in the interests of the domination of the 'pleasure principle' and the money form and, therefore, is extremely comfortable with the de facto notion of the 'sterility' of structure. The transition from the would-be blocked libidinality of social democracy and state socialism is the very fulfilment of the avant-garde of capital.

As we stressed the critical language of a de-sublimated libidinality frustrated by state capitalist relations of production is no longer appropriate, given that domination is no longer synonymous with the 'repression' of desire. We live under a global regime in which the access to pleasure through the wage form (and outside of it) is accompanied not just by a sense of compensatory release, but by *an active investment in the techniques of self-love or self-reliance as the constitutive form of social reproduction and its 'friendly' control*. The intersection of the ego-ideal and ideal ego under the demands of detoured desire, realizes, therefore, a particular form of mature libidinal economy: one in which the continuum of the producer and consumer is invested in a relentless attention to the labour of self-realization and sovereign self-development. Indeed, during the years of the classical workers' movement, such expectations in the workplace and the sphere of consumption were minimal. So, neoliberalism, in one key respect, represents, therefore, a massive explosion of individuated-de-individuation under the expansion of real subsumption since the 1970s. As such, this presents us, as we discussed in Chapter 1, with a situation in which the libidinal economy works in two conflicted and intersectional ways: on the one hand, the production of an economic and social system in which the pleasures of least resistance – increasingly sophisticated forms of individuation–de-individuation – continue to threaten and dissolve the autonomy of the producer (the 'happily' dominated producer), and, on the other hand, the creation of a libidinal subject across production and consumption that is increasingly attached – under the regime of individuation–de-individuation – to the desire for self-realization as a claim on this limited autonomy. If, the dream of autonomy was once connected to the modern fantasy of de-sublimation and increased access to consumption, today it forms a kind of daily struggle across the pain and pleasure of consumer adaptation/disadaptation. There is a sense, therefore, that the libidinal economy of surplus *jouissance* sustains the prospect of autonomy, as much as it threatens it, as if the subject was running towards an experience of individuation that mystifyingly it never seems able to achieve, yet always seems to be in reach of (the object *a*).

Something of this paradoxical tension lies in Adorno's late work on bourgeois interiority and the sovereign subject. Under capitalism's destruction of autonomy and subjectivity the pursuit of autonomy, in its alienated individuated-de-individuated forms, returns in a delimited, estranged capacity as sovereign desire, *as* a resistance to subjective ruination.[10] In other words, the fictiveness of sovereign or constitutive subjectivity provides the very means by which a subjectivity free from subjectivation is to be achieved; there can only be a struggle for individuation through the pursuit of individuation, even if this individuation is subject to forces of de-individuation that weakens the capacity of the subject to distinguish its experience of individuation from de-individuation. This immanent model admittedly has its limits in Adorno, given Adorno's attachment to a moral economy of individuation whose understanding of de-individuation is all encompassing; but it does foreground, what subtends and drives resistance under mature capitalism, and what we outlined earlier in Marx's concept of the 'ego' and declination: resistance is the working out of individuation via the working through of de-individuation as a struggle for new forms of individuation that ultimately cannot be mistaken for 'individuation'. But this process involves an explicit reflection on individuation itself and therefore the subject's attachment to a range of critical goods and practices, in which desire is not tied to the pleasures of least resistance; and this has limited traction and efficacy for all the reasons we have outlined on 'adaptive preference' and the crisis of the dianoetic in the previous chapters. This is why neoliberalism is the epoch of 'individuation' first and foremost.

What distinguishes the 'ideal image' of neoliberalism is the conscious and active belief that the system can resolve the question of individuation through self-reliance and the market's expansion of 'difference'; if capitalism 'laughs at critique' (laughs at critical reason) it does so in the belief, that difference in these terms is the greater 'good', insofar as it is able to meet the *adaptive* needs of all – the 'real' needs of all, as neoliberals might say – even expand the range of these adaptive needs; and therefore the meeting of these needs always and necessarily overrides the 'lesser' academic questions of: why *this* pleasure? Why *these* attachments? For, the lesser question of *what* pleasure only serves to create a moral hierarchy, which benefits the few who feel they can make judgements about the pleasures of the many. This is why, paradoxically, popular pleasure and difference serve power and domination well under mature capitalism: they define democracy as the place where all desires as pleasure are accounted for and where new desires as pleasure are welcomed and encouraged. The drive for self-realization, consequently, offers an image of happiness that is based on the availability of a multitude of cultural, moral, physical and spiritual goods, that may or may not fit the needs of the subject, but, nonetheless, in the very spirit of democracy, provides the subject with the space and opportunity to find what goods do have value for them; indeed, this multiplicity of spiritual and material goods creates space and opportunity for individual 'growth' and change.

From this perspective neoliberalism's libidinal economy is shaped and driven by a particular adaptive account of perfectionism: the logic of detoured desire and pleasure as least resistance are incorporated into a perfectionist ideal that places, for the many, the development of certain attainments and possession of certain material goods, in competition with, and at the expense of, the attainments of others as the basis of this growth and change. On this basis the love of the love of self here is an adaptive version of perfectionism, in which the desire to be the 'best I can be' finds its *raison d'etre* in what serves the desire for desire best. Thus, significantly, there is a truth that lies buried in Lyotard's miasmic exaltation of *jouissance*, that meets the early and late Marx, Adorno and Lacan's critique of *jouissance* coming the other way: mature capitalism does not repress self-realization through the 'master's desire' but adapts it as the engine of individuation-de-individuation, and this is where, in Lacan's terms, surplus value and surplus *jouissance* intersect. For across libidinal economy and the libidinal economy of the self, stability for capitalism is the threat of *destabilization*, meaning, conversely, that it is precisely destabilization that secures stability, the stability or continuity of the desire for desire. This is fundamental to the contemporary capitalist project; (Western) capitalist governments may act in order to provide stability and security for the many in the developed zones, but workers and non-workers have to find the measure of their 'creativity' and self-realization through the political–economic forces of an 'ideal' destabilization. Hence, capitalism brings all of its dominative and libidinal power to bear on the production of a sovereign self that is equal to this process of permanent destabilization, as the site, we might say, of a *utilitarian* perfectionism: the making of happiness from the rational pursuit of individual pleasure. Utilitarian perfectionism as 'happiness', consequently, is the thing neoliberalism needs most in order to make the desire for desire as least resistance and surplus *jouissance* 'pay their way' creatively. For, capitalism is a system that cannot afford a perfectionism that leaves self-realization to the virtues and knowledge alone. In this sense utilitarian perfectionism has deep historical connections to power and 'good order'.

Eudaimonism and perfectionism

Capitalism has been inseparable from the legacy of the classical perfectionist tradition from its inception, as the development of market relations encouraged questions of best practice amongst the aristocracy and the bourgeoisie, as an expression of their domination and their desire to distinguish themselves as sovereign subjects absolutely from the peasantry, artisans and workers; and, concomitantly, as an expression of their desire to secularize moral principle as the basis of their place in new commercial and competitive world. For the aristocracy this was accomplished principally through the re-invention of classical Greek virtue and 'taste', and for the emerging bourgeoisie, through the pursuit of a range of scientific, technical, cultural and artistic attainments that defined their central administrative, commercial and cultural position within the epoch of 'progress'. But, if perfectionism, in the high bourgeoisie period, tended to detach perfectibility from moral principle alone, perfectionism's attachment to religious proscriptions and moral order was no less influential in the development of the capitalist subject. Indeed, moral perfectionism initially served two different masters: God *and* capital. That is, in some instances, moral proscriptions and principles were defined in opposition to the emergent capitalism as a condition of maintaining the purity of tradition and the sanctity of faith. All the major monotheistic religions (Christianity, Islam and Judaism) have at some point opposed the spiritual degradation of capitalism as being consistent with the demands of a perfectionism made in the image of God and, as such, in some instances, expressly opposed capitalism itself (particularly the 'sin' of usury).[11] But this opposition was rarely overarching and consistent, outside of cenobitic or apocalyptic sects, for it was not the job of ecclesiastical faith to contest what could not be contested, particularly when sanctioned by royalty and heads of state. Hence, in most instances moral perfectionism is held to be compatible with capitalism; indeed, when monotheistic religions are not heaping praise on the convergence between religious self-stewardship and the prudential worker, they are claiming capitalism as that fallen realm of spiritual and mortal struggle (against concupiscence and evil), where moral perfectionism is to be tested and attained; in fact, capitalism is the perfect disciplinary training ground in the virtues for the believer and non-believer alike.

If capitalism historically has been happy to see God and capital as partners, nonetheless, it readily finds good reason to oppose eudaimonism (the art of living well or 'doing well' in Aristotle's sense)[12] to perfectionism, when perfectionism oversteps its 'ideal' and 'pastoral' role and actually threatens the interests of capital and the sovereign pursuit of pleasure. This is why capitalism has overwhelmingly preferred perfectionism when it is attached to eudaimonism or, rather, preferred a version of perfectionism that is attached to a utilitarian and materially goods-based eudaimonism; and, therefore, is explicitly defined by the link between human flourishing and the accumulation of material wealth. For the late-nineteenth-century bourgeoisie, driven by secular achievement and accomplishments, and the pursuit of wealth and influence, the question of self-realization, consequently, found itself confronting an old premodern philosophical question: can pleasure alone secure happiness? Can a person be happy without being morally virtuous or wise? As Augustine says in *On the Happy Life*: 'to be happy is nothing else but not to be in need, that is to be wise ... For wisdom is none other than the measure of the mind, that is, that by which the mind balances itself.'[13] The bourgeoisie as a class, of course, provided no univocal answer to Augustine's admonition; the bourgeoisie, split as it was by various traditional pious attachments and modern hedonistic, pragmatic and agnostic sympathies, was neither anti-utilitarian nor utilitarian in ideology, in any strict sense. Ecclesiastical religion served its interests where it saw fit. However, overall, its class interests and moral interests did have to submit to their primary master: the anomic logic of capital, as the very condition of its pursuit of wealth and influence; and, therefore, the perfection of the virtues was not just a hindrance to the pursuit of material wealth and pleasure, but a flagrant contradiction of the bourgeois spirit and self-identity. There was no place for intellectual accomplishment and spiritual development when they constrained wealth creation. This is why the European bourgeoisie had such a conflicted relationship to the classical 'virtues' as mediated by eighteenth- and nineteenth-century Christian piety: in the end, self-restraint, moderation and propriety best served those who were compelled to serve those who ruled – as the common ground for the interests of all, and for the creation of 'universal wealth' – but were not consistent as values with the interests of those who had to lead and make difficult decisions in the pursuit of prosperity for 'all'. And this is why the nineteenth-century bourgeoisie took eudaimonism as the basis for its perfectionism; classical, pure perfectionism was fine for those who took their measure of achievement from the religious imagination, but not for those who laboured to make or remake the world. Indeed, perfectionism in the ecclesiastical religious traditions was seen as a deformation of the classical spirit of self-discipline and self-realization: all perfectionisms made solely in the image of God and piety tended to submit the powers of the self to the demands of faith, dissolving self-realization into the self's realization in God. One can see, therefore, why Marx in his early Epicurean voice in his *Dissertation* and late Adorno were so compelled by the secular bourgeois construction of the sovereign self: it not only enabled producers to fully participate in the making of the world, without moral reserve, and unthinking submission to God or King, but actually enabled producers to take some pleasure from the outcome of their daily labours, however alienated.

But, Augustine's question was not easily dismissed by the bourgeoisie's utilitarian eudaimonism, insofar as his account of perfectionism opened up a powerful disjunction between happiness and material wealth, self-realization and truth, that capitalism and the libidinal forces of modernity were in the business of closing down as the basis of bourgeois class domination and progress. Indeed, Augustine could be said to be the first perfectionist of note – following, Aristotle, Cicero, Seneca and Plotinus – who establishes a critique of pleasure as a *primary condition* of the critique of power, in the pursuit of the individual's self-realization and human flourishing. In Aristotle, Cicero, Seneca and Plotinus, the perfectionist development of the virtues is an intra-aristocratic matter, insofar as it acts as the basis for good leadership; slaves, women and artisans have obviously no part to play in this ideal of moral and ethical development.[14] In Augustine, in contrast, the perfectionist virtues are a concern of all: 'not everyone who is miserable is in need'.[15] That is, the common assumption that the poor lack the capacity for wisdom (intellectual attainment), because they have no access to material goods that would support such pursuits, is false. This, famously, is the distinction that attracts Frederick Engels to the 'revolutionary' nature of early Christianity's development of the perfectionist moral virtues; finding 'happiness' in misery – because one has found a wisdom of self-reliance through God – is, of course, at one level, the hideous language of Christian supplication and pacification, that Nietzsche ridiculed so well[16]; but, for Engels it also configures a means of resistance to 'master's desire' through the rejection of the automatic association of virtue and knowledge with wealth.[17]

The modern perfectionist, tradition, then, in its liberal bourgeois form, attaches perfectionism to largely utilitarian eudaimonistic ends as a means of distinguishes its immediate needs, power and self-identity from the abstract 'virtues' of the aristocracy and the unformed passions of the peasantry and working class. This is why the bourgeoisie's demotion of the perfectionist virtues through its attachment to eudaimonism so preoccupied Rousseau. Eudaimonism is for Rousseau the very ideology of *amour-propre*, in as much as its conception of the 'happy life' submits itself to *amour-propre*'s logic of competitive distinction and hierarchy, and the pursuit of status through the accumulation of material wealth. For Rousseau, consequently, there is no possibility of universal perfectionism under the social division of labour; on this basis there can only be exclusion of the majority from the prospects of perfectionism and, as such, widespread material and spiritual immiseration for the poor. Rousseau, accordingly, treats perfectionism as bounded and constrained by social determination in a way that radically alters the 'balance', so to speak, of classical and bourgeois eudaimonism and perfectionism. If in Aristotle, the eudaimonist 'happy life' is firmly attached to secular perfectionist virtues (pleasure is the pleasure taken in self-discipline and the development of intellectual attainment and, in particular, athletic prowess); and if in Augustine and Aquinas the 'happy life' is attached to the rational perfection of oneself as a subject of Christ 'without need' (in the image of God); and, if in the bourgeoisie the 'happy life' is the competitive and secular pursuit of the intellectual and professional virtues and of material success; in Rousseau the 'happy life' is attached neither to 'godliness' nor to the cultivation of intellectual and cultural achievement and the accumulation of wealth, but to what might we might call the 'lower' civic virtues: artisanal craft skills and occupational accomplishments and martial self-discipline; virtues that serve and protect the life of the community, before, that is, the development of those individual intellectual attainments and pursuit of spiritual enlightenment that secure the individual's advance and competitive admiration within the sphere of the higher virtues. Pleasure, thereby, is attached to the contribution that the individual makes to the 'common good'. So, bourgeois utilitarian eudaimonism and the perfectionist intellectual virtues are both suspect for Rousseau on two equally important counts: they diminish the part practical reason plays in any eudaimonist concept of the virtues and a 'happy life' (virtues that emphasis practical attainment are of no less importance to human flourishing than the intellectual virtues and would-be 'godliness'); and they disconnect the development of capacity, intellectual and practical, from its social and *non-competitive* sources of collective support; the individual accomplishments a person might achieve is the result of the sharing of skills and the socialization of good practice. Thus, for Rousseau the development of such skills and practices – such as those connected to martial self-defence and the artisan's workshop – are co-operative matters, supported and maintained by the active participation of the popular citizenry and its institutions; virtue, in this sense, is a civic matter not a secular or religious individual 'mastery' of the passions.

Of course, the Greek and Roman development of the virtues was based on a model of civic virtue; for Aristotle the mastery of the passions and the pursuit of self-governance was always a question of public concern: my good is the basis of my concern for, and interest in, the good of others; Rousseau derives his civic critique of bourgeois *amour-propre*, precisely, from these Greek and Roman notions of self-governance. But for Greek and Roman aristocrats this self-governance was always a way of distinguished themselves *from* the 'people'; the idea of slaves, artisans and women fully exercising their capacity for eudaimonia would have been an affront to aristocratic reason. Rousseau, in contrast, rejects this aristocratic hubris out of hand, locating the development of the virtues not in the maximalization of individual capacities available to the most capable and powerful – as exemplars of human achievement – but, in the widest possible distribution of the 'lower virtues' as the basis for public virtue and the pleasure taken in shared achievements.

Rousseau, thereby, introduces a fundamental break into the eudaimonist and perfectionist tradition: that is, he radically shifts eudaimonism and perfectionism away from its elite class impositions and anti-egalitarian horizons. On this basis, he not only has a profound influence on Marx but on the liberal/social democratic tradition, which unlike orthodox Marxism in the twentieth century (which we will discuss below), developed a strong philosophical and political interest in non-maximalist or egalitarian concepts of perfectionism, particular in relation to public education, as was the case in Britain and other European countries: the expansion of mass education, state-funded schools, and state-funded workers' education are all indebted to late-nineteenth-century and early-twentieth-century commitments to notions of egalitarian perfectionism, in which the intellectual and cultural gains of the least able are favoured over the maximalist, perfectionist advancement of the most able.[18] Indeed, this practical eudaimonia forms the re-distributive basis of European social democracy and the classical workers' movement from the 1920s to the 1970s, and as such, represents the core values of workers' collective self-advancement that neoliberalism has successfully dismantled, in its recovery and (radical) advancement of a utilitarian eudaimonism, as the basis for self-realization. Marx, though, was not an anti-maximalist; he distrusted egalitarianism when it limits workers' advancement to the development of mere 'practical reason'. This is because it substituted workers' unmet needs for those needs determined by the immediate interests of wage labour and the labour–capital relation, ultimately confining workers to their received identity as workers. As Agnes Heller notes: such unmet needs are the opposite of necessary needs: 'Such needs will not be fixed – at least in the future – by their position in the division of labour, because they are *individual* needs (they cannot be expressed by any average), and because their satisfaction is not purchasable (all the more so, since there will be no money).'[19] And this is why Marx is dismissive of Rousseau's *völkism*: it undoubtedly frees the less able from the oppressive hierarchies of bourgeois accomplishment and the self-mastering sovereign virtues of ancient Greek philosophy; but, nevertheless, as a eudaimonia that submits the less able to practical reason alone it fails the test of human flourishing in any demanding non-parochial sense; levelling down is not universal emancipation or the creation of new needs. This is why the social democratic notion of 'distributive neutrality' was never a part of Marx's vision of perfectionism. The ending of the bourgeois division of labour for him was always consistent with the universal expansion of needs, not with the management of 'reasonable expectations'. But Marx's version of perfectionism in *The German Ideology* was, of course, a 'research programme' for the future, and not a working model of working class and non-workers' attainments under capitalist conditions and, as such, was rarely consulted by Marxists, socialists and social democrats as part of radical vision of politics and self-activity *in the present*. Its vision was always attached to a post-capitalist future; in the present, perfectionism, even in a restricted form, was considered utopian and incidental to class identity and class struggle. 'The idea that that the individual can fully bring to actuality all the powers and abilities he possesses is one of the more Utopian elements in Marx's thought.'[20] The argument is accordingly: workers are primarily interested in maintaining their living standards, not in developing their intellectual and cultural capacities, beyond a level, that is, that enabled them to secure their livelihood.

But, as we have demonstrated in this book, eudaimonia and perfectionism as living and pressing questions have becoming increasingly attached in the late twentieth century and twenty-first century to issues of self-realization, as workers find their lives and desires dissociated from the old ethnographic, workerist and corporatist identities and their conservative presumptions; and, conversely, as a result workers have increasingly become exposed as producers and consumers under the advance of real subsumption to the demands of libidinal investment in the expansion of individuation-as-de-individuation and surplus *jouissance*. The emancipatory demands, consequently, of individuation (as opposed to 'individuation') are not easily excised from the working practices and imaginary of a new politics and the 'consciousness of capital', in the name of the future or of class pragmaticism. In this way, eudaimonia and perfectionism have become pressing issues for all as a condition of making the future, here and now; indeed, eudaimonism and perfectionism are the philosophical horizons that turn individuation into a politics with universal implications. Yet, nevertheless, there remains a great deal of confusion about perfectionism and its relationship to the left and Marx's legacy. As such in the next section I want to look at a major contribution to the debate, Thomas Hurka's *Perfectionism* (1993). Hurka's concept of perfectionism sits loosely within the North American social democratic tradition, and methodologically, therefore, has much in common with mainstream analytic philosophical rationalism (Hurka, as in the case of Elster, Przeworski, Jerry Cohen and Lordon, has no working relationship to psychoanalysis); yet he has interesting things to say about the long-standing philosophical tension between maximalist and practical-distributive accounts of perfection, and as such, enables us to examine notions of self-realization that stretch far beyond present political realities, at the same time, allowing us to reassess Marx's model of perfectionism in the light of today's libidinal economy.

Hurka's perfectionism

In his introduction to *Perfectionism* Hurka outlines why a robust definition of perfectionism has significant things to say about both the limits to utilitarian pleasure and the mere equitable development and distribution of human capacities across the less abled and most abled. For Hurka, perfectionism has been constrained by both its utilitarian and its narrow moral definitions of self-conduct and self-realization, weakening the normative and holistic dimensions of perfectionism as an ideal. In this respect: 'its acceptance of *self-regarding duties* is a great strength of perfectionism. A too narrow conception of the moral has impoverished recent moral philosophy and helped to limits its influence ... To study perfectionism is to study part of what is most lacking in current philosophical morality.'[21] (And crucially what is most lacking in contemporary political theory and political philosophy.) As such, perfectionism in Hurka's account points away from what we should do or not do, so as not to frustrate the desires of others, but what we should *chose for ourselves* (in the spirit of the early Marx) in relation to what is best for ourselves *and* others. In this, Hurka adopts a mixture of Aristotelian, Augustinian, Marxist and Rousseauvian elements: perfectionism encourages us to pursue our own capacity for self-realization as one part of the varied capacity for self-realization of all humans.

Hurka offers a model of perfectionism, therefore, that broadly combines, Rousseau's critique of the privileging of rational perfectionism and Greek self-mastery, with Marx's maximalist perfectionist critique of specialisms *and* Rousseauvian artisanal consciousness, and an Aristotelian conception of self-realization in which excellence should be pursued irrespective of whether it promotes immediate pleasures and comforts and the well-being of the individual. In this sense he detaches perfectionism from eudaimonism on the grounds that eudaimonism confuses perfectionism with a particularist understanding of what increases the pleasure of self-attainment for the individual. The ideal of perfectionism should be pursued regardless of whether it brings immediate rewards or not; indeed, the idea of excellence should be pursued in its own right as a condition of excelling, in and of itself. Thus, the pursuit of excellence may be determined by inordinate difficulties and struggles and, as such, provide little pleasure or sense of well-being in the short term (or even in the end fail or disappoint), yet, without these struggles and difficulties there is no self-realization and sense of achievement to talk of and correspondingly no sense of pleasure beyond immediate satisfaction. But for Hurka this is not to be confused with the development of the intellectual virtues; following Marx, the attachment of a normative notion of excellence as the basis for human flourishing is not grounded in the development of intellectual excellence alone. The pursuit of excellence can find its realization in both abstract and practical reason, in fact, they offer comparable perfectionist rewards:

> It is wrong to focus only on the highest goods and ignore ones lower down the scale of value. More modest practical achievements are possible in gardening, child rearing, and carpentry … Otherwise, only a few people would have talents worth developing; as it is, there are serious practical goods to be sought for all.[22]

Yet, nevertheless, some notion of excellence on holistic grounds has to mark perfectionism off from mere eudaimonistic satisfaction. That is, perfectionism must involve the pleasure of seeing a plan or programme of training or action come to fruition, as opposed to the development of skill or facility as a localized solution to a given problem or the pursuit of a set of interests; self-realization certainly involves the passage from a state of 'not knowing' or absence of accomplishment to a state of 'knowing' or accomplishment, but it is also something done in the long-term for its own and non-instrumental ends, with all the difficulties this entails. Thus, *perfectionism harnesses self-discipline as a condition of self-realization.* The upshot is that self-realization is not simply the struggle for technical or disciplinary mastery, as if it was merely a higher kind of schooling or advanced academic accreditation. If perfectionism mobilizes the capacity of humans to develop their powers of excellence across a range of practical, creative and intellectual interests, it does this in the interests of the rewards of self-directed activity first and foremost, and not as formal exercises in accomplishment. Accordingly, the acceptance of struggle in the pursuit of excellence is certainly defining of any lasting sense of individual achievement, beyond mere satisfaction; but, self-directed and long-term struggles can just as easily be attached to a narrow, self-aggrandizing and hierarchical vision of accomplishment. The struggle for mastery can just as easily be put towards socially regressive and oppressive ends, attaching notions of excellence to the achievements and advancement of the most privileged and able and at the expense of the least privileged and able. In these terms, the pursuit of excellence can comfortably find its rationalization in the exclusive and anti-egalitarian idea of 'peak' achievement, as the defining exemplar of self-realization.

> Perfectionism could also be anti-egalitarian if it aggregated using the single-peak principle. When single-peak governs individual feats, there is value only in [the highest of] new achievements – new scientific discoveries or new climbs of mountains – and no value in repetitions.[23]

And this is where the Rousseauvian elements of Hurka's perspective are at their clearest: if the pursuit of excellence finds its sole rationalization in the idea of 'peak' achievement, perfectionism excludes the majority of those practices and domains where most people excel, or seek to excel, undermining the abilities of the majority. Hence for Hurka there are not just different kinds of perfections, but different routes open to achieving them, drawing on very different capacities, skills and access to resources, given peoples' interests, inclinations and histories; just as excellence may require a great deal of routine application over the long-term in the pursuit of one activity or practice or, may require relatively little routine application in other activities and practices.

However, the varied routes to excellence and the very different sense of what is excellent, based on the development of different sets of powers, is not the whole story for Hurka. If this was the case perfectionism would simply be an elaborate version of occupational development, as if perfectionism was a kind of glorified form of preferred 'skill-enhancement', in which incremental improvement in a particular activity, pastime or discipline over the long term, was satisfaction enough; as such, in these terms, this would appear to be little different from capitalist exhortations about 'self-improvement' – such as, 'getting back into the gym' or 'eating healthily'. On the contrary, the defining content of perfectionism is not that there are different routes to excellence across the intellectual, practical and creative, but rather that the most able and least able have a comparative investment in a notion of self-realization that is larger than the divisions and hierarchies of the prevailing social division of labour. This is why perfectionism is a theory of the 'general good': perfectionism is what is good for the self-realization of the human being in toto – across all capacities – as the self-realization of human beings universally. Hence, if perfectionism is to be more than simply the advancement of 'well-being' or the cultivation of various pleasures, it is also, has to be a theory of self-realization that raises and develops the intellectual and practical capacities of all. Hurka calls this an *agent-neutral* perfectionism: the pursuit of perfectionism forms the rational potential of all humans – or what we've been calling, in a slightly different register, the potential of radical unmet needs. 'Our project', he says, is to develop a perfectionism:

> That accords best with our considered judgements, and central among these judgements are one's forbidding harm to others' good. Aristotelian perfectionism cannot capture these convictions if it is fully agent-relative, but it can if it is agent-neutral. Then each agent's duty to develop his own rationality is constrained by an equal duty to preserve and promote rationality in others.[24]

In other words, there is a duty to develop one's own talents as the basis for the development of the talents of all; the development of one's own talents are derived from, and supported by, the talents of others as a condition for the pursuit of individual excellence. Therefore, the idea of a group of individuals defining their achievement of excellence at the expense of others is not a theory of universal excellence at all, but, rather, a theory of exclusionary merit that aggregates achievement in one social direction only: the achievements of the most able as the most exemplary. In this way, Hurka's perfectionism takes on two interrelated aspects: firstly, perfectionism is the social form human flourishing takes *beyond* mere 'satisfying'; and, secondly, the pursuit of self-realization – as the development of excellence – finds its fulfilment in the maximalization of one's own talents as part of the maximalization of those resources able to secure the development of excellence for all.

This is why Hurka's model of perfectionism here is closest to Marx's concept of 'all-roundedness'. 'Peak' achievements may define the very highest form of excellence within certain disciplines and domains, and, as such, set certain standards of achievement overall, but, these achievements are not compatible with the flourishing of excellence in the many across a range of interests and capacities. In fact, these levels of achievement are unrealistic for the majority, and in many instances, through their elevation of specialist achievement and the resource-rich support of such forms of excellence, prevent, the variegated pleasures that come with the integration of intellectual reason and practical reason in all-roundedness. 'I will assume that we are to seek variety not just among excellences but among aspects of each excellence, so a fully rounded life is developed, knowing, and active in many fields.'[25] As such, Hurka prefers a spread of excellences across the intellectual and practical: 'In my view the most appealing ideal, especially when we consider the value in whole lives, is that of well-roundedness.'[26] Thus, all-roundedness is the perfectionist form that secures a richness of needs that frees the subject from the separation between intellect and practical reason and consequently the valorization of specialist achievement over that of practical skills, both of which are inscribed into the division of labour; yet all-roundedness also protects the respective value of intellectual and practical reason within a non-hierarchically integrated maximalization of multiple skills and capacities.

So, Hurka rejects a narrow conception of perfectionist excellence, dismissing perfectionism's classical attachment to both the pursuit of moral virtues and/or intellectual achievement. He refuses the idea that perfectionist self-realization is defined solely by the very highest achievements of human (specialist) skill and capacity, and therefore, that perfectionist standards are crucially determined by 'peak' achievement in the singular. But his model of perfectionist self-realization is not purely eudaimonist either, or *völkisch* like Rousseau; self-realization is not, in contrast to 'peak' perfectionism, simply an issue of the utilitarian pleasures of self-development and the pursuit of the 'happy life'. Perfectionism must retain some normative link between self-realization and excellence and the struggle for a purposeful life, which, means, that whatever capacities and skills the individual develops intellectually and practically, they must be grounded in an active and assiduous notion of self-development and self-excellence as part of the 'common good'; the equalization of intellectual and practical skills is merely decorative if attached solely to the pleasures of 'satisfaction'. In these terms what perfectionism excludes from its scope is not the lesser practical achievements, but the adventitious, dilettantish and arbitrary. It is of greater perfectionist value to know a fundamental law of the universe, or how to tie a range of nautical knots that might save lives, than it is to know the number of blades of grass in your front lawn or the number of roundabouts in every town and city in the UK. This is because your knowledge of a fundamental law of the universe or a range of nautical knots will have, under most circumstances, a stronger bearing on transformative practice and the realization of your rational and creative powers in the interests of a range of values outside of yourself, than the extension of your numerical and geographical knowledge of roundabouts in the UK. It is not that a life devoted to recording roundabouts in the UK, or any other country for that matter, has no value – you may enliven the lives of those around you through your passion (and humour) and bring considerable enjoyment to your own life – but that lives devoted to counting such things as roundabouts are less likely to produce transformative outcomes, than, those devoted to mastering a range of intellectual and practical accomplishments. In this sense, certain accomplishments, or a mix of certain accomplishments, encourage a capacity for pleasure greater and deeper than satisfaction alone: the knowledge that the pleasure taken in the realization of things can point to a notion of pleasure beyond pleasure as an end in itself. 'You're not just pleased, you're pleased *that* something is the case.'[27]

But if the issue of 'well-roundedness' or 'all-roundedness' erodes the hierarchical distinction between intellectual reason and practical reason, creativity and praxis, it is not free of problems itself.

This centres on the notion that the maximalization of multiple skills and capacities across the intellectual and practical may encourage a broad or balanced approach to perfectionist excellence and the realization of one's rational and creative powers, but this approach does not necessarily provide any direct link to emancipatory practice and discourse. Hurka's model of 'all-roundedness' is largely indifferent to the possible connection between perfectionism and emancipation. This is because, although he separates the *realization* of pleasure (as autonomous endeavour and reflection), from the mere attainment of pleasure (in roundabout counting, for example), in order to distinguish his perfectionism from eudaimonia, Hurka, nevertheless, disregards the production of pleasure – or new kinds of pleasure – as an act of non-compliance or resistance. The realization of pleasure seems to have very little at stake, culturally, therefore, in relation to the struggle against perfectionism's principal enemy, what we have been calling here pleasure as 'least resistance'. The pursuit of pleasure is dissociated from a wider notion of confrontation or negation as way of redefining pleasure's attachments, of exposing dominant or settled notions of pleasure to scrutiny. Thus, although Hurka may possess a critique of eudaimonia and self-realization as prudential happiness, and, therefore, some understanding of pleasure and least resistance (pleasure beyond pleasure as an end in itself), this critique it is not expressly attached to a theory of subjectivation and domination.

Hurka's philosophical subjects, as in the analytic tradition generally, exercise their creativity and rationality and capacity for self-reflection and pleasure to the best of their ability, in world that offers them an opportunity to do so, despite the worst. This leads him to produce an odd range of social examples to illustrate his non-hierarchical thesis, revealing how accommodating his concept of perfectionism is, overall, to the social division of labour and political economy, contradicting those points in his argument where perfectionism is defined as the pursuit of human flourishing beyond mere 'satisfying': 'Many money-making activities including business activities, demand sophisticated rationality and can therefore, given formal measures of quality, embody perfection.'[28] The idea that sophisticated models of the money form offer a different route for perfectionist values is bizarre, to say the least, as if these forms of sophistication were sovereign aesthetic options and not forms of domination. Similarly, as he says, from an opposite position within the division of labour:

> The best practical endeavours have varied subplans, requiring actions of different types. This variety is often found in politics, where a reformer may have to master economic theory, negotiate agreements, raise funds, and deliver speeches, all as a means to a final political goal. By contrast, variety is absent from repetitive manual labour. A worker on an assembly line makes many movements as the means to earning his day's pay, but all are essentially the same. All are movings of this lever or pushings of that knob.[29]

The assumption being, that repetitive waged labour is somehow a free career choice, and therefore workers have made a poor decision in accepting a job that fails to provide them with resources for skill development. Hurka's radicalism is far better than this; but, nevertheless, it reveals how much Hurka identifies self-development with access to certain professional occupational skills, and as such, how he over-identifies repetitive labour and the diminishment of perfectionist resources with factory work alone, rather than showing how repetition and the narrowing of 'all roundedness' is the constitutive form under which all wage-labour operates.

Hurka's concept of perfectionism, consequently, is strangely disconnected from those social–psychic forces of subjectivation that actually define why perfectionism is not simply a form of eudaimonia. It is because eudaimonia is attached to the pleasures of repetition and least resistance under mature capitalism that perfectionism's critique of eudaimonia as mere 'happiness' finds itself as a critique of the social division of labour rather than just an exercise in moral law or the balancing of intellectual and the practical accomplishments. As Hurka rightly says: 'perfectionism should never be expressed in terms of well-being. It gives an account of the good human life, or what is good in a human, but not of what is "good for" a human in the sense tied to well-being.'[30] Yet at no point in Hurka's account is the ideal of what is good for all humans attached to an anti-capitalist programme or, more precisely, part of a working transitional strategy. What is 'good for' the subject is shaped by what capitalism can pragmatically provide; not how what is 'good for' the subject might exceed these provisions. So, in this sense, this is where Hurka establishes his politics, and where he also takes his distance from his own analytic-rationalist model. Perfectionism broadly may defy the imposed limits of capitalist individuation, but its capacity for defiance is limited by the deep historical crisis of moral perfectionism, the same crisis that Lacan identifies with Aristotelian reason and empirical psychology and analytic philosophy. This takes Hurka, then, into the territory of Elster and Lordon, if not into psychoanalysis proper.

> Moralism is present in the perfectionisms of Aristotle, Aquinas, and Green, and it dominates that of Kant. In my view it is a fundamental error. Humans are by no means necessarily virtuous, and if moralism implies that they are, it embodies a clear falsehood ... it is not plausible that conventionally moral humans are always more rational than immoral ones. Here rationality connotes deliberation and the effective pursuit of ends, which can be found no less in a successful burglar than in a philanthropist.[31]

In other words, perfectionism is only plausible, at all, as a form of self-realization under present conditions if it disconnects itself from a moral perfectionism that is out of reach of the many. But as a moral economy, as opposed to simple and eudaimonistic libidinal economy, perfectionism has to retain some notion of what is universally 'good' (in the Aristotelian sense) rather than what is simply 'satisfying'. It has to find some moral and critical leverage against the forces of de-individuation and heteronomy that stakes a claim on human flourishing and emancipation beyond the social division of labour. This leaves Hurka, then, in a quandary, as do all accounts of self-realization and perfectionism under capitalist conditions. What are, and where are, the resources that will produce a self-realization beyond mere 'satisfying'? How can such resources become a politics or shape an emancipatory politics and agency? Hurka doesn't answer these questions directly, because, at the time of writing the book, it is clear he has already mostly made his peace with the market and social democracy after the collapse of state Communism. 'No one can develop nuanced sensitivity or abandon self-concern who must always be worrying about his physical survival'[32]; yet 'I have no settled view of whether the economy most likely to promote the perfection of all is a market economy with the redistributive elements of the welfare state or some non-market, socialist alternative.'[33]

This is why Hurka's critique of pure, moral perfectionism and defence of all-roundedness, might be said to take on a *maximalist form under minimalist conditions*: that is, the placing of a mix of intellectual and practical values *down the scale of achievement* – which he advocates as a model of excellence for the many – is the best we can presently hope for. In these terms, this lower-scale maximalism is designed as a practicable and balanced ideal for social democracy rather than acting as a model for an emancipatory politics as such. The well-formed life that strives for excellence under present conditions of capitalist self-reliance and limited possibilities for self-realization, can at least achieve a balanced and ameliorative range of intellectual and practical goods.

It is possible to see the pragmatic or defensive virtue of this as a means of forestalling some of the ravages of mature capitalist de-individuation and should be defended; but the social democracy, he imagines as securing this mix of values, is long past. Thus, if we were to compare Hurka's *Perfectionism* to Stiegler's *Symbolic Misery* trilogy, with its mass proletarianization of cognitive capacity, and to Lordon's *Willing Slaves of Capital*, with its 'joyful alienation' and 'voluntary servitude', it seems as if Hurka, and Stiegler and Lordon, are talking about different worlds. And, in a sense they are. In Stiegler and Lordon the question of perfectionism, in either a programmatic form at the level of state provision or on an individual–social basis, as a process of non-eudaimonist self-realization (through political struggle, intellectual excellence and critical practice), would appear to be phantasies, derived from a misreading of desire and subjectivity under libidinal economy. The subjects of self-realization that Hurka picks out are not just delimited in the pursuit of their powers of excellence under mature market conditions – in the analytic philosophic sense – but, are attached to desires that are thoroughly eudaimonistic; are indissociable from pleasure as least resistance.

One can see, then, why perfectionism has on the radical left in the modern period appeared to be a false dawn for emancipatory politics, and, hence, why Marx saw it is a post-revolutionary horizon for all, and not a requirement of class struggle. Marx's concept of all-roundedness is a state of accomplishment, a harmonious situation of repose and resolution, even stasis, for perfectionism is not a form of praxis or part of the struggle for communism but its end state. Marx assumed this because he believed that collective workers' struggle would open up a historical space for such all-roundedness to flourish. But if self-realization was of little import for workers during the workers' movement in the twentieth century, today, it defines the very means by which workers and non-workers negotiate the demands of surplus *jouissance* and the desire for desire. Perfectionism, thereby, takes on a directly emancipatory role: the limits of capitalist eudaimonism are exposed as the outcome of the pursuit of mass (utilitarian) self-realization. This essentially is the theme of Stiegler and Lordon. In this way, a range of perfectionist virtues are necessarily and urgently re-attached to an emancipatory politics. But this cannot be a newly moralist version of perfectionism. The exercise of these virtues has to have some libidinal attachment to what we 'should choose for ourselves',[34] as a condition of the collective good and a new, non-utilitarian conception of pleasure. The call for a perfectionism that talks of the 'decline of reason', or of mass narcissism, leaves pleasure exposed to moral censure and the akratic dissociation of action from desire. Hence Hurka is right to loosen the ties of perfectionism to the classical diktats of moral improvement and the moral condemnation of those forces that would prevent self-realization. The classical or religious mastery of the self not only compounds the elitist distinction between the most able and least able, but also destroys the very thing that perfectionism elicits under mature capitalism: a new account of pleasure, given workers and non-workers direct libidinal, self-pleasuring, investment in their own material reproduction. That is, the *moralistic* disapproval of (de-individuated) pleasure, as a politics, means little or nothing to those who labour under capitalism and who take pleasure from this process of de-individuation. This is why, Hurka is at least right to note that in choosing 'for ourselves' what carries meaning and value as the 'good', the question of perfectionism has to link self-realization and moral theory to the question of pleasure when moral theory has little leverage on its own. Pleasure and moral theory require some common ground in the critique of adaptive reason; they both need to look out for each other's interests, so to speak.

But the pursuit of non-instrumental reason in this sense does not just involve the merely cognitive or reflective *realization* of non-adaptive pleasure. Pleasures have to be realized, certainly, through practice, in contradistinction to their passive acceptance in consumption, as a basic condition of perfectionist autonomy, but the realization of pleasure, if it has to have any emancipatory content, has to be connected to a desire that puts adaptive pleasure in jeopardy *as such*, and, therefore, is linked, above all else, to a logic of negation; that is, the realization of pleasure cannot simply be an *affirmative* process adjusted to the desire for desire. Rather, the realization of this kind of pleasure is produced by the desire for non-compliance and non-reconciliation; the pleasure taken in those values *not* supported by 'master's desire' – in Lacan's sense. In other words, the realization of pleasure as a form of non-adaptive reason is defined by the struggle for a pleasure actually worthy of autonomy: that is, a desire that is identifiable with the pursuit of individuation as opposed to that of 'individuation' or individuation-as-de-individuation. It is only through this struggle that desire and agency can break through the pleasures of least resistance. So, in this respect, the realization of new pleasures under libidinal economy have to find their immediate orientation in a *recourse to unpleasure*, to those perfectionist virtues that delay or deny the rationality of least resistance, that dis-accommodate the reason of such pleasures. It is only through this acceptance and assimilation of unpleasure as pleasure, as a different claim on pleasure and reason, that the link between pleasure and political economy can be negated as a practicable working through of least resistance. Indeed, this is where the emancipatory transition under libidinal economy is located: through the *refunctioning of pleasure as the refunctioning of values*. Or, co-extensively, *the refunctioning of values as the refunctioning of pleasures*.

Hence, perfectionism's critique of eudaimonism's 'happy life' is not strictly the issue here in any absolute sense. Perfectionism is a critique of de-individuated and heteronomous pleasure, and not a critique of pleasure as such. We need, accordingly, to distinguish between *utilitarian eudaimonism* (adaptive pleasure) and *non-utilitarian eudaimonism* (non-adaptive pleasure) in any workable theory of perfectionism. For, on the basis of this distinction the realization of pleasure as a non-utilitarian and emancipatory set of values shifts the focus in perfectionism philosophically away from the development of the virtues as the rational, akratic control of heteronomous passions – as a claim on autonomy and freedom – to the notion of exercise of the virtues as acting on desires, and, thereby a claim to pleasure. Deliberative desire defines moral motivation, and not a threat to its realization, underlying what I say above: virtue is not independent of desire (non-moral values), and, therefore, self-realization under these revised 'perfectionist demands' enables the subject to desire what offers little or no immediate reward and, as such, take pleasure from the vicissitudes of this struggle. Thus, we might say, this intersection of virtue and desire is the form that the *working through* of pleasure as least resistance takes. However, under libidinal economy perfectionism has little to say about this process politically. When it does so, its orientation is unwarrantably abstract. So, the key issue of perfectionism – to become the best one can be – is certainly a moral matter, but not a moral matter in which, desire and pleasure, threatens self-realization and the moral virtues themselves.

Self-love and perfectionism

On this basis one of the strengths of Hurka's model of perfectionism is that it attaches the moral economy of perfectionism and the critique of eudaimonism to the issue of self-love. There is no actual discussion of self-love in *Perfectionism* in any detail or, for that matter, any discussion, specifically, about the relationship between pleasure and self-realization. This is because self-love is too attached to the psychoanalytic critique of the libidinal subject for comfort for Hurka. Nevertheless, Hurka's insistence that perfectionist virtues are inoperative unless based on 'what we should choose for ourselves' is nevertheless clearly sensitive to the question of what he calls *self-regard* or, more precisely, the *pleasure* of self-regard. Self-regard and self-love are not the same philosophically, but they do share an understanding of self-affection or self-worth as being crucial to the pursuit of perfectionist 'goods'. In this section, therefore, I want to return to the issue of self-love (*amour-propre*) as a means of thinking through the 'working through' of perfectionist excellence and the pleasures of least resistance under libidinal economy. For it is through a reconsideration of what we might gain from self-love as a perfectionist concept of excellence, that we can further develop what we mean by individuation, self-realization, autonomy – and importantly for this section – non-identity. In turn, we can see how self-love has to be part of any emancipatory logic under libidinal economy, if desire, pleasure and moral accountability are not to be separated.

As we outlined briefly earlier, self-love or *amour-propre* in Rousseau's language – in its conventional evaluation, that is – represents a kind of failure of moral perspective and action. Indeed, it appears as source of existential threat to virtue, insofar as it takes the sovereignty of the self as primary: in

Seneca's sense *one is answerable only to oneself*.[35] Or rather, to qualify Seneca's stoicism here, one is answerable to oneself as a *utilitarian pursuer of pleasure and status*. Self-love, therefore, is defined principally as form of heightened self-attention in which the pursuit of self-evaluation and the development of one's capacities and advantages is the priority. This is what traditionally we might call: inflated self-interest. And, as such, crucial to this self-attention is a primary concern with how one compares with others, particularly those who appear to be equally 'abled'.

Fundamentally, self-love is driven by 'comparative desire'; one needs to make clear to oneself and to others that one's capacities and advantages have high worth. Hence self-love in this respect combines a number of motivations and desires that exceed mere *amour de soi* (self-preservation). Self-love sees self-realization and self-development as relative to the admiration and acceptance of others. But because the admiration and acceptance of others is never guaranteed or stable, the desire for greater rewards from comparative judgement, becomes insatiable, unsatisfiable, placing a heightened emphasis on the pursuit of those 'goods' (property, influence, fame) that appear to offer the greatest opportunity for both advancement and admiration and therefore for self-realization. Moreover, these actions find a rational justification in the necessary protection of one's own self-esteem and social standing. Given the demands for self-advancement faced by all under competitive market conditions, occupational skills and social distinction and personal accomplishments, have to be continually developed and refined in order to sustain advantage and difference.

This heightened model of self-attention is what some philosophers call 'inflamed' *amour-propre*[36] and, as such, is remarkably close to what we have been calling surplus *jouissance* and the desire for desire. But self-love is also attached to a different economy of pleasure, in which notions of self-attention and self-regard provide the psychological ground for what we defined above as: a *non-utilitarian eudaimonist perfectionism* – the interconnection between desire, pleasure and moral agency. This is not strictly Kantian (desire and pleasure are not moral imperatives), but it does recognize, like Kant, that a respect for one's own accomplishments irrespective of how they measure up against the accomplishments of others, is one of the means by which desire, as opposed to the desire for desire and individuation as opposed to 'individuation', can find some notional point of detachment from pleasure as least resistance. In this sense self-love here is the autonomous pleasure taken in one's own accomplishments, irrespective of how of successful they are judged to be by those with authority and power. As Simon Blackburn argues:

> Far from being a selfish concern, [self-love] as it might appear, this is thought to be the foundation without which it is impossible to respect others as morality requires. And we have already noticed that the converse, self-disgust or self-hatred, is unlikely to co-exist with any great feeling for others and what they deserve. A cynical view of oneself is much more apt to consort with a similar view of others. Kant himself held that without duty to oneself, there can be no duties to others.[37]

This duty of care to oneself, however, is not a sophisticated version of 'self-empowerment', with all its therapeutic and identitarian baggage about the 'power of affirmative thinking'. Self-love is not a form of benign self-ratification once it dissociates itself from heightened self-regard and the pursuit of recognition; a comfortable exercise in accommodation. As Alain Badiou says, as a way of reminding ourselves of what is stake philosophically: any materialist theory of the subject is 'diametrically opposed to all elucidating transparency. Immediacy and self-presence are idealist attributes … The subject does not overcome itself in any reconciliation of itself with the real or with itself'.[38] And the concept of self-love is no different. In this form, self-love offers a pathway through self-regard to the critique of self-identity. This is because crucially it is no less indebted to comparative desire than 'inflated' *amour-propre*. That is, in this instance, comparative desire is not designed to heighten self-regard at all but, rather, subject it to critical reflection. The subject's reliance on comparative judgement does not serve to promote self-affection as an act of pure self-will and self-aggrandizement but, on the contrary, open up the subject's self-affection to the scrutiny of others, as a means of testing the value of its conduct and accomplishments. In order to make good the value of one's own accomplishments, then, one respects one's own accomplishments by 'submitting [one's] own conduct or [one's] own work to criticism'.[39] For, criticism is the means by which the pleasures taken in one's own accomplishments and one's powers of realization are sustained, as opposed to criticism being the agency whereby they are withheld or cut-off, in order to protect one's self-identity. Without the socialization of judgement there is no possibility of self-realization or excellence at all (beyond a pure and phantasmatic notion of eudaimonia, that is); no point of connection between one's own self-love and the self-love of others. Consequently, self-love is an invitation to knowledge and evaluation and not simply a form of self-admiration.

This sense of self-love as a (critical) care of the self has little purchase in the modern period and the epoch of capitalism, for all the reasons we have outlined in relations to the legacy of perfectionism. This is reflected in the predominantly pejorative accounts of self-love that have derived from a partial reading of Rousseau, and in the failure of the orthodox Marxist tradition to open the debate on ethics and self-realization as a contemporary politics, rather than leaving it to the work of the future. (Agnes Heller's *The Theory of Need in Marx* is one of the few books in the Marxist tradition in the twentieth century to address questions of perfectionism and self-realization as a problem of contemporary praxis; written in Hungary in the early 1970s her book, essentially, is an oblique defence of the 1960s counterculture and critique of Stalinist workerism.) This is why in his own engagement with the question of self-realization and perfectionism in the early 1980s, Michel Foucault had to return to the long premodern history of the debate in order get some critical purchase on the chronic self/society binarisms and positivisms, Althusserian 'subjectless subjectivations', and Kantian and neo-Christianized ethics that dominated the social sciences at the time. All these positions conspired to limit, diminish or ignore how capitalism continues to produce various modalities of self-governance (or self-realization) as the necessary means of mediating between the interests of the governed and the power and demands of those who govern. His notion of the governed here is a very narrow one, admittedly: the unmet needs of the governed here are obviously not those attached to women, slaves, free peasants and artisans; self-governance is principally an intra-aristocratic pursuit and ideal; a reflection, as in ancient Greek philosophy generally, on the norms of male, aristocratic conduct and virtue. But, nevertheless, in his discussion, in *The Care of the Self* (1984), of a range of literatures on marriage, sexuality, public conduct, Foucault presents various ancient Greek and Roman diagnostics and technics of the 'care of the self' in oblique relationship to the ruling set of aristocratic Stoic assumptions about self-governance as a diligent withdrawal from the passions. Foucault notes in his extensive research, that the exercise of ruling power in these terms, as a retreat of the individual into himself, was not a stable process and certainly not one defined by virtue as self-abnegation alone. As he argues:

> It is true that in certain philosophical currents one finds the recommendation to turn aside from public affairs, from the troubles

and passions to which they give rise. But it is not in this choice between participation and abstention that the principal line of division lies; and it is not in opposition to the active life that the cultivation of the self places its own values and practices ... The important political transformation that took place in the Hellenistic and Roman world may have induced certain withdrawal behaviors. But, above all, they brought about, in a much more general and essential way, a problematization of political activity.[40]

The exercise of power was not fashioned from the privatized and individualistic withdrawal of the self, but from the notion that the governance of oneself should be the basis of taking one's place among others. Thus, far from the care of self being a matter of pursuing an exacting solitude, the relationship of oneself to oneself finds its orientation in social practice. The development of the 'ideal self' as an exercise of power for Foucault is formed by its critical constitution as a mode of political and social mediation between the exercise of power and the conflicts of power inside the polity, and the exercise and maintenance of power outside of it. And, therefore, obviously this is far from being a harmonious process. 'We need to think in terms of a crisis of the subject, or rather a crisis of subjectivation – that is, in terms of a difficulty in the manner in which the individual could form himself as the ethical subjects of his actions.'[41] In this sense the vicissitudes of the care of the self are produced out of this very crisis of subjectivation: of how, and what to do, as someone who exercises reason in the name of power. But crucially for Foucault this exercise of power is also an exercise in civics and, as such, is not separate from the cultivation of the self and the formation of the place of the individual and the exercise of reason in the 'good life'. Thus, at the heart of power for Foucault the ideal 'care of the self' finds its virtue in the art of living well and not egregiously as a form of self-predation or pious self-renunciation. 'It is the development of an art of existence that revolves around the question of the self, of its dependence and independence ... of the connection it can and should establish with others.'[42]

Foucault's quasi-eudaimonistic defence of the 'care of the self' as a making of the political and of civic society, then, is not simply an induction into ancient male ruling class politics. It forms an account of politics and self-realization that has some resonance in relation to questions of autonomy and individuation under libidinal capitalism, that avoids, Lyotardian paeans to *jouissance*, voluntary submission to the unidirectional force of 'master's desire', and the usual, conventional moral condemnations of self-love as self-aggrandizement. Consequently, Foucault's reading of the Hellenistic and Roman debate on the 'care of the self' contributes a singularly important aspect to our understanding of self-love and *non-utilitarian eudaimonist perfectionism*: politics and emancipatory struggle need to find a point of convergence between the modalities of self-governance and pleasure; or more precisely a pleasure taken in, and pursued through, the vicissitudes the conflicts and struggles of self-governance. As we have noted in our discussion of the intersection of desire, pleasure and moral action, this convergence is not a new version of Kantian virtue; but, it does, at least, instate that virtue is not the obverse of pleasure, and, therefore, that reason does not operate at the exclusion of desire. Our relationship to Kant here, accordingly, is based precisely on what Kant fears and knows: that it is not morality that enjoys our primary favours; just as contra Aristotle it is not the teleology of reason, that commands our desires.

Self-love and 'selflessness'

Thus, the definition of self-love at stake here, to recall the distinction between Rousseau's 'inflamed' self-love and the notion above of self-love as pride in one's own accomplishments and struggles, is a place where pleasure in virtue finds an attachment to the 'care of the self' as an act of resistance or non-compliance. To love oneself is neither the language of narcissism, nor that of therapeutic self-affirmation, but, rather, an attachment to making oneself true to one's interests as a means of making oneself available to others and the world. As Harry Frankfurt argues: a person exhibits self-love in this way, 'by protecting and advancing what he takes to be his own true interests, even when doing so frustrates desires by which he is powerfully moved but that threaten to divert him from that goal.'[43] Hence self-love conforms more closely to the ordinary modalities of love than we might assume: in loving oneself one loves oneself as particular individual, as one would love someone else for their particularities, and therefore not as an abstraction or ideal. In this sense, self-love provides a space for the realization and support of individuation, given that our capacity for self-affection and self-attention find their greatest autonomy and pleasure in the resistance to the designs and purposes imposed on us by others; we love, as an act of self-love what we claim for ourselves. There is therefore a purposeless purposiveness at work in the concern for individuation that self-love promotes: the interests of the subject, irrespective, of their value, or merit, are their own.

Only rarely do we seek our own well-being primarily because we expect that it will lead to some other good. In the love that we devote to ourselves, the flourishing of the beloved is sought – to a greater degree than other types of love – not only for its own sake but for its own sake alone. Perhaps it would [be egregious to flirt with the notion] that self-love may be *selfless*. It is entirely apposite, however, to characterize it as *disinterested*, in the clear and literal sense of being motivated by interests other than those of the beloved.[44]

But, 'Selflessness', 'disinterestedness'? This is a strange way to talk about self-love, as if the idea of self-affection and self-attention were not tightly coiled into – as we have seen in detail – a libidinal economy that attaches self-love to the love of the love of self, the demands of surplus *jouissance* and the desire for desire. Isn't selfless self-love a misrecognition of the subject's investment in the 'joyful labour' of capitalist self-realization? A misrecognition of 'individuation' for individuation? Frankfurt's model looks conspicuously like a Kantian inflation of the sovereign powers of the self (despite his identification of pleasure and the passions with virtue and its struggles), and therefore, ultimately, of little value for a *non-utilitarian eudaimonist perfectionism*. Yet, Frankfurt provides an interesting, or at least potentially interesting, further move; a Rousseauvian move: the love that people have for things as a manifestation of the love we owe ourselves, be they virtuous or meretricious, cannot be identical with the sovereignty of the self. That is, a 'person cannot love himself except insofar as he loves other things'[45] – other things than 'himself' or 'herself' as a sovereign subject. To act in the interests of self-love is therefore to love what exceeds the limits of my own identity as a would-be sovereign, desiring being. Here, then, the tendentiousness of the notion of selfless self-love reveals its truth value: self-love in this mode acts as the basis for a non-identitarian split with self-affection as self-identification: I love what is *not* of me as a means of making and giving value to what is particular to me and what is true to my interests, and in turn, therefore, what is true to my interests is what I find true in the interests of others; my particularities are mine insofar as I have made them from particularities which are external to me – opposed, that is, to just desiring what I lack as the means by which I can continue to freely desire what I lack. Consequently, self-love's love of what is not of me as a means of making what is of me is a constitutive part of what we called earlier: the process of making good the value of one's own interests and accomplishments by submitting oneself to criticism. Self-love, in other words, is the mode by which the subject's non-instrumental attachment to his or her interests and goals are formed; indeed, without this love of oneself, such interests and goals are invariably subject to the heteronomous interests and goals of others. So, self-love, in these terms, is a struggle for self-governance, in which, paradoxically, non-identity and self-critique prevail over identity.

I have pushed Frankfurt's argument here somewhat further than he allows, given, the fact he doesn't expressly follow his own critical intuitions on self-love. For, rather than associate self-love openly with non-identity, with the critique of the sovereignty of the subject, as I do here, he attaches its volitional rationality as a mode of autonomy to an 'integral' model of the self: it is self-love, as 'autonomy' and 'undivided will',[46] that will release the subject from instrumental desire, from *jouissance*. This gives self-love a metaphysical power completely out of keeping with its merely local powers, so to speak: the fact that it is one part of the socialized 'working through' of individuation under libidinal economy and not a discrete mode of non-alienated conduct or action. Self-love in this form, then, is a not magical antidote to de-individuation and surplus *jouissance*; the source of true self-regard, or 'wholeheartedness' as Frankfurt oddly calls it.[47] Psychoanalysis tells us otherwise; under conditions of general de-individuation we cannot *secure* our autonomy as a sovereign act, because we are unable to freely pursue this autonomy in concert with the autonomy of others. But, nevertheless, acting *for* autonomy breaks the circuits of de-individuation through the grounding of self-love in the subject's non-instrumental attachment to its interests; and this has critical and social outcomes, principally that the self finds its libidinal attachment through what is not me (non-identity): namely, Lacan's non-sovereign, 'I am he who is thinking.' Thus, self-love, from this perspective, is not about establishing a bond or communion with oneself, of establishing 'oneness' (of imputing sovereignty to oneself through the desire for desire) but, in fact, the opposite: the means by which the subject finds some notional place, a conflicted place, a decentred place, in the struggle for autonomy and the pursuit of individuation.

Two Forms of Self-Love; Two Forms of Self-Governance

What I've traced out so far in this chapter, essentially, is a long-standing debate on the relationship between self-governance and self-realization. For pre-capitalist social formations, as we have touched on, this was solely a preoccupation of ruling classes as a condition of their self-proclaimed possession of reason and desire, hence their investment in 'peak' perfectionist notions of excellence; the subjects of the oppressed classes were assumed to be too enfeebled by their subordination and therefore had no need of the subtle dialectic of self-governance and self-realization: for there was nothing of note to 'realize'. Yet, nevertheless these ruling classes could not but rule through encouraging the self-governance of the ruled; the demands enforced on rulers could not be served by violence and coercion alone, although this violence and coercion was terrible and ubiquitous and held the high ground; the rulers needed the ruled to find some notional point of psychic attachment and pleasure in their submission, certainly when the masses were mobilized for warfare or punitive taxation. For the slaves and popular classes of ancient Greece and Roman society, this was knowing that they were part of an Empire and hierarchically governed universe, in which serving, unquestionably, defined their best and only interests. Under feudalism Christianity destroyed aspects of this secular ideology of service, given its displacement of unquestioned faith in secular power. This is why it was held to be a threat. But Christianity also served to limit and repress the beginnings of a consciousness of individuation beyond service, that had been released by the development of the social division of labour. Hence, the fact that Christianity found its mature *raison d'etre* in the destruction of secular interiority and the eudaimonistic cultivation of the self, through the submission of the passions and material self-interest to self-realization in God. And of course, if the church saw this as a way of protecting its flock from secular influence, secular power was happy to support this submission to God as a means of protecting its own material interests.

Under early capitalism, however, the servants of God lose their immediate command over the self-governance of the ruled, as workers and artisans are required to find a set of attachments that define their interests first and foremost as capitalist producers and consumers; Christian proscriptions can only guide capitalist desires so far, they cannot challenge them, without delimiting capitalism's need for pliant and willing labour power. In turn, the emergence of the European bourgeoisie as the class that governs and shapes this global labour power, marks its rise to power with an unprecedented investment in these desires as a new age of progress, in which self-realization for those who rule overrides self-governance as religious restraint; self-governance is now principally for those whose self-discipline is required to 'serve' the interests of capital. But serving productive capital is not like serving the church or landowners: the self-discipline of wage labour brings the self-governance demanded of the worker into tension with the possibility of a self-realization not controlled by direct moral jurisdiction; workers' desires and needs begin to expand, as their capacity for independent action outside of the factory and office begins to widen as they are transformed into consumers and citizens. This is why Rousseau's work on self-love is so important to this history: it defines that moment when the question of self-governance and self-realization takes on their modern forms: self-realization begins to appear as a horizon for all; and self-governance begins to re-attach itself to self-realization as a secular condition of resisting the new forces of domination that the transformation of workers into biddable consumers creates (what we have called, in its late modern form, libidinal economy).

This is why the concept of self-love takes the two forms that we have analysed above: self-love as the worker's and dominated response to the demands of the 'master's desire'; and, conversely, self-love as a 'care of the self' and struggle for autonomy. This distinction of course is artificial, as we have stressed; neither are pure categories: the self-love attached to 'master's desire' is never fully subordinate to this desire; just as the self-love attached to a 'care of the self' never escapes the heteronomous reach of 'master's desire'. Both forms of self-love co-exist, unevenly, depending on class location, occupation, gender and race etc. Yet, despite this artificial opposition, they nevertheless provide a taxonomy of distinctions that foreground the conditions under which social reproduction and the struggles around de-individuation/individuation take place in the current period, bringing into relief what these two forms of self-love both share and what separates them.

Both forms are driven by self-governance; one form, however, facilitates immediate pleasure and 'master's desire'; the other resists this desire. Both forms encourage self-reliance, but one form seeks access to 'master's desire' as a means of self-advancement, the other its foreclosure. One form closes off self-love to transindividuality as a belief in sovereignty, one form sees transindividuality as fundamental to the exercise of one's autonomy and capacities; one form seeks comparative judgement in the pursuit of social status; one form seeks comparative judgement as a means of self-critique; one form acts as a psychic barrier against non-identity; one form opens up self-attention and self-regard to non-identity; one form squanders desire in *jouissance*, one form acts to protect desire against *jouissance*; one form pursues a utilitarian 'care of the self'; one form encourages a non-utilitarian 'care of the self'; one form submits to the pleasure of least resistance; one form seeks to break its logic; one form pursues the love of the love of self as a means of securing sovereign pleasure; one form pursues the love of the love of self as a means of negating sovereign pleasure; one form channels a narrow, eudaimonist perfectionism compatible with capital; one form establishes perfectionism as an emancipatory horizon, incompatible with capital.

In a way this taxonomy is a crude exercise. None of these oppositions are functionally stable; they are not 'negatives' and 'positives'. Yet, crucially, it shows how contemporary capitalism produces an increasingly powerful dialectic of investment/disinvestment around competing notions of individuation, that bring an unprecedented self-consciousness to bear on the capitalist subject as libidinal subject that is inseparable from normative claims of human flourishing. The libidinal subject is increasingly sensitized to the costs, passing rewards and false dawns, of the desire for desire and surplus *jouissance*, through boredom, inertia, ill-health, self-hatred, anxiety and distress. The issue, consequently, is not that emancipatory politics is able programmatically to attach itself to an ethics of self-love, as a form of radical self-governance (autonomy). This is to assume that the notion of a non-utilitarian eudaimonist perfectionism could be passed on like an exercise in Christian homiletics, or that, simply, the 'care of oneself' might re-attach itself to a critical auto-didacticism that we associate with the highest cultural achievements of the communist tradition. Capitalism has mostly destroyed the relationship between critical knowledge and desire in these terms, and, therefore, has diminished knowledge's powerful supplementary force on those lives who need it the most, knowledge becoming a burden and luxury. This is one of the outcomes of what we have called subjective ruination and the destruction of workers' parties and institutions. But this is precisely the point of my argument: under these conditions the perfectionist pursuit of self-affection is not ethical recompense for this loss of collective action and orientation and the deflated status of the militant. Rather, in its respite from de-individuation and cultural proletarianization it opens up new forms of libidinal attachment to values that expose the costs of surplus *jouissance* as the basis for establishing new connections, new meanings, new unities – the basis, in fact, for new forms of passion and militancy. And, therefore, whatever practicable merits this might or might not have as the basis for collective political and cultural practice ('the consciousness of capital'), it functions residually, at least, as a space of (determinate) autonomy in action and thought, in precisely the same way that in the psychoanalytic session desire is recovered from repetition. It connects the subject to those capacities and affects which prioritize individuation as a claim on desire and the pursuit of individuation by all, in spite of the chronically diminished opportunities for such individuation; it marks the beginning of a new affection. And the 'consciousness of capital' more than anything else needs new affections, for there is no critique of capital worthy of the name that does not recognize and accept the cost of the diminishment of this individuation.

Hence the fact that, virtue accords here with the link between desire, pleasure and moral action; and therefore, with the necessary connect between pleasure (my desire) *and* reality, pleasure *and* struggle – what Lacan calls the interrelationship of the 'pleasure principle' and the 'reality principle'; pleasure does not escape or precede reason; pleasure is a claim on reason, just as reason is a claim on pleasure. In this Lacan follows Freud's wider insight that reason is not reducible to repression. As Bernard Stiegler argues:

> Pleasure ... is what constructs reality (insofar as fantasy arises through the individuation of psychic beings, who, incomplete, pursue themselves in their fantasy, and who, through this transindividuating pursuit, transform reality, and are themselves conversely and transductively transformed through it): pleasure cannot be *opposed* to reality, nor life to death, freedom to repression.[48]

This is why the pleasures of 'adaptive preference' and 'least resistance' are judgements based on 'best reason' and not evidence of a failure of reason, particularly, when we note that the rewards of 'adaptive preference' and 'least resistance' seem greater when the subject is threatened by forces that appear to diminish his or her pleasure. These are the constant and powerful rewards of surplus *jouissance*. Thus, from this perspective self-love, in resisting the separation of self-affection (desire) from struggle, is able to give subjective shape to the challenge against these rewards as 'best reason' and therefore the regression of desire to the drives.

Self-Realization, Perfectionism and the Transition Problem

Consequently, perfectionism is not simply an abstract problem of moral philosophy: it is crucial to the establishment of a new subjective orientation for emancipatory politics in the present period, where surplus *jouissance*, the desire for desire and the love of the love of self are our ruling reason and therefore so powerful at determining the content of our self-affections. For the conception of the 'good' life, pleasure and self-realization have not just found influential allies in the defenders of capitalist eudaimonism, but are the means by which capitalism encourages us all to be self-reliant as the best means of accessing pleasure (as least resistance). In this sense, the debate on self-realization, as we have constructed it in the modern period, marks a long period of adjustment to the crisis of self-interest – or rather, more precisely, to workers and non-workers concepts of self-interest. As we have acknowledged, the rise of a post-Kantian, anti-akratic model of reason in a modified analytic philosophy, and in a Hegelianized and psychoanalytically based Marxism and critical theory, has made Aristotelian claims on 'best interest' compromised or defeasible, once desire is shown to split reason open. As Michel Rosen declares in a representative fashion: 'Why do the many accept the rule of the few, even when it seems to be plainly against their interests to do so?'[49] Indeed, this is the overwhelming and defining question of modern political theory, post-Freudian psychoanalysis and the new critiques of libidinal economy that have their modern origins, in many ways, in Wilhelm Reich's writing on fascism in the 1930s – the point where desire and reason fed voraciously on each other. Why, Reich asked, do the majority find pleasure in servitude?[50]

The intellectual damage done to the perfectionist legacy, then, has been enormous under the failure of an Aristotelian conception of reason to offer a convincing account of why 'best interests' have invariably deferred to a reason of 'adaptive preference' and 'voluntary servitude'. But if we have shown why there is good reason for workers to accept (the rewards) of adaptive preference as being in their best (pragmatic) interests, we have also shown why 'adaptive preference' and 'voluntary servitude' don't work consistently as concepts, particularly when they are attached in the literature to the notion of 'free-riding'. Workers find pleasure in self-reliance under the dictates of 'master-desires', but workers' desire is not a mirror of that of 'master's desire'. Perfectionism, therefore, has found little resonance in a period where the pleasures of finitude appear to have most of the answers. Perfectionism seems largely surplus to political requirements, even an embarrassment to a left attached to defending what remains of the old workers' movement, as a threadbare attachment to what remains of the politics of the wage form. That is, given the fact self-realization is seen to be a collective problem, and that the resolution of this collective problem is no longer a living possibility, questions of self-realization remain superfluous to the immediate problems of social reproduction and workers' fair reward for their labours. In fact, there is a mismatch between resources and possibilities: if self-realization in its ideal form, in Marx's sense, is the full and free actualization of powers, the pursuit of self-realization under a system that prevents and destroys individuation as a fundamental condition of the system's reproduction, is self-defeating as both an immediate and long-term problem. To concentrate on self-realization in the long-term might be an interesting philosophical exercise, but to concentrate on it in the short term is impractical and wasteful. Thus – and this is perhaps more telling – the pleasures and achievements of perfectionist excellence appear abstract and unbearably strenuous, irrelevant, even obtuse, against the mass cultural pleasures and occupational satisfactions and achievements, provided by a modern capitalist democracy that is the sole horizon of progressive change.

It has been easy, then, for the left to abandon self-realization, 'care of the self' and self-love as self-affection – in their expanded sense – from the question of transition, for they appear, in many of their intellectual forms, as elitist and attached to modernist notions of negation and corrective distance. That is, they are thought of as elitist precisely because they are attached to an ideal horizon that is no longer available, in any practicable sense. The revolutionary notion of perfectionism as the subjective form of an anti-capitalist transition that mobilizes self-affection as a militant and non-compliant socialized individuation is seen as an ideological remnant. This is why the recent construction of new emancipatory 'post-work' transition programmes is light on self-realization as subjective investment and the pursuit of individuation. The transition problem is invariably thought of more practicably as a problem of greater democratic management, as we outlined in model 2 in the introduction, dominated as it is by the Technology Solution and the Third Disruption. And, as such, when self-realization does come up it is not attached to the critique of the social division of labour as the basis for the expansion of perfectionist goods; rather, self-realization is simply a technical and welfarist or 'culturalist' problem, dictated by greater, more refined, more efficient access to mass technologies and 'personal technologies' that further relieve us of the burden of necessary labour and enhance 'creativity'. In fact, in these terms, subjectivity is simply a formal attachment to the technological mediation of difference and, therefore, is no more than a crass eudaimonist response to the post-capitalist 'happy life' and self-development. In other words, freedom becomes little more than an increase in passionate identifications and their mediated pleasures, as opposed to, the production of new attachments as part of the socialized expansion and development of human powers. This leads to an old confusion between emancipation – after the release of the subject from necessary labour and the commodity form – with 'free time', as if 'free-time' is the same as self-directed autonomy. 'Free-time', without the strengthening of self-affection and self-directed autonomy, is vacuous.

This confusion, in fact, reproduces, in a range of the 'post-work' writing, some of the problems in Lyotard and Marcuse in relation to de-sublimation and the liberation of pleasure and the instincts from reason. Indeed, there is a de-sublimation hangover in Aaron Bastani's writing on 'fully-automated luxury communism' and, most perplexingly in Fredric Jameson's contribution to the debate: *An American Utopia: Dual Power and the Universal Army* (2016). Philosophically, Jameson's long essay reads like a leftist anti-perfectionist manifesto, given its strange indifference to self-realization as a maximal realization of human powers. The temporal sequence of its utopic vision is quite muddy, so one is not too sure whether Jameson's vision of the future is actually a mature post-capitalism in the making, or a picture of the uncertain beginning of a state of transition – as in the classic formulation of dual power (the book's title would suggest the latter, but it is still not self-evident). Yet, nevertheless, his anti-perfectionist argument is certainly clear enough. After a few hours of necessary labour, daily, the post-capitalist individual:

> [I]s as free to be a recluse as a party person, to practice hobbies or to live out existence as a couch potato, to be a family man or professional mother or to struggle with drug addiction, to gamble on the stock market [?] (some new form of value competition to be invented here) or to write books, to conduct services, to become a saint, or to live whatever underground life can still be invented.[51]

And to continue the theme of 'radical permissiveness'[52]:

I have no particular revulsion [to addiction] and such pleasures, whether those of consumerism or of cocaine – indeed, we must rigorously exclude all moralism from the analysis from their analysis as well as from that of a given society as a whole – but their construction leads on to no further production any more than a poetic figure generally would.[53]

The guaranteed minimum wage, the freedom to do nothing at all and drug yourself into oblivion, obviously makes such a utopia into a paradise for slackers; yet this society is wealthy enough to let them go their own way.[54]

Today no utopia is viable that promises Thomas More's monasticism or the left puritanism of so many modern revolutionary traditions: rather it must necessarily aim at reducing the inevitable repressions – libidinal as well as security-oriented – that any society interiorizes in order to cohere. The new utopia, indeed must welcome the most outrageous self-indulgences and personal freedoms of its citizens in all things.[55]

This is depressing and a mess; indeed, Jameson is ill-met by pleasure here; his society of 'fundamental permissiveness'[56] reads like a mixture of classic American libertarianism, heated up by Lyotardian '68ism, and a Fourieresque celebration of our mad, bad, beautiful, heteroclite passions. (Jameson, in fact, discusses Charles Fourier briefly: Fourier is the great philosopher of desire and the harmonizer of our 'anti-social drives and feelings'[57]). Indeed, Jameson's libidinal form of post-capitalism seems to be much like the old libidinal (American) capitalism: 'this new world will look exactly like the old one, but with a few minor modifications'[58] – that is, with greater opportunities for us to pursue our 'sad passions' (and perhaps less ecclesiastical piety and day-time TV). The issue in question here is not that the increased opportunity for our passions are irreconcilable with the post-capitalist dissolution of de-individuation and instrumental power (this is the great abiding vision of modern eudaimonism); but that emancipation is relativized across the intellectual, practical, libidinal and non-libidinal, without any recourse to the questions of excellence and self-realization. Defeating moralism seems to be the key emancipatory figure, and not the socialization of our capacities, or of self-love and self-affection; the passions of identity override the passions of individuation, as if the latter is too boring for a new American century. This is reflected in the acceptance, even celebration, of the inevitable pathologies of this de-sublimated landscape, as a kind of bracing welcome to this brave new world of pleasures.

Committed to the primacy of the 'well-chosen' or 'ill-chosen' passion alike, Jameson offers a vision of the passions in which the pleasure of the post-capitalist subject will be carried along, monitored, tended to, and therapized by various agencies and institutions; the state will wither away into 'some enormous group therapy'.[59] Passions, however, are not *released* as a spontaneous expulsion; they are *produced and refined as social practice*. This is why Jameson's social relativization of drug addiction is particularly revealing. Jameson's repeated introduction of drug addiction into his range of post-capitalist non-moral passions is a way of testing and spooking the would-be emancipatory (welfarist) discourses of the parliamentary left, given that drug addiction is the very opposite of self-directed autonomy; a passion that, in its modern forms is almost indissociable from capitalism and its intensities and joys of least resistance. He seems to be saying therefore: if post-capitalist cannot assimilate drug addiction as a form of eudaimonia, then, post-capitalism is just more of the same, more, that is, of the old mortal excuses for bodily displeasure; and no fun. Jameson may be thinking of Aldous Huxley here: no system of governance has yet constrained humans' desire for 'artificial paradises'.[60]

In this respect, he clearly sets out his anti-perfectionist stall, based on, what I assume to be his generation's antipathy to the state socialist 'perfectionism' on offer in the post-1950s Soviet Union (where everyone was encouraged to read the classics and feel uplifting thoughts about the individual's small but calculable contribution to the health of the state), and that, similarly, was so much part of the standard welfarism of the social democratic and socialist humanist traditions. As such, Jameson offers a radical eudaimonistic demolition of cultural development and liberation as moral improvement. The individual is released – as a mark of equality – from the responsibility of providing for the welfare of others – in a spirit of Foucault and Gilles Deleuze's critique of radical paternalism, in their famous dialogue from the early 1970s on intellectuals and power; only the cultivation of one's own passions and the passions of others has true moral purpose.[61]

But this relativization of the passions through a (marginalist) defence of drug addiction produces a raft of problems that cannot be solved simply through allowing these passions to 'go their own way' as an aesthetic viewpoint. This is because such passions cannot, in fact, 'go their own way' at all, given that once they become the acceptable as social practices they become justifiable as part of a general range of emancipatory goods, subject to public scrutiny. In other words, they become a commendable and purposeful state of achievement along with a range of other commendable and purposeful narcotic dispositions, and, as such, have moral and practicable outcomes that define what has value or not: why seek the pleasures of 'self-transformation', 'intellectual and creative excellence' and 'moral improvement', then, when the pleasures of such narcotic eudaimonist goods are of equal value to those that seek least resistance? Hence, this is not simply an issue of passion versus the spectre of moralism; there is nothing immoral about the pursuit of states of narcosis – unless that is they are inflicted on others, without their consent. However, in a situation in which these states of narcosis are marked out for emancipatory approbation they serve to weaken the relationship between pleasure and excellence, given that such pleasures under the protection of the emancipated 'happy life' has few enemies once they are defined as 'life enhancing'. (And the notion that narcotic eudaimonia and perfectionism might cohabit does not resolve the problem.) Consequently, if narcosis is valued as a legitimate eudaimonist route out of perfectionism and socialized individuation it means that pleasure is able to continue to serve the most limited notions of self-affection and self-attention, without fear of contradiction. The attachment to non-moral values becomes not so much the pleasurable apotheosis of 'post-work' self-affection than an abandonment of self-realization to a weak eudaimonia and, indeed, to nihilism. Jameson's indifference to the perfectionist legacy, therefore, removes what distinguishes a maximalist conception of emancipation from all accounts of 'radical permissiveness': *the creation of forms of sublimation* that are not based on repression and anxiety. It is sublimation, therefore, that is crucial to any non-reductive account of desire and self-realization, because it is sublimation alone that provides those psychic defences that enables human powers to flourish beyond the exercise of mere 'satisfying'. Yet, Jameson's de-sublimated vision of emancipation is toe-curlingly cavalier about this, as if the rewards of such self-realization are ultimately thin when placed up against the plenipotentiary passions, for it is the plenipotentiary passions, Jameson seems to be saying, that release us into an *unmediated* state of emancipation, that is, into a state free from the burden of the intellectual 'thought' and pursuit of emancipation as opposed to its 'doing'.

Sublimation represents the form of agency by which self-directed actions achieve their autonomy, enabling the subject to develop their capacity to see through a goal or project, short term or long term, to a worthwhile conclusion or outcome. Sublimation, in this sense, is the armature of non-identitary self-love and self-affection, and, as such, the means therefore, the means by which individuation finds its socialized forms and attachments. As Stiegler argues sublimation has been fatally weakened, though, through mature capitalism's destruction of the super-ego and its capacity for ideality, and the hostility generally towards the very idea of civilization as an infinite realm of universal human powers (which would include class struggle as the defining agency of these civilizing, super-egoic powers): in short: 'sublimation is what enables elevation'.[62] Stiegler's notion of symbolic misery is, essentially, the outcome of this crisis of the super-ego and ideality and the rise of mass proletarianization and, accordingly, represents the civilizational failure of workers to achieve meaningful struggle as a break with value production. Consequently, for these emancipatory powers to flourish sublimation as non-repression also needs to flourish. And this can only occur through the processes of self-love, self-attention, 'care of the self' and so on, attaching themselves to, and reshaping, a new reality principle, to new processes of socialized individuation. Importantly, then, these processes need to play an active perfectionist counter-symbolic role in contemporary politics as opposed to being mere abstract attainments or loose attachments to 'self-improvement'. Indeed, these processes must play a decisive philosophical role in post-capitalist theorizing generally. This is why the relationship between sublimation and emancipation is fundamental to post-capitalist, 'post-work' perfectionist discourse, because sublimation as 'non-repressive self-governance' foregrounds, specifically, the relationship between the passions and the refunctioning of the question of necessary labour, which is fundamental to any deep and psychically transformative and satisfying sense of emancipation. That is, it is in relation to what remains of necessary labour within the restructuring of the social division of labour where a new libidinal economy – new forms of self-attention and self-love – will be defined, beyond, that is, the non-labouring pleasures of self-directed autonomy.

Sublimation and Necessary Labour

One of the fundamental issues facing a 'post-work' emancipated world is what we do with what remains of those forms of necessary labour (those occupations not assimilable to machinic innovation and algorithmic technique), that people will continue to need to perform as a new regime of reproduction; and, therefore, how these forms of labour, might or might not be incorporated into a new economy of libidinal attachments and passions. The weak accelerationists and Jameson have little interest in this problem; technology and the mass industrial provision of basic goods, will obviate any residual moral or libidinal investments in necessary labour; necessary labour will be something done and forgotten. Jameson's Fourieresque celebration of the passions and 'auto-intoxication' sets up a clear division between a new world of passions and a dead zone of remnant necessary labour; necessary labour is where we go for a couple of a hours a day to take a break from our passions.

This is reflected more broadly in both the accelerationists and Jameson's subjective indifference to a holistic account of the passions across necessary labour and self-directed activity, as a means of bringing ideological coherence and creative self-consciousness to this new world, a world that is not capitalist. So fearful are they of the old communist languages of 'consciousness raising', 'the collective' and 'ideological struggle', that questions of subjectivity and 'post-capitalist' world-building are barely visible. But this, we might say, is all of a piece with the retreat from perfectionism; in Jameson's vision, the post-capitalist transition appears to be mostly accomplished through the expansion of the libidinal passions, and necessary labour is a mere technical problem.

In Volume Three of *Capital* Marx devotes a lengthy reflection on necessary labour under post-capitalist or communist conditions:

> The realm of freedom actually begins only where labour which is determined by necessity and mundane considerations ceases; thus in the very nature of things it lies beyond the sphere of actual material production. Just as the savage must wrestle with nature to satisfy his wants, to maintain and reproduce life, so must civilized man and he must do so in all social formations and under all possible modes of production. With his development this realm of physical necessity expands as a result of his wants; but at the same time, the forces of production, which satisfy these wants also increase. Freedom in this field can only consist in socialized man, the associated producers, rationally regulating their interchange with Nature, bringing it under their common control, instead of being ruled by it as by the blind forces of Nature; and achieving this with the least expenditure of energy and under conditions most favourable to, and worthy of, their human nature. *But it nonetheless still remains a realm of necessity* [my emphasis].[63]

Communism still remains a realm of necessity, and therefore necessary labour still remains a source of non-reconcilability. In this Marx takes his distance from his earlier Schillerian Romanticism, in which the destruction of the division of labour will produce an integral incorporation of what remains of necessary labour into a newly aestheticized and individuated realm of self-realization ('all-roundness'). But, as the last line of the quote makes clear, because all economic systems are ultimately reliant on necessary labour, even a system in which necessary labour is taken up by machines and reduced generally through technological and technical innovation, cannot reduce necessary labour to a mere technical residue. Necessary labour will still dictate how general needs are met, and how the 'working/non-working' day is divided up, and its various affective attachments distributed. This, however, is not evidence of a political retreat secreted at the end of Marx's labours on the capitalist system. There is nothing to suggest in *Capital* Vol 3 that anything short of the ending of private property, the end of the division of labour, and the dissolution of the value form will release humanity from the burdens of capitalism's recurring and chronic crises, and capital's instrumental destruction and delimitation of human powers. But these late reflections on necessary labour do stress that not all forms of labour will be subject to creative redirection or incorporation – nor, more importantly, *should they be*. How might aesthetic incorporation redirect street cleaning, garbage disposal, sewage maintenance, and the care of the elderly, and a hundred other difficult, demanding, or unpalatable activities – that is activities that lie outside of the domain of highly specialist occupations and activities that cannot be wholly replicated by machines (such as certain forms of brain surgery and mathematical and high-end scientific research etc.) and, therefore, are open to the efforts of the majority? In these terms, the dismantling of the social division of labour will remove necessary labour from traditional patterns of career structure allowing people to change, if they so desire, the nature of their contribution to the totality of necessary labour after relevant training. Indeed, the switch over from necessary labour to autonomous self-directed activity, and back again, will constitute the re-temporalization of labour generally, breaking up the primary and fetishized link between professions and social identity for the majority. That is, only a part of each day or each week will be devoted to necessary labour, where required, and the rest of the day or week will be given over to self-directed activity. As such, this re-temporalization means that by requiring that all workers contribute equitably at some level and where possible to necessary labour, necessary labour is removed from its inherited subordinate position within the new regime of self-directed activities and self-realization as a whole.

Thus, in the above passage from *Capital*, collective control over nature and the productive process is quite separate from the control and reduction of necessary labour, which is irreducible. The irreducibility of necessary labour then blocks the full incorporation of this labour into the unalienated labour process and the regime of self-realization, in as much as certain kinds of labour are determined by pre-given instrumental outcomes and direct human input, and, as such, are 'non-aestheticizable' or non-transformable into machinic/robotic outcomes. Marx doesn't discuss the implications of this blockage. In fact, it appears that he does not consider such implications at all, leaving the early Romantic model in political and philosophical abeyance (this is why when the subject of emancipation and the critique of the division of labour comes up, the famous quote about hunting, fishing and criticizing from *The German Ideology* tends to be revived, and not the quote from *Capital* Vol. 3.). Indeed, one of the problems with Marx's concept of 'all-roundness' in *The German Ideology* is, in fact, its limited active sense of perfectionism; his concept of 'all-roundness' provides only an abstract and formal distribution of skills and dispositions, and, as such, presents a limited attachment of a range of perfectionist goods to a new emancipatory regime of the passions. Marx's 'suite' of intellectual and practical perfectionist goods is strangely passive and 'balanced' (which Jameson in an inverted eudaimonist form reproduces).

Yet, the consequences of this passage from *Capital* are clear enough. In a system freed of the hierarchical and competitive demands of the value form, the dismantling of alienated labour will, nonetheless, experience its own limitations and constraints. That is, there will remain forms of labour that will be impervious to the creative de-alienating of labour power and remain so. But this does not mean that they will be excluded from a new realm of passionate attachments. And, therefore, in turn, these passionate attachments will take their place in a wider regime of passionate attachments. (The stewardship of technical and repetitive processes, cleaning and other forms of simple manual labour, will become part of vast array of new libidinal affects and self-affections; these indeed will produce their own individuated rewards.) In other words, in a system where sublimation takes a 'non-repressive' form, workers may actually take a passionate pleasure from the disproportionate exertions of necessary labour, knowing that their brief daily labours are contributing to the primary reproduction of the new society and the generation of new use values. This is not as utopian as it may first seem; nor is it a subtle reinvestment in the 'nobility of labour'.[64] For, as Marx recognized, not all necessary labour can be dissociated from pleasure. Indeed, if there was not pleasure to be had from different kinds of 'freely alienated labour' under capitalism, capitalism would not be able to secure its reproduction and the continuing adherence that it does, as we have analysed in detail (and of course Lyotard captures, in extremis, in his invocation of pleasure through masochism). A post-capitalist system will need to draw on this adherence to the passionate 'pleasures of displeasure', as an important source of transformative energy for all those involved in maintaining the forward movement of the new system.

This is a more substantive way of looking at the re-attachment of the passions than accelerationism and Jameson. For sublimation as 'non-repressive self-governance' provides perfectionism – as a mix of intellectual and practical goods, and the pursuit of 'all-roundness' – with a greater psychological depth and range of passions and pleasures than those associated simply with a utilitarian eudaimonia. It, therefore, also, importantly links pleasure not just to desire (a desire for a new world), but links the passions to new and broader attachments and thus to the pursuit of forms of individuation across a range of intellectual and practical accomplishments and dispositions. The expansion of the passions across both necessary labour and self-directed activity opens out individuation to a wide compass of self-affections and modes of attention. This means that the quality of any 'post-work' transformative process will be decided by the richness of its subjective investments in both necessary labour and self-directed activity, for it is on the basis of this mix that a new world of pleasure and knowledge, pleasure and praxis, will be created. Accelerationism and Jameson's 'bitter-sweet' eudaimonism fail to do this, reproducing all the miseries of de-sublimation as *jouissance*.

But, as we have argued, non-utilitarian eudaimonist perfectionism is not just a post-transition problem; an exercise in futurology. The emancipatory horizons of 'non-repressive self-governance' are immanent to the perfectionist struggles for self-affection and individuation that will define the political and collective outcomes of the 'consciousness of capital' and future class struggles. There is no harmonious suite of perfectionist goods waiting for us; the pursuit of perfectionist goods has to exercise a claim on the future now. The question of transition, consequently, is not just a struggle at the level of ideas, or even worse, the embrace of hope, that feel-good standby for idiocy. It is a struggle defined by the exercise of non-instrumental practices, modes of attention, sublimated desires and non-utilitarian pleasures, as means of producing attachments that are worthy of a future neither dominated by 'master's desire' or de-sublimation. For such efforts will give practicable and 'elevated' shape to what a liveable 'post-work' future might be, to a new 'reality principle', that is, to a world in which new passions will attach themselves as much to what is unforgiving and intractable as that which is pliant and giving, and, therefore, as much to what remains of necessary labour as to the pleasures (and difficulties) of self-directed activity.

Individuation and self-affection

I want to end this final chapter with the discussion of a remarkable story from seventeenth-century China, which brings to life what self-love, self-attention and socialized individuation presage, for a world not dominated by capital and 'master's desire'. The story also feels as if it has wandered in from Marx's modern 'village' commune imaginary at the end of his life; and, therefore, as a story about the premodern world would seem to offer some purchase on our wider historical concerns about individuation and de-individuation and Marx's mature concern for what is 'newest in the oldest'. The story is 'The Old Gardener Meets Fairy Maidens', which is set in the Song dynasty (960–1279) and derives from a mix of written and oral sources from that period and older periods and put together for publication in the Ming dynasty (1368–1644) by the writer and scholar Feng Menglong (1574–1646). The story was first published in Chinese in 1627 in Suzhou in a compilation of forty vernacular stories, *Stories to Awaken the World* (*Xingshi hengyan*), edited and rewritten by Feng.[65] Feng is as important to world literature, as are William Shakespeare (his near contemporary) and the Brothers Grimm, in their respective reclamation and introduction of popular literary forms (written and oral) and folk themes and myths generally into the public domain. What is remarkable about the popular stories Feng collects and 'rewrites' (and his own stories, included in his edited collections) is their extraordinary candour on issues of money, sex, relations between men and women, peasants and landowners, and violence, and their rich mix of psychological naturalism and fairy-tale fantasy, producing an 'uncanny' modernity. Their capacity for a (seventeenth-century) 'modernity' or relevance is certainly what interests Feng about these older stories of marriage, warlords, family duty, honour and passion, given his moral and political concerns. But these stories also provide for our own avid contemporary eyes, an access point into the everyday conflicts and power struggles under dynastic Chinese rule, no more so than in the story 'The Old Gardener Meets Fairy Maidens'.

'The Old Gardener Meets Fairy Maidens' concerns the life's work of an old gardener, Qiu Xian, who lives alone in Eternal Happiness Village outside Pingjiang Prefecture (contemporary Suzhou) south of the Yangzi river, during the reign of the Song Emperor Renzong. Having retired from farming, he has devoted himself fulltime to horticulture, and a love of flowers, interest that he had acquired when he was a young boy, when he first grew flowers and fruits. Indeed, his passion for flowers is all consuming:

> Whenever he chanced upon some rare flower, he was happier than if he had found a jewel. Whatever pressing business he had, if he happened to pass a house and saw trees or flowers in the yard, he would maneuver his way into the garden with an apologetic smile to take a better look at them ... Whenever [he] saw a flower vendor with a good plant, he just had to buy it, whether he had money on him or not. In the latter case, he would take off his clothes and pawn them.[66]

In fact, his concern and care for flowers extends to overwhelming tenderness for their welfare and their non-living form after they have died. He refuses to pluck them and at all times protects other flowers being plucked or damaged by other people; and once the petals of dying flowers have fallen to the ground in his garden he would gather them up and put them on plate for his own pleasure, to look at their beauty for the last time, before he placed them, as they finally dried out, into a jar.

> When there were people plucking flowers, all would be well if [he] was not there to witness the act, but if he were, he would try to talk them out of it. If he was ignored, he would lower his head and sink to his knees to beg for the flowers' lives ... To boys who wanted to pick the flowers and sell them, he offered his own money so as to protect the flowers. If the flowers were damaged in his absence, he would turn sick at heart and try to seal the damaged spots with soil in what he called an act of 'curing the flowers.'[67]

His garden, then, was a beautiful place of repose – 'beautiful in all four seasons, rain or shine'[68] – where a vast array of flowers bloomed under his protection and careful and loving eye. The variety was stupendous, the work of fifty years of devotion and attention. There were roses, banksia roses, roseleaf raspberries, thorned plums, hibiscus, kerria, broom, hollyhocks, touch-me-nots, coxcombs, mallows, poppies, day lilies, campions, creeping phlox, gladioli, cannas, azaleas, galangals, irises, purple-red pentapetes and twisting-stem peonies; along with – completing the splendour:

> Dainty mei plum blossoms, elegant orchids,
> Graceful camellias, demure li plum blossoms,
> Apricot flowers that could hardly stand the rain,
> Chrysanthemums that defied frosty chills,
> Narcissuses in all their refinement,
> Tree peonies in all their grandeur,
> Scholartrees that towered over the steps,
> Water lilies that graced the pond,
> Garden peonies nonpareil in their elegance,
> Pomegranate blossoms unrivaled in their charm,
> Cassia whose fragrance rose to the moon,
> Lotuses whose icy beauty chilled the river,
> Pear blossoms aglow in the moonlight,
> Peach blossoms aflame in the sun,
> Mountain camellias shaped like precious pearls,
> Wintersweets in the form of alm bowls,
> Crabapple flowers of the best dwarf species,
> Winter daphnes of the choicest gold-rimmed kind,
> Roses and azaleas resplendent as scrolls of brocade,
> Hydrangeas and brush cherries adding charms to the scene....[69]

One day, however, this beauty is shattered by the arrival of Zhang Wei, son of a highly placed official and local landowner: a 'perfidious, crafty, cruel, and ruthless man emboldened by his family's influence, he bullied the neighbors and brought affliction to innocent people.'[70] He and his cronies notice the garden and its luxuriant foliage peeping over the garden's fence as they are passing. Zhang Wei, having asked a local peasant who owns the garden, knocks on the gate to gain entry. Qui opens the gate to find six drunk men standing there 'reeking with alcohol,'[71] and Zhang, without ceremony, insists on being let in. Qui politely demures, trying to convince Zhang Wei that there is little to see in his garden. Zhang pushes Qui aside and the gang storm in. The group walk around the garden with Qui trailing behind and Zhang notices that one of the most beautiful flowers in bloom is one of the magnificent tree peonies, the Lyoyang tree peony, 'the queen of queens',[72] the blossoms hanging as large as plates. Zhang steps forward to smell the blossoms and Qui objects, fearing the flowers might be damaged. This gives Zhang the opportunity he has been waiting for; he attacks Qui for his overprotectiveness and aggressively bends each of the flowers closer to him, and asks for wine and a rug to be brought so he and his gang can appreciate their beauty in comfort. Wei then reveals his true purpose: 'Is this garden of yours for sale?'[73] Qui is shocked and refuses – 'This garden is my life'[74] – yet Zhang presses his case with menaces: he ridicules the gardener's pretence of lifelong attachment to the garden, and threatens that, if he doesn't agree to sell he will write a complaint to the county yamen (the official residence of the local mandarin). Full of suppressed anger at the intrusion and the violence of the request and threat, Qui tries to calm the situation by asking for a day to think about the offer. Zhang reluctantly agrees but says defiantly that the garden will still be his anyway the following day. Now even more inebriated and emboldened he and his gang direct their attention back to the tree peonies and try to pick them. Yet, bravely, Qui steps in and holds Zhang in a 'tight grip': 'Even if you kill me, I'm still not going to let you pluck these flowers!'[75] But the gang persists, and 'pluck the flowers with abandon',[76] mocking the gardener for his attempted interjection – 'What a horrible old scoundrel!'[77] This is Qui's tipping point and physically confronts the gang, charging into Zhang Wei, who falls over. A member of the gang helps him to his feet, and, in mixture of 'anger and shame',[78] Zhang attacks what remains of the blossoms until every petal is scattered to the ground, which in a final gratuitous act of violence he tramples on. On hearing the commotion and Qui's loud wails of grief, a group of his peasant neighbours rush into the garden to see the gang in the final paroxysms of their destruction of the flowers. All the neighbours are appalled at the violence, but three of them, who also happen to be tenants of Zhang apologize on 'behalf' of Qui, for the inconvenience and diplomatically usher Zhang and the gang off the property, then return to comfort the gardener and lock the gate. Two, peasants, though, as they walk away from the garden offer contrasting views of the situation: one man is appalled at the wanton destruction of flowers that blossom for only ten days, and yet take a year to cultivate; but another man bemoans the fact that Qui, in permanently closing his garden to others has kept such beauty to himself: 'This old man is indeed way too eccentric. That's why this happened. He needs this lesson.'[79] But in the garden, unaware of the thoughts of his neighbours good or bad, and immured in his grief, the gardener is startled by the appearance of a beautiful sixteen-years-old girl. The girl asks him why he is so sad, and says, she has a magic formula that can replace all his lost flowers. She asks for a bowl of water and when Qui returns all the blossoms have been replaced, with greater beauty and lustre than before; and she has disappeared. He delights in the flowers' return assuming that he has been honoured by the visit of a garden fairy; yet, realizes that it is, indeed, his own selfishness that has brought about the calamity. The following day, though, after the malicious Zhang Wei returns to complete the sale and sees all the blossoms restored to their former glory, Qui is accused of black magic and is called up before the prefectural magistrate. Zhang now not only wants to buy the garden but destroy Qui's reputation. Disbelieving of Qui's account of Zhang's violence, and accepting the story from others about the restoration of the flowers as proof of his powers of black magic, the magistrate locks Qui up for the night before the case goes to trial. Whilst in his cell, however, the garden fairy reappears to comfort and counsel him. She says, it was because of his profound love of flowers, that she the Great Fairy, was requested to restore them and that he has nothing to worry about regarding his false accusers (they will come to a sorry end); and tomorrow he will be released from gaol. But she also says that he should do well, to consider, in the spirit of Daoism, devoting more attention to *self-cultivation*.

The beauty and perspicacity of this story lies in its extraordinary dialectical reflections on individuation and de-individuation. The gardener, with a lifetime's devotion to the cultivation of his garden and the protection of flowers of all kinds, is presented as an admirable figure, committed to the maintenance of horticultural skills and practices, with a long history of achievement and refinement behind them. In addition, he is shown to be a devoted innovator, someone who finds new ways to be creative inside this long and venerable history; a man who fashions new and arresting floral arrangements and patterns and new garden vistas. As such his capacity for self-affection and quiet self-reliance and self-regard reveals a person who is highly attentive to the particulars of nature and the demands of creativity, and their importance in the development of techniques of self-governance; he's, in short, a master of individuation. But it is also inferred that he is a man full of anxiety, and perhaps disappointment, who chooses to lock his capacities and achievements behind closed doors; who is fearful that the cultivation of beauty will be destroyed or defiled by others. His cultivation of the flowers, therefore, hides a fear of people, and perhaps even a condescending view that they are not really worthy of appreciating his achievements. Hence, the story shows a man who has 'privatized' his self-governance, even though his own skills are derived from the skills, labour and experience of many others.

The violent intrusion, by Zhang Wei, then, represents two sets of forces: firstly, and perhaps most obviously, the permanent threat and violence of primitive accumulation in premodern landlordist and warlordist China to appropriate and destroy all independent signs of wealth and status not protected by clientelist relations; and secondly, and less obviously, an external 'reality principle', that in this instance, appears in an inverted form: Zhang's violent desire to appropriate the garden without thought or care for what is involved in its cultivation and the achievements of the gardener, nevertheless, hides his own desire for such powers of self-governance. His anger and disregard are therefore full of anxiety and resentment for a life lived without recourse to appropriation and possession; he hates the idea that someone who has lived outside of his sphere of influence and power, could live so well and so unassumingly and so contentedly. His own anxiety, consequently, not only reflects a class resentment, but a recognition of the value of something that lies outside of his command and reach as a landlord; thus, he is willing to destroy the garden, despite its magnificence, because of its affront to his own sense of autonomy.

But Zhang's violent and destructive breaking of Qui's 'righteous circle' is also a way of speaking for the desires of Qui's neighbours, for the peasants who have seen glimpses of his garden, but never been allowed in to share in its uplifting beauty. The garden has been a tantalizing spectre for the neighbours; something everyone couldn't help but admire, but that which they have had no access to. The story stages, then, within a classical Daoist framework the ease with which the pursuit of individuation and self-governance can collapse into self-corruption; into conceit and self-isolation. The garden is gradually shown to be a de-socialized pressure cooker of self-regard within the village; a visible break in solidarity between the pursuit of individuation, self-affection and the community. In this sense, Qui's life's work reveals the psychic trauma of a perfectionism not open to the common development of human powers: the anxiety and violence that self-affection and intense self-realization create in those who are not in a position to match such achievements and self-governance. What Qui fails to understand, accordingly, is that the labour of individuation produces the labour of individuation in others, that is, it produces both the labour of attachment to the individuated achievements of others, but also the opportunity to find in the achievements of others the means to pursue one's own powers of creative self-governance. But Qui has closed this possibility down out of a misplaced desire to protect the beauty he has cultivated. Thus, for modern readers the story offers a philosophical insight into the pursuit of perfectionist excellence and virtue: self-governance produces resentment and violence in others when it is made a matter of private achievement and reflection, indeed, when it is detached from its social consequences. So, Qui's tragedy is that, in failing to fully socialize his pursuit of individuation he reaps the violence and resentment of those who feel locked outside of it. Justice, however, is served in two ways in the story: the flowers are restored and the perpetrators of violence are dispatched (Zhang Wei is discovered dead ignominiously in the garden's stinking cesspool with his two legs sticking out); and Qui, lifted from this righteous self-enclosure is asked to consider, in his conversation with the fairy, the wider implications of his pursuit of self-cultivation. Self-cultivation is corrupted when the self alone takes pleasure from its own achievements. But more pointedly, the pursuit of individuation loses its bearings with the world, when the cultivation or appreciation of inanimate things is fetishized as living things. Qui's perfectionist virtue and powerful self-affection lay in his willingness to treat flowers as equivalent to humans, but his sadness lay in believing this truly to be so.

Conclusion

Thus, to put Feng Menglong's story in the context of our argument: without the pursuit of socialized individuation the cultivation of perfectionist goods leads to various pathologies; both for those who seek perfectionist goods and those who feel excluded by them. And this has been the central concern of this book, as a critique of libidinal economy. In the tradition of Rousseau and Marx socialized individuation offers a way through the eudaimonist limits of 'satisfaction' and the privatized 'happy life'. But, we live in a world where socialized individuation and the pursuit of perfectionist goods find little room to flourish, for capitalism is a system in which self-realization is sundered from sublimation and non-repressive self-governance. As we have discussed in detail capitalism is overwhelmingly involved in a 'friendly war' against the cultivation of perfectionist goods through 'creativity', surplus *jouissance* and the desire for desire. The dominant function of de-sublimation under capitalism is to identify pleasure with reason and freedom, and self-realization with the love of the love of self. This, indeed, is the core logic of libidinal economy: the maintenance and continuity of pleasure against the discontinuities and destabilization of desire. This is why real subsumption after the 1950s is not simply the completed integration of wage labourers into the science and technologies of production and distribution, but also their integration into consumption as regime of pleasure that is indivisible from action and belief and the cultivation of self-affection; this is what we mean by subjectivation. Real subsumption is the overarching structure by which subjectivation – as the continuity of pleasure – is sustained: the means by which the subject's access to pleasure through the wage form is integrated into the sovereignty of the self and its defence mechanisms.

Consequently, at the political level it is the means by which 'self-interests' are measured *against* 'collective interests', and, therefore, the means by which adaptive preference calculates the costs of emancipation and freedom. 'Collective interests' certainly shape self-interests across class lines, but 'self-interests' are not isomorphic with class interests. Both class interests as 'self-interests' and the conflict between 'self-interests' and class interests are unstable, as we have outlined. And, this is why pleasure is structured around the intersection of 'adaptive preference' and least resistance, particularly, under mature capitalist conditions where least resistance derives its force from surplus *jouissance* and the love of the love of self. 'Adaptive preference' and least resistance are tightly coiled into a utilitarian or eudaimonist conception of pleasure. Furthermore, this is where workers' self-interests re-define themselves in the post-war period as a rational exercise in delimitation. That is, through the rational calculation of the costs of self-realization the majority find good reason *not* to exercise their desire. And this is where the relationship between state power and reason comes into play. Where the social and material costs are higher, the greater reason appears to be in alignment with the power of the few. The power that supports the reason of the few is assumed in these circumstances to be inexorable, particularly given the control that the few possess over the means and instruments of violence and the means of access – through the wage form – to pleasure. This is why the alignment between reason and state power serves a defensive function for the majority: by accepting the overwhelmingly coercive character of the state forces that prevail against the realization of the majority's interests, the majority adapts and delimits its desires in order to preserve what is already won. This of course is the definition of dependency (master's desire) and the pleasure of least resistance.

The postponement of desire and two forms of dependency

Thus, to underline our previous discussion, the acceptance of delimitation produces two forms of dependent pleasure: 1) the acceptance of pleasure as the stable measure of desire (surplus *jouissance*); and 2): pleasure as the *postponement* of desire – the immanent resistance to pleasure. The former – the strong form of adaptive preference calculation – dissolves pleasure into the passions of de-individuation, and, therefore, lacks any self-consciousness about autonomy and self-governance, whereas the latter – the weaker form of adaptive preference calculation – experiences lack (desire) as a negation in the pursuit of pleasure. As a result, the subject experiences a loss of autonomy through *jouissance*; he or she feels some asymmetry between *jouissance* and identity. Yet, the greater reason of individuation-de-individuation threatens the realization of this autonomy and its emancipatory and transindividual attachments. Hence, this asymmetry is not an automatic exit point into reflection and action: the experience of lack forces the subject to pursue further pleasure in order to dispel this anxiety; and, therefore, both forms of dependency share a certain homology on the basis of the 'return to pleasure' (neotony). But the return to pleasure of the second form of dependency introduces the recognition of pleasure *as a postponement* of something other than pleasure – a desire, that is, other than the desire for desire. This produces a pleasure that is split between realization and negation.

As the postponement of desire, pleasure secures the continuity and validity of one's actions; yet at the same time this protects one's desire from the perils, disappointments, and duties of action; desire finds compensatory forms in the continuities of pleasure. So, desire is not exactly repressed, but, rather, finds its sublimated 'agency' through the pleasures of non-realization. This finds its most obvious expression in the role of adaptive preference in the conflict between 'self-interests' and 'collective interests'. Adaptive preference speaks in the name of desire (collective interests), but, acts in the name of pleasure (self-interests, or self-interest as an adapted version of collective interests). By accepting that an impediment is immovable, yet persisting in the desire that it can be removed and should be removed, the belief in the removal of the impediment is preserved; adaptive preference sustains desire in the act of suspending it; desire as other than desire for desire is thereby maintained. But, crucially, this postponement eventually *changes the nature of the object itself*; no object of desire can survive the postponement of desire forever. With the extended postponement of desire, the impediment increasingly doesn't seem like an impediment at all; it becomes indistinguishable from that which is not an impediment. The postponement of desire doesn't just produce widespread pacification, but the *naturalization* of pacification itself, thereby removing pacification as a *cause* of postponement. Postponement as *blocked desire* disappears and, as such, postponement and the impediment become invisible.

This transformation of the postponement of desire into the disappearance of desire – and the convergence of the two forms of dependent pleasure – is the fundamental aporia of our age. *As the postponement of the end of capitalism is endlessly extended, the actual desire for the supersession of capitalism weakens.* Pleasure blocks desire, making it far easier to find pleasure in dependency. Indeed, the disaggregative forces of mature capitalism have fatally compromised the dialectic of desire–praxis, that marks the logic of emancipatory struggle: that is, the bringing of desire to bear on reality in order to change reality, as the basis for *changing the nature of desire itself*. As Mao Tse-Tung recognized, praxis without desire is empty (for Mao immiseration and abandonment are not guaranteed factors in, or precursors, to emancipatory struggle; neither are they the spontaneous and transparent gateway to 'consciousness raising'). Praxis is only functional and transformative when it is mobilized by desire and the possible transformation of reality. And this is why, as Lacan recognized, desire as reflective agency is so powerful: people *will* give up their old lives for it, if they see their own life and other lives changed by it. This is how new unities are born, as the early Marx also understood. But when, desire is blocked by feelings of (structural) impotence, 'elevation' and the transformative powers of the super-ego are squandered, and no amount of the exposure of the 'real conditions of the majority' or the 'real conditions of my own life' will shift this blockage. This is the weakness of emancipatory politics when it is confined to explanatory outcomes alone; the struggles of praxis are as much the struggle *for* desire, that is, for a desire that creates the possibility of a praxis that changes desire. So, yes, we languish in a state of postponement – there is no doubt; it fills all the clefts of the global capitalist experience. And this is why there is a perceived crisis of agency far wider than the 'free rider' problem and adaptive preference in the current period, because action from below seems to be inefficient or unreliable in removing the things that need to be removed, for action from below appears to lack the capacity to do so. As a consequence, there is still a greater pleasure in postponing the possibility of the freedoms of non-repressive self-governance – given the freedoms already enjoyed – than exposing all freedom to jeopardy.

Perfectionism and Desire

The key question, then – the question that defines the very basis of emancipatory thought since the Second World War – would appear to be: how to unblock desire for praxis? How do we shift these conditions of dependency? Yet, the asking of the question in this way is part of the problem, for it is to defeat the very aim of the question. There is no unblocking of desire as such, no 'release' of desire from the black pit of inaction, de-individuation, adaptive preference, and subjective ruination, as if desire was an act of sheer will (as we noted in Lyotard). The critique of voluntarism is correct on this matter, as is Gilles Deleuze's dismissal of desire as a 'locked in' force waiting its appointment with destiny. But Deleuze's notion of desire as a virtual, subterranean carrying stream is no solution either,[1] for desire, in this instance may destabilize and electrify the inertia of capitalist reification and heteronomy, but as an act of counter-actualization or resistance it is divorced from concrete techniques and practices of self-realization and self-affection; indeed, it functions more like a flux of pulsions and incandescent bursts of energy, than a 'care of the self' (much like capitalist *jouissance* itself) – hence the central importance of the perfectionist legacy to my critique of libidinal economy. Perfectionist goods exercise a moral claim on desire: that is, they ask of desire: desire for what, under what conditions, and to what ends and with what resources? But to ask these questions is not to seek some satisfactory answer about what actions are worthy of human flourishing, and those that are not. This is purely a *moral* perfectionism – the domain of abstract virtue and homiletics. As Thomas Hurka says, perfectionism's aim is not to *justify morality*: 'Perfectionism is not a magical entrée into morality, but a substantive position within it. It assumes a general willingness to act on moral ideals and propose a specific ideal to follow [a quite different matter].'[2]

The moral claim on desire is grounded, therefore, in an account of what 'makes best' for all, that is an analysis of what – all things considered – represents the most propitious conditions, aspects and circumstances under which desire might be pursued and *exercised*. Desire presupposes a normative claim on the widest development and exercise of intellectual, practical and creative human powers, and, therefore, what kinds of attachments and passions best shape and fulfil these powers – in the lieu, obviously, of those forces that prevent or diminish these powers. Desire, thereby, is not a *subjective* category, that is, a category simply coeval with notion of the 'freedom of the desiring subject'. As Jean-Paul Sartre argues: 'There can be a free for-itself only as engaged in resistance. Outside of this engagement the notions of freedom, of determinism, of necessity lose all meaning.'[3] Thus freedom may require and demand quick exits, but it is also defined by how, and in what ways and under what conditions, it passes through a series of obstacles that render the removal of constraints as the means by which the newly achieved state of freedom is brought to realization and given form.

So, freedom, like desire, is not an 'undetermined' power[4]; it is linked to the development of socialized individuation, skills, technique, reflection and to innovative and creative forms of struggle. This is why to be confronted with desire as underdetermination is to suffer the trauma of indecision and excess: if everything is possible and conceivable and available without obstacle or limited obstacle, freedom becomes a de-sublimated tyranny, and destroyer of self-affection and self-governance, as we have analysed in our discussion of the 'walk to freedom' paradox. Whereas, conversely, to be free as a condition of 'freedom from' is to pursue a wide range of self-directed ends as the condition of 'freedom to'.[5] But the maximalization of 'freedom to', as a future possibility or promise is not a concrete actuality. Hence the pursuit of this 'freedom to' is governed by previous struggles to exercise 'freedom from', that is, the development of practices and forms generated by perfectionist goods. In this respect, desire is the freedom to desire as a condition of desire's dependency on its conditions of possibility and emergence; and this is why desire, like pleasure, is structured by the social and libidinal conditions of its dependency and conditions of constraint. Individuation and de-individuation are parts of a single process.[6] This is why pleasure is invariably confused with desire; both are subject to the forces of iteration (surplus *jouissance*). But desire's dependency on its conditions of possibility, unlike pleasure, is able to detach from its conditions of emergence given its capacity to exercise pleasure *as displeasure*, and therefore dissociate the pursuit of its ends from mere adaptation and iteration. In other words, desire has the unconditioned capacity to figure and assimilate pleasure as displeasure, even pain as pleasure, as a social and *emancipatory* claim on desire (in this sense, struggle can be defined, then, more appropriately as *pleasure taken in displeasure*). This is what is meant broadly by the pleasure–displeasure of self-governance.

But under the libidinal regime of capitalism this emancipatory claim is of course weakened by the subordination of the powers of desire (of self-realization) to the dependencies and iterations of pleasure – the repeated submission of the immanent resistance to pleasure to the primary pleasures of dependency. Yet, this is crucially where the stakes of desire–praxis–desire lie, and therefore, points precisely to what I mean by *working through*: that is, the exercise of desire *through* its conditions of dependency (or the forces of real subsumption). Working through these conditions of dependency consequently does not mean desire discovers its practicable limits, but rather, that, it is not de-cathected from its conditions of possibility – that is immaterialized. And this is why the realities of blocked desire, contrary to Deleuze, remain central to emancipatory discourse under present conditions. Because to recognize the facticity of blocked or postponed desire is to acknowledge why desire is not an elemental force of freedom – the vitalist force that flows through all humans – but, rather, the discursive and practicable encounter with, and outcome of, its heteronomous conditions of emergence, as an active but delimited set of powers. Therefore, this is not simply a question of desire being latent, as opposed to being a living substance, but, how individuation and self-actualization are formed from out of the social, derived powers of self-governance and care of the self. Indeed, we need to reverse Deleuze's creative 'becoming'. As opposed to inhabiting desire we need to possess it (as a set of practices, intellectual and practical capacities, creative skills, resources, and transindividual conditions) *in order thereby, to inhabit it*. Then we may acquire the means to release desire–praxis–desire from the bounds of its postponement as a transformative programme of new affects, new attachments. Desire is not an ungovernable becoming, but a determinate 'making' derived from the collective and transindividual potentials of the 'ego'.

This is why desire is the name we can give to the transindividual capacity of the 'ego' to break or dissolve de-individuation and its reified unities, as a working through and rejection of old attachments and affects. *Individuation is a claim on socialization, and socialization is formed through individuation.* Jean-Luc Nancy is the one philosopher, since Marx, who has been most sensitive to this issue: the making of new unities, a new community, a new collectivity, is articulated through the interruption of singularities as forms of sharing. 'There is voice of community, articulated in the interruption, even out of the interruption itself.'[7] In other words, individuation carries with it the *transindividual conditions and possibilities of its production*. 'Singular beings are themselves constituted by sharing.'[8] There are no discrete states of individuation, just as there are no pure communities or communities composed of pure singularities. Community is an open or inaugural condition that is formed from a succession of interruptions, revisions and displacements that produce new and shifting forms of belonging and connection. It is a non-fusional whole of transindividually articulated singularities that creates, through their non-identity with other transinidividual singularities, new points of connection and new unities. Thus, in short, individuation is constituted from sharing and splitting, and the splitting of sharing; the singular being is neither the common nor the individual; and, individuation is what the subject makes of its transindividual formation and possibilities (under conditions not of its own choosing). As Jason Read argues in *The Politics of Transindividuality* (2016):

> It is because the individual subject is never complete, never identical with itself, that every individuation is both an individuation of subjectivities and collectivities, a transindividual individuality. Transindividuality is not intersubjectivity: it is not a relation between constituted subjects, but rather a relation between the constitutive conditions of subjects ... Transindividuality is not a relation between individuals but a relation of individuation.[9]

But this making of individuation from the individuated-common is, in addition, enriched by memory, as the historical basis of good practice. The making of individuation is formed from the materials and potentialities of the past that have been swept away or made invisible by being called on to serve the de-individuated interests of the present. And therefore, these processes of disruption, refunctioning and recovery are at their most vital when they are attached to those forms of self-affection and attentiveness that link self-realization with the pursuit of perfectionist goods. For, these perfectionist goods provide the transindividual means by which these processes of actualization and recovery are secured autonomously and affectively *over time*. The production of desire is as much the outcome of the development of forms of self-love and self-affection in the interests of non-repressive self-governance, as it is the pursuit of new attachments and affects; as much a function of maintaining individuation in continuity as inviting discontinuity (of disruption) into continuity. Indeed, these processes are essentially co-extensive. In fact, it is precisely through the co-extensity of the production of forms of autonomy and the drive for new attachments and affects that the production of new subjectivities will emerge – subjectivities that disinvest the pursuit of self-realization from the proprietary and competitive attachments of de-individuation.

The possibility of these subjectivities presently may be theoretical, even abstract, but their analysis is far from marginal or inopportune; and not simply because they have explanatory and prefigurative value in the classical sense: that is, the perfectionist realization of such capacities is the means by which the 'essential' powers of humans are a preparation for a 'maximal' emancipation, under a new mode of production; on the contrary, they are opportune *now*, given the fracturing of capitalist subjectivation. This is why perfectionist goods cannot be locked into a future mode of production alone; they are a part of present set of struggles against de-individuation and least resistance, given that they are the necessary underlabourers for new attachments, new affects, that will create a new 'reality principle'. They are therefore key to the production of new subjectivities that the 'post-work' transition and horizon announces.

New subjectivities

Capitalism needs to produce new subjectivities. It has to produce – on the pain of the extinction of the production of value – new forms of self-attachment and self-affection that link pleasure and freedom to the reason of political economy. It cannot allow competing subjectivities to interfere with this process and break the circuits of consumption, and the desire for desire. Historically, the workers' movement, partly – and in a very limited way – filled this role of circuit-breaking: its institutions and practices served as threat to this continuity – but no longer. In this respect neoliberalism has won the interim battle in the war of subjectivities, by shifting all its libidinal energies to the maintenance of the link between capitalist freedom, self-realization and pleasure: that is the 'war for pleasure' that we discussed earlier. But if the 'friendliness' of this war strains the bounds of credulity (the love of capitalism, is an unstable factor in the production in the subject's subjection to 'master's desire'), it nonetheless, has been relatively successful, and brought about extraordinary levels of attachment to this regime of pleasure, despite the relentless disappointments of *jouissance*-as-desire. These disappointments in pleasure are constitutive, in fact, of the role least resistance plays in social reproduction. Irrespective of levels of income, conditions of life, career prospects, the routinizations of immiseration, people find some greater attachment to the pleasure of 'personal development' that the sovereignty of the self provides under mature capitalism. Workers find a greater attachment to their identity as non-workers than they do as workers, even in poverty.

Since the 1930s these new disciplinary conditions have generated an extensive critical literature on the incorporation of workers and their interests and the workers' movement into capitalist desire, or 'master's desire'. All the work done on 'pacification', 'adaptive preference', 'voluntary servitude', and 'joyful alienation', from Wilhelm Reich to Frédéric Lordon, has assumed a limit to worker's agency under parliamentary democracy;

workers have been willing to accept the guarantees of short-term gains for the uncertainty of possible long-term gains. Critical theory built this form of adaptive preference into its own instrumental and totalizing account of post-war capitalism, that found a new (and reactionary) life in the emergence of postmodernism in the 1980s. Orthodox Marxism, in contrast, during this period largely stuck to its guns, and argued, that 'adaptive preference' was merely the result of workers' leaders' and workers' parties' failure to defend the real unmet needs and long-term interests of workers.[10] Moreover, it asserted, that the end of the working class is myth; there are more wage earners globally than there were at the beginning of the twentieth century. Both positions today, though, appear without much leverage. Not because capitalism today is any less administered in a totalizing fashion that yesterday, or that 'adaptive preference' no longer holds workers tightly to libidinal economy and 'master's desire', or, furthermore, that, it is wrong to believe that there are more wage earners now globally than they were at the beginning of the twentieth century. There are, indeed millions, millions, more wage labourers. But, the key issue, rather, is that capitalism is no longer a system in which instrumental reason works uninhibitedly in the interests of 'progress', or that, conversely, workers' struggles have any meaning as a workers' culture or set of oppositional values. It is, rather, a system, now that is wholly devoted to the administration of dead desires, the diminished advocacy of dead worker practices (wage struggles) and the maintenance of dead capitalist antinomies: work and non-work, the city and the countryside, growth and increased consumption and the 'protection' of nature; this is why the labour–capital relation is barely functional as a clash of class-based interests; its crypto-stasis as generator of political fault lines signifies the deepening erosion of collective labour as the mediator of either working-class interests and identity or the future. Thus, numerically, we see a vast global working class, but little or no, working-class self-consciousness, insofar as working-class self-consciousness has no functional relationship to the 'collective worker'. But if the system and the official opposition don't work according to their own lights, the system still reproduces itself relatively successfully. Large working majorities still take comfort from what the system delivers; non-working majorities outside or on the edge of the system want to enter the system fully, and find its values conducive to their dream of self-realization. And this is what has concerned me in this book. Why, and in what ways, does the postponement of desire continue to prevail? Capitalists don't think too hard about this question – they don't have to, because, the wage form guarantees continuity. But they do recognize that the greater is the range of libidinal attachments that are made available, the easier it is to link pleasure, freedom and self-realization with economic reason; no capitalist can, and wants to, see misery in 'individuation'. (Adorno spent his life's work showing why they should.)

De-attachment and dis-attachment

The deadening conditions of social reproduction and libidinal attachment, however, produce a subjective gap, between the continuity of pleasure and unmet needs – a gap that has come in and out of critical focus in this book. This subjective gap may be weak politically, but it exists, nonetheless, for it is where workers and non-workers live when the anxiety that accompanies surplus *jouissance* gets too much. This gap, indeed, is where the second weaker form of dependent pleasure finds its hesitant and conflicted realization, and therefore where a 'consciousness of capital' may arise and where desire is able to separate itself from desire for desire. It is the place where new attachments begin to grow; a nascent moment of desire–praxis–desire. Thus, these moments of self-affection and self-love stabilize and develop when they objectify themselves in suitable forms of transindividual connection or socialization, opening up new relations, new identifications. But to return to the issue of dependency, these new attachments are still framed by the pre-selective choices of adaptive preference derived from the predeterminations of ideology (new attachments weaken older forms of adaptation; there are no pure exits from adaptation – this is why freedom is not undetermined), however, with the emergence of new attachments these predeterminations and older adaptive preferences *are now under threat;* they appear less convincing than they did, more open to other considerations; weaker in their assurances. And, therefore, with the arrival of these new attachments autonomous self-activity feels more feasible and less onerous. The important consideration, then, is that these new attachments do not necessarily lie in the direction of what is in reach – although, as we have seen, this is how desire 'resolves itself' as pleasure. These attachments may also seek some wider set of connections, some point of identification with values that *don't follow* the line of least resistance, that appear, indeed, to accept the gap between pleasure and desire as something that diminishes autonomy.

So, if these less new attachments feel less onerous, it is not because they provide feelings of stability. For, the point here is that these new attachments when they cathect to desire as unmet needs, are forms of *dis-attachment* or *de-attachment*. What has changed in this instance is not that the subject has worked himself or herself free of adaptation, but that a different economy of pleasure has come into play, in which pleasure in displeasure becomes a measure of the subject's dissociation from pleasure as least resistance. The re-calibration of displeasure as pleasure, thus, conversely, foregrounds capitalism's libidinal regime of pleasure as *collective displeasure*.

It is the primary task of any anti-capitalist politics to open up the consequences of these nascent attachments, intuitions and affections to a new reason, or 'reality principle', that gives material and strategic shape to these forms of de-attachment–attachment, a New Naming of Things. For, if politics is as much about cathecting desire to ideas as it is the judicious assessment of ideas themselves, then the production of new subjectivities is not simply about 'competing' with capitalist attachments (a competition which capitalism will invariably win on the terrain of daily needs), but of generating attachments, affects, forms and practices that exceed the identification of capitalism with pleasure and freedom. And this can only be done through forces and practices of de-attachment that offer pleasures that are deeper and more satisfying. But these de-attachments/re-attachments have no agency unless they appear psychologically connected to the real conditions of the experience of the majority and to the major fault lines of political economy. Hence the four interconnected conditions I listed earlier are crucial to this: the space freed up by the dissociation of workers from the corporatist logic of social democracy and trade union 'consciousness' and the old industrial, ethnographic identities; the sensitivity to questions of autonomy in light of the expansion of new forms of self-differentiation and new forms of 'individuation' as a consequence of real subsumption; the critical acknowledgement of the growing global expulsion of living labour from production as a threat to the meaning and continuity of work and waged labour; and the critical awareness of the chronic ecological crisis as an immediate threat to the actual metabolic reproduction of capitalist growth itself.

As Éric Alliez and Maurizio Lazzarato have argued, this requires a new political and cultural front, beyond the old political force fields: 'the invention of anti-capitalist, democratic war machines capable of taking as their strategic tasks civil wars and the struggle on the front of subjectivation.'[11]

Since 2011, anti-capitalist movements have multiplied the modalities of subjective rupture. But they have quickly found themselves faced with an unavoidable alternative. Either "disappear" and dissolve as organized forces or establish themselves in new forms of representation by resuscitating the modalities of modern political action that are in the process of dying off. Extraction from the relation of governmentality requires using both sides of the relation. Not only to exit the state of subordination (of the "governed") but also to refuse to become the new "governing", new pretenders to a better *representation* of the "interests" of the dominated than the one performed by the "elites." The "new parties" born of these movements plaster over parliamentary representation by reproducing·the illusion that this "politics" can change something, when "another politics" within governmentality is impossible.[12]

Beyond party, beyond revolutionary groupuscle and non-hierarchical, transversal alliance, this new 'united' front re-inhabits a post-representational actionism from the 1970s, albeit in conditions where the crisis of productivism and economic growth have increased the majority's capacity for 'another politics', even if this moment also continues, defensively, to strengthen workers' reinvestment in the libidinal continuity of political economy. Thus, it is hard to avoid the fact that their new front faces the same problems faced by the anti-capitalist groups, parties, alliances and forces it criticizes. *However*, beyond the uncertainties and intangibilities of strategy, Alliez and Lazzarato do point to a fundamental difference and orientation than the millenarian technists and the accelerationists demote, and that marks out the current crisis as a necessary working through of subjectivation and 'individuation' as the beginning of a new set of attachments: the need to put in place an anti-capitalist politics and culture on a subjectively adversarial 'footing', in order to clear a definable space for a new rationality, a New Naming.[13] Their 'war machines', therefore, are an expression of what I've been calling de-attachment and dis-attachment as re-attachment; and, as such, are – without me wanting to tie myself to the Guattarian-Deleuzian origins of their 'war machines' – subjectively linked to the exigencies of a new desire–praxis–desire. And, thus – as I read their argument – the primary function is to open up a new adversarial pathway through two interlinked, if politically disconnected, forces of capitalist subjectivity and dependency: firstly, and most directly, the creation of a space of disaffection/affection beyond both the axioms of liberal governmentality (parliamentary participation; economic and cultural entrepreneurialism and social competitiveness); and secondly, a critique of the fetishization of radical politics as network thinking; that is, a rejection of the current widespread phantasmatic and overbearing attachment to change through the affirmation of identity and creative inclusion, that ties the extra-parliamentary left and post-social democratic left and 'weak accelerationism' to the norms of capitalist democracy, technological development and the sovereignty of the self. As Alliez and Lazzarato say: 'thinking in terms of the war machine means confronting what we see as the limits of '68 thought: its inability to think of war in all its components as total form of value creation of capital relegating its reformist "moments" to strategic parentheses in the grand capitalist utopia of the free market.'[14] Exactly. Lyotard's libidinal pulsions lead to the graveyard of subjectivity and action. Indeed, governmental norms of 'representation' and network participation form the axiomatic core of libidinal economy: the ameliorative resolution of division through identity and the distribution of democratic affects, and, in turn, the attachment of identity (and identity politics) to eudaimonistic notions of self-realization.

Civilizational struggle

The combative concept of non-martial 'war machines' is important, then, in re-foregrounding the production of new anti-capitalist unities, based as they are on the clear demarcation between neoliberal and social democratic norms and subjectivities and the potential self-activity of the majority, and the pursuit of non-capitalist autonomy and individuation. But more crucially the combative concept of 'war machines' as the primary site of the struggle over subjectivation and individuation, also significantly marks out emancipatory struggle as *civilizational struggle*, something that the communist tradition in its most advanced forms took for granted, and the left today, in most of its centres of influence, finds embarrassing. This is because for these centres of influence civilizational struggles have come to be attached to all the baggage of high culture and cultural improvement, and, indirectly, capitalist and imperialist apologias. Civilization should be thought no more highly of than the barbarism it veils, to echo Benjamin. And, therefore, civilizational struggle and the idea of 'war machines' is a tricky mix; for it puts workers and non-workers on the defensive immediately (as is evident in Jameson's thinking, who hitches his colours to a notion of freedom that escapes all normative attachments to the defence of intellectual standards and pursuit of perfectionist excellence). 'Am I being asked to fight the good fight?' is not an appealing question to many, even on the left. Similarly, this is why in recent autonomist and liberationist thought there has also been a growing disaffection from the notion of 'struggle' itself, as opposed to revolt and resistance. Struggle appears to be impacted with arduous and demanding forms of self-scrutiny and self-negation, that default to self-sacrifice, virtue, and the veneration of historical precedent. As Richard Gilman-Opalsky argues in *Specters of Revolt* (2016):

> A politics that valorizes struggle is something no one wants to do; people struggle because they must. Struggle is an apt description of the default position of so much daily life. Therefore, we explore more ecstatic and less insufferable dimensions ... The possibilities for activities other than those called 'struggles' is at the same time the possibility for making a more desirable mode of action, or many more desirable modes. The old idea of class struggle runs contrary to an autonomist praxis, according to which we might develop new and joyful forms of contestation.[15]

In one sense, this offers a valuable insight into the current crisis, and, in a way, touches on the core arguments of this book; but as a pronouncement from the left, it is odd nonetheless, and misleading, and as such a limited response to the current civilizational crisis of humanity. Gilman-Opalsky, seems to be saying, in a way comparable to the early Deleuze and Foucault and late libertarian Jameson, that those involved in inexorable struggle, should, indeed, be those who struggle inexorably, given that their needs are indivisible from those struggles; and those, that are not engaged directly in such inexorable primary struggle, or obligated to struggle as an intellectual or creative commitment to emancipation or the primary struggles of others, should find attachments that are less onerous. Firstly, because, those involved in primary struggles do not need support through the active involvement of secondary parties (what they need, invariably is material support, and intellectual solidarity); but secondly, that the martyrdom of revolutionary (sectarian), politics, leaves the activist in a state of painful disconnection and dereliction, particularly when the options for collective action are limited; indeed in the valorization of struggle, without deviation or hesitancy, the activist and revolutionary inflates their own and comrades moral strength and intellectual perspicacity, as way of compensating for the impotence that the struggle repeatedly encounters. The solution to this Gilman-Opalsky appears to be saying, is that if anti-capitalist struggle is to be sustained and expanded beyond a small devoted core and beyond the singular actions of workers involved in particular struggles, it has to detach itself from narrow and exclusive notions of virtue (supported by party discipline, or intellectual tradition and training). In a marginal sense this is true: under conditions where the exercise of virtue or the passing on of revolutionary thought and its disciplinary protocols and expectations is merely ritualized adherence, the widest point of access to anti-capitalist politics is required. In one sense, this is what Alain Badiou means by a new movementism, and what Jodi Dean means by the reconstruction of the 'Party' as an open forum that is equal to the non-militant consciousness of the majority: that is, a case, not of enough 'never being enough' but of 'enough', of whatever you can contribute, being fine;[16] and, as such, this reveals the increasing impact of anti-akratic approaches on the left – an anti-akratic leftism – to reason and agency under mature libidinal economy: the critical demands placed on political consciousness cannot be defined by the ideal figure of the militant alone, or, indeed, at all. As I have stressed, an anti-akratic conception of reason and desire allows us to model a greater psychological realism when it comes to assessing why workers don't act in their own (ideal) best interests, or deny that future universal freedoms are more worthwhile than present pleasures, particularly when history appears to tell us that this is so, certainly for workers. The critique of 'struggle' (or specifically class struggle) as an attenuated, disciplinary and theorized mode of action; and, as a consequence, the valorization of the indeterminate, heterogeneous, under-theorized and even playful notions of 'revolt' and 'resistance' are the outward manifestations of the crisis of the classical workers' movement and the subjective ruination of workers *as* workers. 'Who *wants* to struggle?'[17] Gilman-Opalsky says, when revolt against capitalism can be, and should be 'artistic, visual, sonic, funny, sexy, disruptive, pervasive and expressed in a million different ways'.[18] 'Revolt', 'insurrection' and 'resistance', then, on this watch, are above all else a counsel of pleasure: go out and enjoy yourself!

Of course, this recourse to artistic avant-gardism as first-order political practice can offer a striking creative counterweight to moral exhortation and the 'mastery of detail' demanded of strategy, that deadens the passions; and this is why non-instrumental conceptions of self-love and self-affection matter and are crucial to the radical destruction of capitalist subjectivation.

Also, we should recognize in a spirit of critical fraternity that Gilman-Opalsky doesn't quite leave action in the realm of post-68 aestheticism:

> Saturnalias of revolt cannot reverse the logic of the capitalist world, and they cannot produce alternative forms of life that can be selected over the capitalist reality. Our opponent, on the other hand, is not temporary like a saturnalia, but deeply entrenched.[19]

In the wake of his intellectual mentor Raya Dunayeskaya, revolt, he asserts, is a philosophical modality: revolt *is* reason.[20] And I have no objections to this. But there is a sense that much of this thought and action that attaches itself to the aesthetic privileges of this version of revolt is in fact functioning on capitalism's terms, indeed, is offering no more than a counter-libidinality to capitalism's libidinality. This is because, despite Gilman-Opalsky's animadversions on revolt *as* reason, the culturalist or aesthetic logics of revolt divorce the reasoning subject from that of the desiring subject; the reasoning subject is constructed, in conventional Romantic or liberationist terms, as a barrier to pleasure. And therefore, the attachments of desire to disciplinary forms of self-love and self-affection – those forms of self-realization that encourage de-attachment *as* pleasure – are diminished and rendered suspect as a result. In revolt – through revolt from struggle-as-determinate action – this kind of thinking, then, weakens the position of the reasoning subject as the subject-in-struggle in the reason–desire dialectic. Reason as the struggle for self-reflective autonomy and the pursuit of forms of individuation and self-affection, based on the widest development of intellectual and practical goods surrenders desire-praxis–desire to an enfeebled account of subjectivity. Consequently, it is not enough to say that revolt opposes rationality with another rationality, when the capacity for rationality as self-directed thought under capitalism is subject to the vast machinery of de-individuation, and therefore, subjectively narrowed by its attachment to purely aestheticist modes of self-realization. Surplus *jouissance* is not miraculously dissolved by reason as revolt. (One can see, therefore, how Lyotard and his generation chased down a mirage of freedom in revolt as *jouissance*). Aestheticized modes of revolt and resistance as *first-order* political strategies is a leftist version of least resistance, in which 'struggle', as a figure for the demands of 'theory' and 'reflexiveness', becomes a stand in for instrumental reason.

Hence these critiques of reason through revolt are complicit with, and operative of, the broader processes of global proletarianization that have arisen in the wake of the deepening crisis of living labour and the hypercapitalist forms of 'individuation' and surplus *jouissance*. The deskilling thesis that Harry Braverman developed in the 1960s[21] is not just a question about the adjustment of living labour to the place of new technologies in the rise of the organic composition of capital, but a reflection of the crisis of the labour-capital itself. The deskilling thesis today, therefore – as a calculation of the input of skilled labour into production on a global scale – is evidence of the fundamental ruination of collective labour as a source of cultural and intellectual opposition to capital; deskilling is now fully confederate with global proletarianization and the libidinal detachment of sense from sensibility. This is why the critique of libidinal economy in the wake of the expulsion of living labour and the efflorescence of surplus *jouissance* and the desire for desire is a struggle on the terrain of civilization, as Stiegler, Alliez and Lazzarato rightly attest, and not just a matter of democratically re-adjusting the labour process to the demands of immaterial and affective labour. For if libidinal economy is engaged, as Stiegler insists, in an 'aesthetic war'[22] against the symbolic, the stakes are those of humanity itself: 'Symbols here being as much the fruits of intellectual life (concepts, ideas, theorems, knowledge) as of sensible life (arts, know-how, mores).'[23] That is, the crisis lies in an increasing state of civilizational annulment: the majority of humanity has little or no access to, or interest in, the concepts, theories, critical and literary traditions, scientific axioms and emancipatory horizons that shape the (super-egoic) ideality of desire–praxis–desire, *because nothing of this ideality is reflected back to them in their imaginary encounter with the world.* Reflexive assessment and the structuring of ideas, the non-instrumental use of knowledge and traditions within critical and emancipatory frameworks and non-mythic histories of emergence, are reduced to the fragmentary remnants of elite education and 'intellectualism', even for those with a higher education: 'we who have access to human works that Kant said were the fruits of the spirit, we are becoming a tiny minority.'[24] One of the temporal functions of the class relation under the division of labour, consequently, is the weakening and destruction of the powers of retention necessary for reflection; this is why the time of consumption under digitalization has become the time of de-chronicity across all classes; and why desire–praxis–desire has become the crisis of memory and the future for workers: the self is 'deprived of [the] possibility of diachronizing itself in unforeseeable ways'.[25]

The aestheticization of revolt and intellectual deflation of struggle, thereby, does little to shift this cultural proletarianization. Far from transforming revolt into a new emancipatory rationality it submits theory and practice to the old liberationist thesis: that the 'pleasure principle' lags behind the 'reality principle', as a result undermining the non-adaptive attachments of super-egoic ideation. It, thus fails to address the radical implications of the anti-akratic debate, given that it adopts the weaker position on the desire–reason dialectic. Revolt may instate a new form of rationality, but the aestheticization of revolt reinstates the privileges of pleasure against struggle-as-desire. It operates, therefore, under the old binarism that pleasure and struggle are fundamentally in conflict. Non-compliance and resistance are defined by the affirmation of those pleasures that defy the good order of reason. This leads, in turn, to the hypostatization of immediacy that leaves little distance between 'actionism' and the reactive formation of the subject under the de-chronicity of libidinal economy; the greater pleasure lies in the adaptation to the moment and inclusive and passing modes of countercultural 'folk thinking'.[26] Accordingly, these modes might be conducive to opening up a new affective space of attachment for those unpersuaded by the disciplinary and sacrificial demands of revolutionary party politics, or intellectual tradition, but it also puts in train the very dissociation between, subjectivity, technique and struggle, that conforms to the capitalist subject of least resistance. Radical spontaneitism + folk thinking + aesthetic action re-attaches the subject to the libidinal rewards of reactive identification, even if the pleasures are held to be contestatory.

Perfectionism and de-attachment

This is why the pursuit of perfectionist goods produces a very different libidinal energy, insofar as it defies the split between pleasure and struggle. Perfectionism's super-egoic dis-attachment from least resistance, its emancipatory claim on desire as pleasure taken in displeasure, ties self-realization to the overcoming of dis-chronicity and the time of the commodity form, and, so deposes those recurring leftist illusions in pleasure-as-freedom; and, consequently, finds in de-attachment as means of avoiding the depressive and nihilistic fall-out and drop of energy after the 'joyful forms of contestation'[27] and tatterdemalion uplift have dissipated. Thus, the real opposition is not between revolt/spontaneous action and collective struggle (they both have their place in a continuum of anti-capitalist actions), but, rather, between subjectivity and self-realization in struggle (self-affection as dis-attachment), and those forms of self-affection that seek a liberationist compromise with libidinal economy's attack on the symbolic, theory and history. (The liberationist compromise is no stranger to the dynamics of 'struggle' as well – so, we also shouldn't forget this). But it is only the former – perfectionist self-realization – that is in a position to provide the subjective resources for any transitional programme out of de-individuation and the creation of libidinal economy of non-repressive self-governance. For, it is only the pursuit of perfectionist 'all-roundedness' that is able to offer the necessary pleasures in struggle of non-adaptive desire. In this respect self-affection, self-love, technique (indisciplinary technique) and critical attentiveness (individuation) combine to form a 'virtuous circle' of de-attachment. However, this 'virtuous circle' is not a new humanism, a homiletics of self-development, a classical mastery of the passions, a moralist exhortation to the 'new man' and 'new women' or a newly minted version of the militant intellectual 'ideal'. But, rather, the means by which the subject is able to pursue a psychologically rewarding detachment from libidinal economy that enables emancipatory technique and practice – as pleasure in displeasure – to find transindividual shape as a New Naming.

The subject, thingness and shame

Finally, then, perfectionism provides a critique of the subject (non-identitary attachments) as a theory of transinidividual subjectivity; and, therefore, a theory of super-egoic defence against desire for desire, and not an idealization of the subject-as-subject. It exposes philosophically the civilizational costs of the capitalist attack on autonomy and self-affection and, as such, the limits of 'post-work' corporate/technist and leftist/technist, accelerationist and post-Kantian responses to this crisis of the subject and agency. (For example, Artificial Intelligence, digital prosthetics, aestheticized actionism, neuroscientific theories of nonconsciousness, countercultural folk-thinking and contemporary object-oriented ontology [the aestheticist wing of speculative realism].) All these meet the vast costs of subjective ruination, blocked desire, and cultural proletarianization and the crisis of the collective labourer, with various kinds of technical and social demotion of the subject and collective agency. Indeed, speculative realism is particularly indicative of this moment, in which the post-Cartesian critique of the subject and the displacement of subject-centred experience are attached to a new post-human de-centring: human agency is limited and is relative to the agency of non-human beings. Humans are only one part of the greater universe of sentient and non-sentient things: humans are one object among other objects.[28]

This invitation to be a stranger to ourselves, to think of ourselves as an object amongst other objects, naturally, deflates our transcendental capacity to see ourselves as external to the non-human and non-sapient objects we live amongst, relate to and rely on; the cognitive powers of human enquiry as a subject-centred explanation of the world are demoted to a kind of de-objectified empathy with the non-human. If non-human things are, ontologically, indivisible from human beings, then, it is our responsibility in our encounter with the discrete, individuated thingness of other living things and the non-living, to avoid explanatory reduction in order to reassess our place in the universe. Unsurprisingly, then, speculative realism accords itself the quasi-Kantian title of a new science of the 'object in itself': philosophy's job is to bring objects both out of their Cartesian reductive invisibility (things explained in the interests of human-constructed taxonomies, categories and itineraries), and, their hermeneutic slumber, into the blazing light of their discrete, thingness. Philosophy, in other words, in comradely alliance with the science of phenomenology, must act to cleanse thought of what ties it to human-centred (anthropomorphized) need and desires. For, it is in recognizing and articulating the ways in which things are independent of ourselves that objects can then be freely restored to a flat ontology of humans and non-human objects; and human thought and action be liberated from the religiosity of human subjectivity.[29] In a way this 'scientism' of the philosophical encounter with the object is full of shame and contrition for philosophy's would-be betrayal of science, and as such the subjection of thought to the transcendental hubris of the philosopher's long love affair – despite all the bad feelings and goodbyes – with the sovereign subject. The isolation of the object from its relational context, causal determinations and human-centred framing is a kind of final purging of philosophy from subjectivism, historicism and metaphysics.

But far from relieving philosophy of the pain of subjectivism and the illusion of the sovereign subject, historicism and metaphysics, it simply enfeebles philosophy by attaching the critique of the subject, to an 'empty' place, as opposed to a conflicted one. For, the idea that subjects need to become more like objects in order to restore their integrity and honour as sapient beings – that is restore their lived relations with the non-human – brings to philosophy, not so much, the clarity of objective scientific distance – 'the way things are' – but the pathos of *jouissance*. Admittedly, speculative realism is not in this way simply a form of self-pleasuring ascesis; but, its thinking does take its place on the side of what the object demands of the subject (the recognition of strangeness; its haecceity), as opposed to what the *subject* demands of the object (pleasure, desire) as a condition of praxis and knowledge and the pursuit of individuation. The result is that the object stands scientistically as a votive substitute for the pain and difficulty of the subject's passionate and distorted (ideological) investment in, and attachment to autonomy and the pursuit of individuation, to the pain and difficulty of being in the world of human and non-human objects, as a participant in a conflictual encounter with all the distortions and misrecognitions this creates. In this sense speculative realism hides a disappointment with agency as much as does accelerationism, and it is important, therefore, to recognize where such thinking stands in relation to desire–praxis–desire: speculative realism thinks of itself as anti-positivist, but it is certainly not a philosophy that re-unites desire with critique. On the contrary, it acts as a post-humanist scourge of desire; a philosophy that advances the critique of the subject, but steps into the de-subjectivized light in order to *hide from the crisis of the subject*. As a philosophy lived out in allusiveness – through the indirect access to the real – it sees philosophy's greatest task as shoring up the 'vulnerability' of objects exposed to positivism and hermeneutics. It accedes, therefore, to the philosopher and to the subject certain contemplative post-humanist privileges, insofar as philosophy's powers of allusiveness are assumed to offer the best resistance to philosophical and political hubris. If capitalism produces a vast surfeit of anxiety, desire for desire and surplus *jouissance*, it is because humans are being asked to be what they cannot be, without inviting pain and confusion: that is, become sovereign agents of their own desire. But if, like psychoanalysis, speculative realism critiques the sovereign subject, in these terms, it is solely a *formal critique*, connected as it is to the idea of a greater destiny for humans than mere 'self-realization': the fact that, with the subsumption of the 'human' under humans' capacity to produce science and its technological and prosthetic outcomes humans can relieve themselves of the transcendental and existential attachments of their would-be 'exceptionalism' (Without exceptionalism why attach philosophy and freedom to the old subject-centred problems?). What has greater value, and as such is distinctive of humans' extraordinary capacities, is that they are able to produce science as a relief from pain and the disorder of subjecthood, and not the fact that human desire is able to invest the world with meaning and struggle.

Jacques Camatte noticed this increasing link between leftist critique and de-subjectivizing technist accounts of freedom in the early 1970s, and as such was highly critical of the progressivist assumptions of technology that underlay them. This was because for Camatte, science and the productive forces were no longer forces being developed in the interests of humanity, but, rather, solely for capital. Capital advances the productive forces in its own interests:

> Present-day scientific analyses of capital proclaim a complete disregard for human beings who, for some, are nothing but a residue without consistency. This means that the discourse of science is the discourse of capital, or that science is only possible only after the destruction of human beings; it is a discourse on the pathology of the human being. Thus it is insane to ground the hope of liberation on science [the growth of the productive forces] ... far from imprisoning the productive forces, capitalism raises them to new heights, because they exist for the benefit of capital, not humanity.[30]

In this respect, Camatte was one of the few writers in the post-68 Marxist tradition in the early 1970s to follow the late Marx in establishing a post-linear, 'progressivist-non-progressivist' conception of modernity, dissociating the industrial and urban-centred development of the productive forces from an account of human flourishing worthy of socialized individuation. Camatte's, focus, like the late Marx, is precisely on the civilizational cost of the unilinear growth of the productive forces: the 'destroyed human being ... produced by class societies'.[31] As such, what is at stake is not just the destruction of worker's subjectivity, but of humanity's relationship to itself: 'the huge movement away from capital is only realizable if human beings rediscover the many potentialities in their past that they have been deprived off.'[32] In this he is very much in accord with Marx's retroactive refunctioning of the 'newest in the oldest' in the present, as a route out of capitalist chronicity. But in Camatte's later writings the 'newest in the oldest' becomes expressly a 'loss of rootedness' and unqualified defence of the premodern commune; an easy temptation in conditions where there seems very little to hold us to the modernity of growth. The identification with Marx's anti-historicist production of the human is transformed into a discourse *of* the human, as if capital loosens us from our essential humanity. This reverses what capital has released, in its pathological forms, for humanity: the development of human attributes and capacities on the basis of humanity's transformation of nature. That this dialectic has broken down, as Camatte (and Stiegler) assert, is correct. Therefore, what capital cannot do *is support this emergence from nature as an emancipatory process*. Consequently, one of the key tasks of the 'consciousness of capital' must be to heighten the civilizational cost of capitalism as an expression of the crisis of the productive forces and modernity. But there is no exit from capital without the work of de-attachment serving as a *re-ordering* of modernity, for it is through this process of de-attachment as re-attachment that the 'huge movement away from capital' will have any chance of subjective success, under conditions where capitalist libidinal economy still overwhelmingly shapes the desires of the majority. This is why the struggle for autonomy and new subjectivities is a struggle that lies presently inside the techno-scientific relations of real subsumption, insofar as there is no site of the development of human powers external to the techno-scientific relation. In these terms, the critique of technology and the development of human powers under capitalism has to possess two aspects: a recognition of how technology controls desire and delimits human powers through the integration of pleasure, facility and de-sublimation, and, conversely, how, non-repressive self-governance under the non-capitalist development of science and technology offers the possibility of new non-dominative attachments between technology and the human, and science and the human, changing the identity of 'technology' and the 'human' and 'science' and the 'human', as a result. The capitalization of technology and the fetishization of 'progress' under real subsumption, however, has currently one primary outcome: the inhibition and degradation of autonomy, even as technology adjusts its inclusionary and democratic logic to the production of 'individuation' as self-realization.

The pathway out of the production of value and the crisis of living labour, then, can only be satisfied through the production and pursuit of forms of individuation that attach themselves to the development of capacity as self-realization (cognitive, intellectual, practical), and not through the eudaimonistic adaptation of the technological distribution of use values and the prostheticization of facility, that fall under the technical notion of creative 'satisfaction'. This is why the emancipatory critique of technology needs above all else to be an anti-eudaimonist critique of facility. The development of technology isn't simply about the advantages and disadvantages of thinking machine–human interface – of humans' reliance on prosthetics as a relief from boredom, pain and inefficiency – but of how the application of cognitive and physical capacities to the pleasures of machinic use, and access to technological use values are allowed passively to define freedom from necessary labour. Indeed, this is the fundamental existential issue for perfectionism and the pursuit of individuation as a present and post-capitalist, 'post-work' horizon. The pursuit of perfectionist goods, is above all else, on the side of the *struggle* for meaning and self-realization, as opposed to passive adaptation. It is therefore, for desire *against* surplus *jouissance* – always.

Notes

Introduction

1   The key text is Nick Srnicek and Alex Williams, *Inventing the Future: Postcapitalism and a World Without Work* (London and New York: Verso, 2016).
2   For an ambitious defence of this position, see Éric Alliez and Maurizio Lazzarato, *Wars and Capital*, translated by Ames Hodges (South Pasadena: Semiotext(e), 2016); and for recent discussions of politics as war, mostly from a position of 'non-violent' resistance, see Howard Caygill, *On Resistance: A Philosophy of Defiance* (London: Bloomsbury Press, 2013), and Étienne Balibar, *Violence and Civility: On the Limits of Political Philosophy*, translated by G.M. Goshgarian (New York: Columbia University Press, 2015).
3   For a discussion of the conflictual form of individuation, see Axel Honneth, *Disrespect: The Normative Foundations of Critical Theory*, translated by Joseph Ganahl, John Farrell Siobhan Kattago, and Mitchell G. Ash (Cambridge: Polity Press, 2007), and Honneth, 'Organized Self-Realization: Some Paradoxes of Individuation', *European Journal of Social Theory*, Vol. 7, No. 4, 2004: 463–78.
4   See, Loren Goldner, 'Once Again, On Fictitious Capital: Further Reply to Aufheben and Other Critics', available at dev.autonomedia.org, 2003.
5   See Endnotes, 'A History of Separation', in *Endnotes 4: Unity in Separation* (2015): 70–192.
6   See in particular, Adam Przeworski, *Capitalism and Social Democracy* (Cambridge: Cambridge University Press, 1985), and Adam Przeworski and John Sprague, *Paper Stones: A History of Electoral Socialism* (Chicago: Chicago University Press, 1986), and Carlo V. Fiorio, Simon Mohun, Roberto Veneziani, 'Social Democracy and Distributive Conflict in the UK, 1950–2010', University of Massachusetts, Economic Department Working Papers, 2013, available at https://scholarworks.umass.edu/cgi/viewcontent.cgi?article=1154&context=econ_workingpaper
7   Aaron Bastani, *Fully Automated Luxury Communism: A Manifesto* (London and New York: Verso, 2019).
8   See, Karl Marx, *Grundrisse*, translated, with a foreword by Martin Nicolaus (Harmondsworth: Penguin Books, 1973). For a discussion of Marx and the

question of workers' unmet needs beyond labour's immediate relation to capital, see Agnes Heller, *The Theory of Need in Marx* (London and New York: Verso, 2018).
9   Alain Badiou, 'Our Contemporary Impotence', *Radical Philosophy*, No. 181 (September/October 2013): 43–7.
10 Endnotes, 'A History of Separation', 127 and 130.
11 Ibid., 139.
12 Ibid.
13 Ibid.
14 For an interesting electoral analysis of the continuing residual position of trade unions as places of political education within the framework of social democratic party politics, see, Line Rennwald and Jonas Pontusson, 'Paper Stones Revisited: Class Voting, Unionization and the Electoral Decline of the Mainstream Left', Annual Conference of the European Political Science Association, Milan, 22–4 June 2017. https://www.cambridge.org/core/journals/perspectives-on-politics/article/paper-stones-revisited-class-voting-unionization-and-the-electoral-decline-of-the-mainstream-left/A3F8C462B34816E36F9ED7AA3BA766A2
15 Endnotes, 'History of Separation', 162.
16 Ibid., 184.
17 Ibid., 164.
18 Theodor Adorno and Max Horkheimer, *Towards a New Manifesto*, translated by Rodney Livingstone (London and New York: Verso, 2011), 4. Indeed, this echoes something Jerry Cohen said in the early 1990s about the greater demands of philosophy in the wake of the crisis of the classical workers movement: the end of the normative and self-evident assumption about the value of workers' mass participation and struggle, 'produces an intellectual need to philosophize which is related to a political need to be clear as never before about values and principles for the sake of socialist advocacy.' (G.A. Cohen, 'Equality as Fact and Norm: Reflections on the (partial) Demise of Marxism', *Theoria: A Journal of Social and Political Theory*, No. 83/84 (October 1994): 5).
19 Nick Srnicek and Alex Williams, *Inventing the Future*, 127.
20 The exit from a state of capitalist belonging to another state of belonging, then, has occurred for the hundreds of millions of unemployed and underemployed already. Indeed, millions of people globally have sought under these conditions of abandonment to forge some life for themselves outside of the exchange economy, or on its edges. Yet, the global poor may be exempt from the exchange economy or forced to exist on its margins in and out of work; they *still live under capitalism*, and, as such, live under the requirement to seek their own means of reproduction and sustenance. They therefore also still live under capitalist subjectivation and its libidinal attachments and constraints. In fact, these forces of pleasurable de-individuation play a disproportionate part in offsetting the endless immiseration. The poor may not be primary producers and consumers, but they are certainly consumers of aspirations and ideas. Consequently, the

experiences of the global poor are far from being uniformly those of the 'poor' in any crude sociological sense; their lives contain experiences and images of individual self-realization through mass communication and its representations of urban life, that link their aspirations to the successful aspirations of others; and, therefore, these experiences and libidinal attachments are no less formative of self-interest as they are for the self-interests of the working majorities in the industrial European and North American metropolises. Even in poverty capitalist ecstasis is no less compelling; poverty doesn't provide a bitter shield against *jouissance*.

21 Aaron Bastani, *Fully Automated Luxury Communism* (London and New York: Verso, 2019), 187.
22 Ibid., 189.
23 Ibid., 193.
24 Ibid., 9.
25 Axel Honneth, 'Organized Self-Realization: Some Paradoxes of Individuation', 467.
26 Georg Lukács, *History and Class Consciousness*, translated by Rodney Livingstone (London: Merlin Press, 1967), 197.
27 Georg Lukács, *The Destruction of Reason*, translated by Peter Palmer (London: Merlin Press, 1980).
28 For a discussion of the Hegelian character of this position, see Adrian Johnston, *The New German Idealism: Hegel, Žižek, and Dialectical Materialism* (New York: Columbia University Press, 2019).
29 John Roberts, *The Reasoning of Unreason: Universalism, Capitalism and Disenlightenment* (London: Bloomsbury, 2018).
30 Frédéric Lordon, *Willing Slaves of Capital: Spinoza & Marx on Desire*, translated by Gabriel Ash (London and New York: Verso, 2014), 49.
31 See, Peter Fleming, *The Mythology of Work: How Capitalism Persists Despite Itself* (London: Pluto Press, 2015).
32 Ibid., 3.
33 See, Ingar Solty, 'Why is There Now Socialist Politics in the United States?', *The Bullet*, 6 June 2019, available at https://socialistproject.ca/2019/06/why-is-there-now-socialism-in-the-united-states/
34 Frédéric, Lordon, *Willing Slaves of Capital: Spinoza & Marx on Desire*, translated by Gabriel Ash (London and New York: Verso, 2014).

Chapter 1

1 Slavoj Žižek, *Living in the End Times* (London and New York: Verso, 2010). See also, Fredric Jameson, 'An American Utopia', in *An American Utopia: Dual Power and the Universal Army*, edited by Slavoj Žižek (London and New York: Verso, 2016), Mark Fisher, *Capitalist Realism: is There No Alternative?* (Ropley, Hants: Zone Books, 2009), and it crops up again, in Bastani's, *Fully Automated Luxury Communism*.

2   See in particular Andreas Malm, *Fossil Capital* (London and New York: Verso, 2015), and Amitav Ghosh, *The Great Derangement: Change and the Unthinkable* (Chicago: Chicago University Press, 2017).
3   Jacques Lacan, 'Du discours psychanalytique', *Lacan in Italia 1953–1978* (Milan: La Salamandra, 1978), and Jacques Lacan, *The Other Side of Psychoanalysis*, Seminar XVII, edited by Jacques-Alain Miller, and translated with notes by Russell Grigg (New York and London: W. W. Norton & Company, 2007).
4   Jean-Jacques Rousseau, *Discours sur l'origine et les fondements de l'inégalité parmi les hommes. Discours sur les sciences et les arts* (Paris: GF Flammarion, 1992).
5   See, for instance, Paul Roberts, *The End of Oil* (London: Bloomsbury, 2004).
6   Andrew Kliman, *The Failure of Capitalist Production: Underlying Causes of the Great Recession* (London: Pluto Press, 2012).
7   Erik Olin Wright, *Envisioning Real Utopias* (London and New York: Verso, 2010), 1.
8   'Notes from the Editors', *Monthly Review*, Vol. 71, No. 7, (December 2019): 65.
9   For an analysis of these conflicts, see John Bellamy Foster, 'On Fire This Time', *Monthly Review*, Vol. 71, No. 6 (November 2019): 1–17.
10 David Harvey, *Seventeen Contradictions and the End of Capitalism* (London: Profile Books, 2015), 253.
11 Theodor Adorno and Max Horkheimer, *Dialectic of Enlightenment* [1946] translated by John Cumming (London and New York: Verso, 1997).
12 Cornelius Castoriadis, 'No God, No Caesar, No Tribune! … Cornelius Castoriadis Interviewed by Daniel Mermet', in *Postscript on Insignificance: Dialogues with Cornelius Castoriadis*, translated by Gabriel Rockhill and John V. Garner, and edited with an introduction by Gabriel Rockhill (London and New York: Continuum, 2011).
13 Joseph Schumpeter, *Capitalism, Socialism and Democracy* [1942] (London: Routledge, 2010).
14 For an analysis of its classical bourgeois form, see C.B. Macpherson, *The Political Theory of Possessive Individualism* (Oxford: Oxford University Press, 1962).
15 Tristan Garcia, *The Life Intense: A Modern Obsession*, translated by Abigail Ray Alexander, Christopher Ray Alexander and Joe Cogburn (Edinburgh: Edinburgh University Press, 2018), 11 and 85.
16 See Robin Mackay and Armen Avanessian, eds., *Accelerate: The Accelerationist Reader* (Falmouth and New York: Urbanomic, 2014). For an overview of the debate, see Benjamin Noys, *Malign Velocities: Accelerationism and Capitalism* (Alresford: Zero Books, 2013).
17 Manfredo Tafuri, *Architecture and Utopia: Design and Capitalist Development* [1973] (Cambridge: MIT Press, 1976).
18 Karl Marx, 'Notebook V11', *Grundrisse*, translated with a foreword by Martin Nicolaus (Harmondsworth: Penguin Books in association with *New Left Review*, 1973), 706.
19 See, for example, Marcel Gauchet, Director of Studies at the École des Hautes Études en Sciences Sociales, Paris, in conversation with Alain Badiou, *What Is to Be Done? A Dialogue on Communism, Capitalism and the Future of Democracy*,

translated by Susan Spitzer (Cambridge: Polity Press, 2016). Gauchet offers a particularly egregious 'democratic' post-neoliberal version of this position: 'it's possible to not to break completely with capital but to bring the economy under political control. I think we can rein capitalism in, destroy its indisputable dominance today, and do so within the democratic model ... ' 66.

20 Slavoj Žižek, *Living in the End Times* (London and New York: Verso, 2010), 133. See also, Žižek, *In Defense of Lost Causes* (London and New York: Verso, 2008).
21 In these terms progressive change is identifiable with a *better* capitalism or a radically ameliorated capitalism, a capitalism that is responsible to the needs of all workers and citizens. As a consequence, this produces – as a matter of policy and everyday common sense – a 'capitalist subjectivity' in which change is always felt naturalistically to be what capitalism does best; *capitalism changes for the best, in the interests of the best.*
22 The standard text on this issue, is of course, Francis Fukayama, *The End of History and the Last Man* (London: Penguin, 1992).
23 This foregrounds the problem of pleasure and causal efficacy, manifest in the classic 'free rider' problem (which I will discuss in chapter 3). See Richard Tuck, *Free Riding* (Cambridge and London: Harvard University Press, 2008), Jon Elster, *Sour Grapes: Studies in the Subversion of Rationality* (Cambridge: Cambridge University Press, 1983) and Cohen, 'Equality as Fact and Norm: Reflections on the (partial) Demise of Marxism'.
24 Slavoj Žižek, *First as Tragedy, Then as Farce* (London and New York: Verso, 2009), 130, and Bruno Bosteels, *The Actuality of Communism* (London and New York: Verso, 2014), 194.
25 For a discussion of these conflicts in the context of the new managerialism, see Fleming: *The Mythology of Work: How Capitalism Persists Despite Itself.*
26 This is in contradistinction to an earlier generation of libidinal political theorists, such as Gilles Deleuze, Félix Guattari and Lyotard, who are all, in their respective ways, strangely transfixed by capitalist *jouissance* as a potential counter-capitalist energy.
27 See Michael Foucault, *The Care of the Self: The History of Sexuality: 3* (London: Penguin Books, 1990), and Julia Kristeva, *The Sense and Non-Sense of Revolt: The Powers and Limits of Psychoanalysis*, translated by Jeanine Herman (New York: Columbia University Press, 2000).
28 Marx, *Grundrisse*, 92.
29 Samo Tomšič, *The Labour of Enjoyment: Towards a Critique of Libidinal Economy* (Berlin: August Verlag, 2019), 15.
30 Ibid., 14.
31 Ibid., 15.
32 Jason Read, *The Micro-Politics of Capital: Marx and the Prehistory of the Present* (New York: State University of New York Press, 2003), 136–7.
33 Ibid., 150–1.
34 Fredric Jameson, 'The Aesthetics of Singularity', *New Left Review*, No. 92, Second Series, (March/April, 2015): 125.

35 Lordon, *Willing Slaves of Capital*, xii.
36 Howard Caygill, *On Resistance: A Philosophy of Defiance* (London: Bloomsbury Press, 2013), 98.
37 For a discussion of this issue in relation to the libidinal analytics of Guattari, Lyotard and Castoriadis, see Keti Chukhrov, 'Desiring Alienation in Capitalism. Zeal to De-Alienate in Socialism', *Crisis & Critique*, Vol. 4, No. 2 (2017): 132–51.
38 Antonio Gramsci, *Selections from the Prison Notebooks*, edited and translated by Quintin Hoare and Geoffrey Nowell Smith (London: Lawrence and Wishart, 1971).
39 Jean-François Lyotard, *Libidinal Economy* [1974], translated by Iain Hamilton Grant (London: Bloomsbury Press, 2015), 124.
40 Nick Dyer-Witherford, *Cyber-Proletariat: Global Labour in the Digital Vortex* (London: Pluto Press, 2015), 59.
41 Thomas Nail, *The Figure of the Migrant* (Stanford: Stanford University Press, 2015). See also, Slavoj Žižek, *Against the Double Blackmail: Refugees, Terror and Other Troubles with the Neighbours* (London: Penguin, 2017).
42 Friends of the Classless Society, 'Workers of the World Fight Amongst Yourselves! Notes on the Refugee Crisis', available at https://endnotes.org.uk/other_texts/en/friends-of-the-classless-society-workers-of-the-world-fight-amongst-yourselves
43 Loren Goldner, *Revolution, Defeat and Theoretical Underdevelopment: Russia, Turkey, Spain, Bolivia* (Brill: Leiden, 2016), 12.
44 Walter Benjamin, 'Capitalism as Religion', in Walter Benjamin's *Selected Writings, 1931–1934* Vol 2, edited by Walter Jennings, Howard Eiland, and Gary Smith, and translated by Chad Kautzer (Cambridge: Harvard University Press, 2005), 259. See also, Dirk Baecker, ed., *Kapitalismus als Religion* (Berlin: Kadmos, 2009).
45 Michel Löwy, *Fire Alarm: Reading Walter Benjamin's 'On the Concept of History'* (London and New York: Verso, 2005) and Giorgio Agamben's book on Benjamin, *Profanations* (New York: Zone Books, 2007). See also Agamben, *Creation and Anarchy: The Work of Art and the Religion of Capitalism*, translated by Adam Kotsko (Stanford: Stanford University Press, 2019).
46 Agamben, *Creation and Anarchy*, 71.
47 See Christoph Deutschmann, 'Capitalism, Religion and the Idea of the Demonic', Max-Planck Institute for the Study of Societies, Discussion Paper 12/2, www.mpifg.de
48 See Elster, *Sour Grapes*.
49 Paul Tillich, 'The Demonic: A Study in the Interpretation of History [1926]', in *Paul Tillich on Creativity*, edited by Jaquelyn Ann K. Kegley (London: University Press of America, 1989), 68
50 Jacques Lacan, *Le Séminaire XVI: D'un Autre à l'autre* (Paris: Le Seuil, 2006).
51 Tomšič, *The Labour of Enjoyment*, 136.
52 Baruch Spinoza, *Theological-Political Treatise*, translated by Samuel Shirley (Indianapolis: Hackett, 2001).

53 Christopher Lasch, *The Culture of Narcissism* [1979] (New York: W. W. Norton & Company, 1991).
54 See Roberts, *The Reasoning of Unreason*.
55 See, for instance, Maurizio Lazzarato, *Experimental Politics: Work, Welfare, and Creativity in the Neoliberal Age*, edited by Jeremy Gilbert, and translated by Ariana Bove, Jeremy Gilbert, Andrew Goffey, Mark Hayward, Jason Read, and Alberto Toscano (Cambridge, MA: MIT Press, 2017).
56 Samo Tomšič, *The Capitalist Unconscious: Marx and Lacan* (London and New York: Verso, 2015), 229. See also Tomšič, *The Labour of Enjoyment*.
57 Bernard Stiegler, *Symbolic Misery: Vol. 1: The Hyperindustrial Epoch*, translated by Barnaby Norman (Cambridge: Polity Press, 2014), 10.
58 Ibid., 5. See also, Stiegler, *The Re-Enchantment of the World: The Value of Spirit Against Industrial Populism*, translated by Trevor Arthur (London and New York: Bloomsbury, 2014). For Stiegler, the current cultural crisis of capitalism is not evidence of the efflorescence of narcissism at all, but rather a profound *lack* of it, insofar as primordial narcissism (or enlightened *amour-propre*) is extremely onerous to pursue, given its constitutive attachment to long-term, self-invested and transformative (transindividual) creative projects.
59 Ibid., 6.
60 Alliez and Lazzarato, *Wars and Capital*.
61 Ibid., 345.
62 Jonathan Crary, *24/7: Late Capitalism and the Ends of Sleep* (London and New York: Verso, 2013). Crary's critique – as do many other critiques currently of the intimacies between *jouissance* and technology – trips over its own radical good faith, insofar it has echoes of the left humanist and CP rejoinders to workers in the 1920s and 1930s newly exposed to Hollywood film and industrialized popular culture to take their cultural pleasures 'elsewhere'. (On this issue of workers and popular culture, see, for example, Stephen G. Jones, *The British Labour Movement and Film, 1918–1939* (London: Routledge, 1987)). Drawing on an impassioned and powerful defence of a de-compressed and temporally generous culture beyond capital and neoliberal accounting and creative demonology, it pulls into view for condemnation all the right things to say, post-Adorno, about the libidinal subject and the cultural crisis of mature capitalism. Yet what the book doesn't address, for all its pointed critique of a capitalist culture in decline – an absence which in itself is very revealing – is that there are actually few people buying into this post-masochistic emancipated vision, as Jameson, Stiegler and Lordon and others acknowledge. It is not that the construction of an 'elsewhere' is incorrect here, emancipatory politics is precisely the construction (non-abstractedly) of possible 'elsewheres'; but nevertheless, it is easy to feel unconvinced by the critical–theoretical puritan tenor of these rejoinders to pleasure, and therefore it is not too difficult to imagine that in fifty years' time Crary's critique will take on the character of the intellectual *folie du jour*, of the high-minded littérateur out-of-time, beset and befuddled by the insensitivities of the age. No more so when we acknowledge

that the radical uptake of new digital technologies, actually offers other, *non-masochistic* forms of 'friendly' power:

> "the recent mass uptake of easy-to-use digital tools [has] lowered the bar for political mobilization, generalizing capacities for active production and dissemination of information". This brought possibilities for countering or bypassing mainstream news agendas, and facilitating processes of questioning the standard practice of simply reiterating police reports within popular media. Other narratives could now be collectively constructed on the basis of relatively little effort on the part of individuals, pulling together particular instances that in previous times would not have been linked. (Endnotes, 'Brown V. Ferguson', in *Endnote*s 4, London and Oakland, 17)

63 Byung-Chul Han, *Psycho-Politics: Neoliberalism and New Technologies of Power* (London and New York: Verso, 2017), 15.
64 Lordon, *Willing Slaves*, 49 and 50.
65 Georg Franck, *Ökonomie der Aufmerksamkeit: Ein Entwurf* (Munich: Hanser Verlag, 1998), and 'The Economy of Attention in the Age of Neoliberalism', available at http://www.iemar.tuwien.ac.at/publications/Franck_2016b.pdf
66 Richard Gilman-Opalsky, *Spectacular Capitalism: Guy Debord & the Practice of Radical Philosophy* (Brooklyn, NY: Minor Compositions, 2011), 19.
67 The love of the love of self is what happens when subjects assume greater individuation to be the answer to what they assume to be their *own* impoverished and limited individuation (individuation-as-de-individuation); and this is on the face of it is hardly unreasonable under the conditions of capitalist surplus *jouissance*. The love of the love of self is not in, and of itself, irrational. Rather, the love of the love of self requires new affects, new attachments to *amour-propre* and creativity as an exit from capitalism's libidinal destruction of autonomy and the compression of reason. Emancipation from capitalist subjectivation, consequently, is not about bringing pleasure under a new moral perfectionism and the harmonious assimilation of individuation into the collective (and, as such, the release of the 'non-narcissistic' personality or pious selfless pleasures), but, rather about disconnecting individuation and pleasure from uxoriousness and the demonic as forms of destructive *least resistance*. (In this respect, how this also relates, philosophically and practically, to self-affection and 'care of one's self' is crucial). The failure to achieve a break with least resistance will not be pleasant, providing yet more 'friendly' authoritarian identifications of pleasure with the identitary drift of the demonic-infinite as the further (and increasingly fascist) exaltation of *amour de soi* and comparative and competitive self-love.
68 Jacques Lacan, *Anxiety: The Seminar of Jacques Lacan*, Book X, translated by A.R. Price, and edited by Jacques Alain Miller (Cambridge: Polity Press, 2014), 14.
69 Ibid., 311–12.
70 Ibid., 325.
71 Ibid.

72 Ibid., 319.
73 Ibid., 76.
74 Ibid., 243.
75 Jacques Lacan, *The Other Side of Psychoanalysis*, Seminar XVII, edited by Jacques-Alain Miller, and translated with notes by Russell Grigg (New York and London: W. W. Norton & Company, 2007), 147.
76 Indeed, how might these counter-moves have any critical grip on the interests of the majority, when 14.5 million people follow Beyoncé on twitter, even though Beyoncé no longer uses it! 'Beyoncé really prefers to communicate in images' (sic): 14.5 million waiting for a message from the void; this truly is the love of the modern votive.
77 Tiqqun, *Preliminary Materials for a Theory of the Young-Girl*, translated by Ariena Reines (Cambridge: Semiotext(e), MIT, 2012), 48, 53 and 56.

Chapter 2

1 For a discussion of the fortunes of this alternative workers' culture, see Mike Davis, *Old Gods, New Enigmas: Marx's Lost Theory* (London and New York: Verso, 2018).
2 See Dave Beech and John Roberts, *The Philistine Controversy* (London and New York: Verso, 2002).
3 See, Jacques Rancière, *La nuit des prolétaires* (Paris: Librairie, Arthème Fayard, 1981).
4 See John Roberts, *Red Days: Popular Music and the English Counterculture, 1965–1975* (New York and Colchester: Autonomedia/Minor Compositions, 2020). In key respects I see *Red Days* as a case study for this one.
5 Pierre Nora, *Realms of Memory*, 3 Vols, edited by Lawrence D. Kritzman, and translated by Arthur Goldhammer (New York: Columbia University Press, 1996–8).
6 Honneth, *Disrespect*.
7 Jean-Jacques Rousseau, *The Social Contract and the Discourses*, translated by G.D.H. Cole, revised and augmented by J.H. Brumfitt, and John C. Hall, with an introduction by Alan Ryan (New York: Everyman Library, Alfred A. Knopf, 1993).
8 Jean-Jacques Rousseau, 'A Discourse on the Moral Effects of the Arts and Sciences', 17.
9 Ibid., 4–5.
10 Ibid., 6.
11 Jean-Jacques Rousseau, *A Discourse on Inequality*, translated and with an introduction and notes by Maurice Cranston (London: Penguin Books, 1984), 68.
12 Ibid., 101.
13 Ibid., 114.
14 Ibid., 114–15.

15 Honneth, *Disrespect*, 9.
16 Jean-Jacques Rousseau, 'A Discourse on Political Economy', in *The Social Contract and the Discourses*, 147.
17 Ibid., 148.
18 Jean-Jacques Rousseau, 'Discourse on the Origin and Foundations of Inequality Among Men', in *The Discourses and Other Early Political Writings*, edited by Victor Gourevitch (Cambridge: Cambridge University Press, 1997), 187.
19 For a brilliant discussion of Lacan and the anti-philosophic tradition, see Alain Badiou, *Lacan: Anti Philosophy 3*, the Seminars of Lacan, translated by Kenneth Reinhard and Susan Spitzer, introduction by Kenneth Reinhard (New York: Columbia University Press, 2018).
20 Aristotle, *Nicomachean Ethics*, revised edition, translated and edited by Roger Crisp (Cambridge: Cambridge University Press, 2014).
21 Thomas Aquinas, *A Summary of Philosophy*, translated and edited and with an introduction and glossary by Richard J. Regan (Indianapolis: Hackett Publishers, 2003).
22 For an extensive and rewarding discussion of the tradition, see Thomas Hurka, *Perfectionism* (Oxford: Oxford University Press, 1993).
23 Thanks to Chris Gomersall for his comments and our discussion on these distinctions.
24 Here I agree with Jean-Luc Nancy. See Alain Badiou and Jean-Luc Nancy, *German Philosophy: A Dialogue*, translated by Richard Lambart, edited and with an afterword by Jan Völker (Cambridge and London: MIT Press, 2018). 'Kant is the first existentialist', 16.
25 Marx and Engels, *The German Ideology*, 47.
26 Friedrich Schiller, *On the Aesthetic Education of Man*, translated by Keith Tribe, with an introduction and notes by Alexander Schmidt (London: Penguin Books, 2016).
27 Jean-Jacques Rousseau, 'Discourse on Sciences and the Arts', in *The Discourses and Other Early Political Writings*, edited by Victor Gourevitch (Cambridge: Cambridge University Press, 1997).
28 Karl Max, 'Economic and Philosophic Manuscripts' (Third Manuscript), in *Karl Marx and Frederick Engels, Collected Works*, Vol. 3 (London: Lawrence & Wishart, 1975), 298.
29 Ibid., 299.
30 Ibid.
31 Karl Marx and Friedrich Engels, *The Holy Family* (London: Lawrence & Wishart, 1956), 267.
32 Ibid., 301.
33 Ibid., 298.
34 Karl Marx, *Difference between the Democritean and Epicurean Philosophy of Nature* (1841) in Karl Marx and Frederick Engels, *Collected Works*, Vol. 1 (London: Lawrence & Wishart, 1975).
35 Ibid., 61.
36 Ibid., 52.

37 Ibid., 55.
38 Ibid., 61.
39 Ibid., 54.
40 Ibid., 52.
41 Ibid., 50.
42 Ibid., 72.
43 Ibid., 52.
44 G.W.F. Hegel, *The Philosophy of History*, translated by J. Sibree, preface by Charles Hegel, and introduction by C.J. Friedrich (New York: Dover Publications, 1956).
45 Schiller, *On the Aesthetic Education of Man*, 27 and 15.
46 Mikhail Lifshitz, *The Philosophy of Art of Karl Marx* [1933], translated by Ralph B. Winn (London: Pluto Press, 1976), 29. Lifshitz's thoughts here touch on the 'subjectivist' controversy in orthodox Marxism, post Lukács's *History and Class Consciousness* (1923) (who was a friend and colleague of Lifshitz's in Moscow in the 1930s) and Karl Korsch's *Marxism and Philos*ophy (1923); Lukács recanted his 'subjective actionism' (in public that is), Korsch didn't; Lukács survived the purges; Korsch was expelled from the Party. The radical and direptive function of 'egoism' therefore was suppressed by the Party on the grounds of 'voluntarism'; one of the few major figures on the left at the time, however, to develop an emancipatory and Marxist perspective on 'egoism' was Bertolt Brecht (through his friendship with Korsch, and his important engagement with classical Chinese philosophy). Brecht's theory of 'egoism' is crucial to his critique of 'dialectical determinism', derived in part from the fifth-century-BCE philosopher, Mo Tzu, who Brecht read in German, in Alfred Forke's, *Me Ti, des Sozialethinkers und seiner Schüler philosophische Werke* (Berlin: Kommissionsverlag der Vereinigung wissenschaftlicher Verleger, 1922). See Bertolt Brecht, *Me-Ti: Book of Interventions in the Flow of Things*, edited and translated by Anthony Tatlow (London: Bloomsbury, 2016).
47 Lifshitz, 29.
48 Karl Marx, 'First Draft' of a reply to Vera Zasulich, February/March, 1881, in *Late Marx and the Russian Road: Marx and the Peripheries of Capitalism* [1983], edited by Theodor Shanin (London and New York: Verso, 2018), 103.
49 Ibid., 104.
50 Ibid., 102.
51 Ibid., 106–7.
52 Karl Marx and Frederick Engels, 'Preface to Second Russian edition of the *Manifesto of the Communist Party*', Karl Marx and Frederick Engels, *Collected Works*, Vol. 24 (London: Lawrence & Wishart, 2010), 426.
53 David Bensaïd, *Marx for Our Time: Adventures and Misadventures of a Critique*, translated by Gregory Elliott (London and New York: Verso, 2002), Jarius Banaji's *Theory as History: Essays on Modes of Production and Exploitation* (Leiden: Brill, 2010), Massimiliano Tomba's *Marx's Temporalities*, translated by Peter D. Thomas and Sara R. Farsis (Chicago: Haymarket Books, 2013),

Goldner, *Revolution, Defeat and Theoretical Underdevelopment*. See also, my '"The Newest in What is Oldest": History, Historicism and the Temporality of the Avant-Garde', available at http://www.neme.org/texts/the-newest-in-what-is-oldest

54 Tomba, *Marx's Temporalities*, 14 and 182.
55 Goldner, *Revolution Defeat and Theoretical Underdevelopment*, 50.
56 Tomba, *Marx's Temporalities*, 53.
57 One can trace out the lineaments of this issue of class relation/class consciousness dissociation, from Marx in the 1860s, then onto a mainly French tradition, from Henri Lefebvre in the 1950s, Jacques Camatte and Cornelius Castoriadis in the1960s and 1970s, André Gorz in the 1970s and 1980s, Jacques Rancière in the 1980s, Théorie Communiste in the 1990s, and on to the UK/US Endnotes today.
58 Endnotes, 'A History of Separation', 166.
59 Ibid.
60 See, Niko Kolodny, 'The Explanation of Amour-Propre', *Philosophical Review*, Vol. 119, No. 2 (2010): 165–200; and for a less sympathetic account of the links between *amour-propre* and the perfectionist tradition, see Simon Blackburn, *Mirror, Mirror: The Uses and Abuses of Self-Love* (Princeton, NJ: Princeton University Press, 2014).
61 Take, for example, the chronic crisis in literacy and (book) learning, particularly in England: there are lower levels of literacy in England in the 16- to 24-year-old age bracket, than in 21 out of 24 OECD countries. See, https://readingagency.org.uk/about/impact/002-reading-facts-1/
62 For a discussion of transindividuality and individuation, and the limits of capitalist individuation, see Jason Read, *The Politics of Transindividuality* (Leiden: Brill, 2015).

Chapter 3

1 Jacques Lacan, *The Other Side of Psychoanalysis*, Seminar XVII, edited by Jacques-Alain Miller, and translated with notes by Russell Grigg (New York and London: W. W. Norton & Company, 2007), 118.
2 Leo Strauss, 'The Crisis of Political Philosophy', in *The Predicament of Modern Politics*, edited by Howard Spaeth (Detroit: University of Detroit Press, 1964).
3 Niccolò Machiavelli, *The Prince*, translated with notes by George Bull, introduction by Anthony Grafton (London: Penguin Books, 2003).
4 See, Costas Lapavitsas, *Profiting without Producing: How Finance Exploits Us All* (London and New York: Verso, 2013).
5 William Davies, 'The New Neoliberalism', *New Left Review*, 101, Second Series (September/October 2016): 132–3.
6 Ibid., 133.

7   Edmund Burke, *Reflections on the Revolution in France* [1790], introduced and edited by Connor O'Brien (London: Penguin Books, 1982).
8   Žižek, *Against the Double Blackmail*, 89.
9   Lacan, *The Other Side of Psychoanalysis*, Seminar XVII, 63.
10 Ibid., 80.
11 Ibid., 45.
12 Tomšič, *The Labour of Enjoyment*, 15.
13 Michael Rosen, *On Voluntary Servitude: False Consciousness and the Theory of Ideology* (Cambridge, MA: Harvard University Press, 1996). The anti-akratic/anti-Aristotelian model of reason, obviously finds its key expression in the 'anti-philosophy' of Lacan and his leading advocate Slavoj Žižek (see in particular, *For They Not What They Do: Enjoyment as a Political Factor*, Verso, London and New York, in 1991) and in Tomšič, but also in some areas of analytic philosophy (Elster, Przeworski) which have been historically adverse methodologically – to psychoanalysis and anti-akratic thought. See, in addition, for example, Lisa Bortolotti, *Irrationality* (Cambridge: Polity Press, 2015).
14 Aristotle, *Nichomachean Ethics*.
15 Jacques Lacan, *Desire and Its Interpretation*, Seminar VI, edited by Jacques-Alain Miller, and translated by Bruce Fink (Cambridge: Polity Press, 2019), 7.
16 Rosen, *Voluntary Servitude*, 275.
17 Lacan, *Anxiety*, 101.
18 Ibid., 174.
19 Ibid., 41.
20 Ibid., 124.
21 Ibid., 102.
22 Ibid., 150.
23 Lacan, *Desire and Its Interpretation*, Seminar V1, 359.
24 Jacques Lacan, *The Formation of the Unconscious*, Seminar V, edited by Jacques-Alain Miller, and translated by Russell Grigg (Cambridge: Polity Press, 2017), 236
25 Jacques Lacan, *… Or Worse*, Seminar XIX, edited by Jacques-Alain Miller, and translated by A.R. Price (Cambridge: Polity Press, 2018), 34.
26 Lacan, *Desire and Its Interpretation*, Seminar VI, 65–6.
27 Lacan, *The Other Side of Psychoanalysis*, Seminar XVII, 2007, 20.
28 Ibid., 46.
29 Ibid., 177.
30 Ibid., 81.
31 Ibid., 105.
32 Lacan, *The Other Side*, 110.
33 Ibid., 119.
34 Ibid., 157.
35 Jacques Lacan, *Television: A Challenge to the Psychoanalytic Establishment*, translated by Jeffrey Mehlman, and edited by Joan Copjec (New York and London: W. W. Norton & Company, 1980), 169.
36 Tomšič, *The Labour of Enjoyment*, 116.

37 Lordon, *Willing Slaves of Capital*, xiii.
38 Ibid., 44.
39 Baruch Spinoza, *Ethics: Proved in Geometrical Order*, translated by Michael Silverthorne, and edited by Matthew J. Kisner (Cambridge: Cambridge University Press, 2018).
40 Lordon, *Willing Slaves of Capital*, 18.
41 Ibid., 20.
42 Ibid., 29.
43 Ibid.
44 Elster, *Sour Grapes*, 1.
45 More specifically this distinction is between endogenous claims (those internal to the subject's own rational powers of action alone) and exogenous claims (the integration of the subject's powers of reason into the social-determinate nexus of class, community, race and gender, and *amour-propre* or identity [that is, what the subject will judge to be 'best reason' will have a basis – through comparison and weak or strong mimetic behaviour – with the would-be 'best reason' of others]).
46 Elster, *Sour Grapes*, 124.
47 Ibid., 152.
48 Adam Przeworski, *Capitalism and Social Democracy* (Cambridge: Cambridge University Press, 1985), 3.
49 Ibid., 146.
50 Étienne de la Boétie, *Slaves by Choice* [*De la servitude volontaire*], translated by Malcolm Smith (Egham: Runnymede Books, 1988), 43.
51 See Erik Olin Wright, *Class, Crisis and the State* (London: New Left Books, 1978).
52 See, Rosen, *On Voluntary Servitude*, 61–5 ('de la Boétie, does form an important background to the theory of ideology by opening up the idea that the political domain is something to be dealt with in its own right, not as an expression or application of theology or moral philosophy,' [65]), and Žižek, *For They Know What They Do*, 263–5. Lordon, also discusses de la Boétie as precursor to the 'self-interest' debate: de la Boétie shows 'a hierarchical structure of servitude, and it is difficult to imagine how any particular "will" would be in a position to overturn it, since the domination that takes place at each of its levels is all the more intense when the local dominators are also dominated and brought to despair through their own dependence' *Willing Slaves of Capital*, 21–2.
53 Žižek, *For They Know Not What They Do*, 264.
54 See Tuck, *Free Riding*.
55 Elster, *Sour Grapes*, 24.
56 Ibid., 166–7.
57 Lordon, *Willing Slaves of Capital*, 33.
58 Eve Chiapello and Luc Boltanski, *The New Spirit of Capitalism*, translated by Gregory Elliott (London and New York: Verso, 2005).
59 Lordon, *Willing Slaves*, 60.

60 Ibid., 63.
61 Ibid., 71.
62 Fleming, *The Myth of Work*, 84.
63 Ibid., 86.
64 Jessica Benjamin, *Like Subjects, Love Objects: Essays on Recognition and Sexual Difference* (New Haven and London: Yale University Press, 1995), 36.
65 Jacques Lacan, 'Slippage in the Meaning of the Ideal', in *Transference*, Seminar VIII, edited by Jacques-Alain Miller, and translated by Bruce Fink (Cambridge: Polity Press, 2015), 329–43. 'Phenomenologically speaking, the ego-ideal and the ideal ego absolutely do not serve the same function', 371.
66 Bruce Fink, *Lacan and Love: An Exploration of Lacan's Seminar VIII, Transference* (Cambridge: Polity Press, 2016), 72.

Chapter 4

1 Lyotard, *Libidinal Economy*, 61.
2 Ibid., 95.
3 Ibid., 61.
4 Ibid., 47.
5 Ibid., 104.
6 Ibid., 109.
7 Ibid., 110.
8 Ibid., 88.
9 Herbert Marcuse, *Eros and Civilization: A Philosophical Inquiry into Freud* (New York: Vintage Books, 1962).
10 See Theodor Adorno, *Notes to Literature*, 2 Vols, edited and translated by Shierry Weber Nicholsen (New York: Columbia University Press, 1991–92). For an extensive discussion of Adorno's critical-redemptive relationship with bourgeois interiority, see Peter E. Gordon, *Adorno and Existence* (Cambridge and London: Harvard University Press, 2016)
11 For a discussion of capitalist/moral perfectionist compatibility across Christianity, Islam and Judaism, see in particular, R.H. Tawney, *Religion and the Rise of Capitalism: A Historical Study*, [1926], with a prefatory note by Charles Gore (Harmondsworth: Penguin Books, 1966), Max Weber, *The Protestant Ethic and the Spirit of Capitalism* [1930], translated by Talcott Parsons, introduction Anthony Giddens (London and New York: Routledge, 1992), Maxime Rodinson, *Islam and Capitalism*, translated by Brian Pearce (London: Pantheon Books, 1973), and Jerry Z. Muller, *Capitalism and the Jews* (Princeton: Princeton University Press, 2010).
12 Aristotle, *Nicomachean Ethics*.
13 St. Augustine, *On the Happy Life*, St. Augustine's Cassiciacum Dialogues, Vol. 11, translation, annotation and commentary by Michael P. Foley (New Haven and London: Yale University Press, 2019), 48. The Cassiciacum dialogues

('Against the Academics', 'On the Happy Life', 'On Order' and the 'Soliloquies') are dialogues, Christian heuristics or inquiries into principles of belief, and were written by Augustine in his capacity as a catechumen, that is, a newly converted Christian (Augustine converted in AD 386) waiting for official baptism. The dialogues were composed two decades before the *Confessions*.

14 See, for example, Cicero, *On the Ideal Orator* [*De Oratore*], translated with Introduction, Notes, Appendixes, Glossary, Indexes by James M. May and Jakob Wisse (Oxford and New York: Oxford University Press, 2001).
15 Augustine, *On the Happy Life*, 43.
16 Friedrich Nietzsche, *The Will To Power*, translated by Walter Kaufmann and R.J. Hollingdale, edited with a commentary by Walter Kaufmann (New York: Vintage Books, 1968).
17 See, Frederick Engels, 'On the History of Early Christianity', in *Collected Works*, Vol. 27, edited by Karl Marx and Frederick Engels (London: Lawrence & Wishart, 1987).
18 One of the most ambitious, if not exactly influential, liberal/early social democratic philosophers within this tradition of 'self-improvement' was T.H. Green – see the, *Collected Works*, 5 Vols (Bristol: Thoemmes Press, 1997). Green develops an akratic, purely reflective model of self-realization, in which the development of one's own rational autonomy (self-governance) is assumed ipso facto, to provide, in common alliance and coordination with the autonomous, self-reflective efforts and ambitions of others, the requisite 'moral reserves' for the mutual flourishing of perfectionist ambitions of oneself and others. Thus, for Green, it is the *virtuous* person who is truly committed to self-love, given that, to attend to the development of one's own moral and practical capacities, is by extension, consequently, to encourage the virtuous development of the self-love of others. For a discussion of Green's co-operative perfectionism and the social democratic tradition, see David O. Brink, *Perfectionism and the Common Good: Themes in the Philosophy of T.H. Green* (Oxford: Oxford University Press, 2003).
19 Heller, *The Theory of Need in Marx*, 34.
20 Jon Elster, 'Self-Realization in Work and Politics: The Marxist Conception of the Good Life', *Social Philosophy & Policy*, Vol. 3, No. 2 (Spring, 1986): 101.
21 Hurka, *Perfectionism*, 5.
22 Ibid., 125.
23 Ibid., 164.
24 Ibid., 62.
25 Ibid., 90.
26 Ibid., 95.
27 Thomas Hurka, *The Best Things in Life: A Guide to What Really Matters* (Oxford: Oxford University Press, 2010), 17.
28 Hurka, *Perfectionism*, 179.
29 Ibid., 118.
30 Ibid., 17–18.
31 Ibid., 19–20.
32 Ibid., 178.

33 Ibid., 189.
34 Ibid., 5.
35 Seneca, *On the Happy Life* (North Shore, Auckland: Vigeo Press, 2018).
36 See, Kolodny, 'The Explanation of Amour-Propre'.
37 Blackburn, *Mirror, Mirror: The Uses and Abuses of Self-Love*, 127.
38 Alain Badiou, *Theory of the Subject*, translated with an introduction, and edited by Bruno Bosteels (London and New York: Continuum, 2009), 180–1.
39 Blackburn, 120.
40 Foucault, *The Care of the Self*, 86.
41 Ibid., 95.
42 Ibid., 238.
43 Harry G. Frankfurt, *The Reasons of Love* (Princeton: Princeton University Press, 2004), 79.
44 Ibid., 82.
45 Ibid., 86.
46 Ibid., 96.
47 Ibid., 95.
48 Bernard Stiegler, *The Lost Spirit of Capitalism: Disbelief and Discredit*, Vol. 3, translated by Daniel Ross (Cambridge: Polity Press, 2014), 51–2.
49 Rosen, *On Voluntary Servitude*, 1.
50 See, Wilhelm Reich, 'What is Class Consciousness?', in *Sex-Pol: Essays, 1929–1934*, translated by Anna Bostock, Tom DuBose and Lee Baxandall, edited by Lee Baxandall, and an Introduction by Bertell Ollman (New York: Vintage Books, 1972), and Wilhelm Reich, *The Mass Psychology of Fascism*, translated by V.R. Carpagno (Harmondsworth: Penguin, 1975).
51 Fredric Jameson, *An American Utopia: Dual Power and the Universal Army*, edited by Slavoj Žižek (London and New York: Verso, 2016), 83.
52 Ibid., 93.
53 Ibid., 90.
54 Ibid., 93.
55 Ibid., 81.
56 Ibid., 87.
57 Ibid., 81. For Fourier, see *The Theory of the Four Movements*, edited by Gareth Stedman Jones and Ian Patterson (Cambridge: Cambridge University Press, 1996).
58 Jameson, *An American Utopia*, 84.
59 Ibid., 82.
60 Aldous Huxley, *The Doors of Perception: Heaven and Hell* [1954] (New York: Random House, 2004). The narcotic infrastructure of libidinal economy – far closer to the realities of the state pacification of desire than the chemical extension of *jouissance* – is increasingly important to global circuits of financial liquidity in the twentieth and twenty-first centuries, from the state-sponsored opium epidemic in 1930s pre-revolutionary China (which supported the developing US air industry; drug smugglers bought aircraft in order to move drugs around China, and to and from China) to the mass addictions in Iran,

India and Afghanistan today, that shape the interests of local economies; where the attachment of pleasure to oppression is required, drugs will follow. See Jonathan Marshall, *The Lebanese Connection: Corruption, Civil War and the International Drug Traffic* (Stanford: Stanford University Press, 2012); Jonathan Marshall and Peter Dale Scott, *Cocaine Politics: Drugs, Armies and the CIA in Central America* (Berkeley: University of California Press, 1991); and Jonathan Marshall, *Drug Wars: Corruption, Counterinsurgency and Covert Operations in the Third World* (Forrestville: Cohan & Cohen, 1991).

61 Michel Foucault and Gilles Deleuze, 'Intellectuals and Power: A Conversation between Michel Foucault and Gilles Deleuze', in *Language, Counter-memory, Practice: Selected Essays and Interviews*, edited by Michel Foucault and introduced by Donald Bouchard and Sherry Simon (Ithaca, NY: Cornell University Press, 1977).

62 Bernard Stiegler, *Symbolic Misery, Vol. 2: The katastrophe of the sensible*, translated by Barnaby Norman (Cambridge: Polity Press, 2015), 117.

63 Karl Marx, *Capital*, Vol. 3 (London: Lawrence & Wishart, 1972), 820.

64 Srnicek and Williams (*Inventing the Future*) are too 'intellectually' sanguine on this question. The 'overcoming of the work ethic' (124) and the demand for 'full unemployment' (127) are psychological detached from the perfectionist need to deepen and widen cognitive and affective attachment and the production of the new passions, that have been narrowed by the conditions of subjective ruination and proletarianization. The non-repressive attachment to necessary labour will play a part in this.

65 'The Old Gardener Meets Fairy Maidens', in *Stories to Awaken the World: A Ming Dynasty Collection*, Vol. 3, compiled by Feng Menglong, and edited by Shuhui Yang and Yunqin Yang (Seattle and London: University of Washington Press, 2014)78–101. © 2009. Reprinted with permission of the University of Washington Press. Many of these stories derive from earlier written materials, known as *chih-kuai* (records of anomalies) and *ch'uan-ch'i* (accounts of the extraordinary) produced mainly in the Six Dynasties (CE 317–589) and the T'ang (CE 618–906). These are collections of narratives of the supernatural and fantastic written by royal servants, courtiers, librarians, and Confucian, Taoist and Buddhist sages, drawing on even earlier written materials and on contemporary oral folk stories and popular observations. See, Karl S. Y. Kao, ed., *Classical Chinese Tales of the Supernatural and the Fantastic: Selections from the Third to the Tenth Century* (Hong Kong: Joint Publishing Co., 1985).

66 'The Old Gardener Meets Fairy Maidens', 82–3.
67 Ibid., 86.
68 Ibid., 84.
69 Ibid., 83–4.
70 Ibid., 87.
71 Ibid.
72 Ibid., 88.
73 Ibid., 89.

74 Ibid.
75 Ibid., 90.
76 Ibid.
77 Ibid.
78 Ibid.
79 Ibid., 91.

Conclusion

1. Gilles Deleuze and Claire Parnet, *Dialogues II* (London and New York: Continuum, 2006).
2. Hurka, *Perfectionism*, 30.
3. Jean-Paul Sartre, *Being and Nothingness: An Essay on Phenomenological Ontology*, translated by Hazel E. Barnes, and introduction by Mary Warnock (London: Methuen & Co, 1969), 483.
4. Ibid., 485.
5. 'Freedom from' (exit) and 'freedom to' (praxis), therefore, cannot be separated. But as the winning of 'freedoms' under capitalism tells us, these two freedoms rarely cohere. What capitalism cannot secure is any holistic correlation between emancipation and freedom; and this is why under mature capitalism freedom finds itself in conflict with emancipation. Freedom is the realization of powers and rights that are constrained by restrictive or regressive market or state/institutional practices, which thereby increase the capacity of a class, group, cohort or individual to flourish as sovereign entities; emancipation, conversely, is the transformation of, and the exit from, the identification of these powers with the social division of labour, on the grounds that the social division of labour acts to delimit and narrow the exercise of human powers. Emancipation, consequently, is the discourse and practice, not of exiting, alone, but of 'working through'; an unfolding process of collective self-action, and therefore not a point of existential arrival. Hence emancipation distinguishes itself from freedom on the basis of an important modal distinction: unlike freedom emancipation has a relationship to the development of powers that fall under the normative demands of the desire for human self-realization, what we have called perfectionism and as such the maximalist mix of intellectual, creative and practical goods. In contrast, freedom, as a point of arrival, is defined by the successful execution of a singular aim or set of aims, in order to secure release from a given privation or oppression. This is why freedom is a deeply malleable and corrupted term under capitalism, yet, it plays an extraordinarily successful part in capitalism's mature reproduction. Freedom, above all else, is what ties I-cracy to the sovereignty of the self, the sovereignty of the self to the desire for desire and the love of the love of self to self-identity.
6. For a discussion of this issue, but in the more classical language of estrangement and de-estrangement, and through the lens of Hegel and Marx, see Ray Brassier, 'Strange Sameness', *Angelaki*, Vol. 24, No. 1 (2019): 98–105.

7   Jean-Luc Nancy, *The Inoperative Community*, edited by Peter Connor, and translated by Peter Connor, Lisa Garbus, Michael Holland, and Simona Sawney, foreword by Christopher Fynsk (Minneapolis and Oxford: University of Minnesota, Press), 62.
8   Ibid., 25.
9   Jason Read, *The Politics of Transindividuality*, 113.
10 See Alex Callinicos, *Making History: Agency, Structure and Change in Social Theory* (Cambridge: Polity Press, 1989).
11 Alliez and Lazzarato, *Wars and Capital*, 384.
12 Ibid., 390.
13 One instance of this is the rise of the *zone à defendre* (ZAD) in France, a semiautonomous area inhabited by a group of activists, engaged in a long-term opposition – supported by the local population – to a particular corporate or state project. For example, the decades-old opposition to a second airport in Nantes, Aéroport du Grand Ouest. What is distinctive about ZADs, particularly the one outside Nantes, is that the local population is directly involved. They are engaged in planning, directing strategies of resistance and materially supporting those who live on the occupied site. This long-term building of new social relations – new attachments and affects – around a core struggle and programme of action, is therefore very different from autonomist 'enclave' communities and actions from the 1990s. Here there is a free integration of those engaged in the action locally and outside activists and supporters; as such, it utilizes a multiplicity of self-directed activities, across a range of skills and interests. The inventiveness, of ZADs, however, should not detract from the fact, that such actions are dependent on governments and corporations persisting with their projects. Governments can easily cancel contracts, find new sites in order to outmanoeuvre opposition or even incorporate their projects, where they affect local ecologies, into a New Green Deal, that offsets criticism. In this respect de-attachment/re-attachment has to also find some generalizable set of provisions and actions, beyond defence zones that link 'consciousness of capital' to the unmet needs of the majority.
14 Ibid., 392.
15 Richard Gilman Opalsky, *Specters of Revolt: On the Intellect of Insurrection and Philosophy from Below* (London: Repeater Books, 2016, 22.
16 Alain Badiou, *The Rebirth of History: Times of Riots and Uprisings*, translated by Gregory Elliott (London and New York: Verso, 2012), and Jodi Dean, *Crowds and Power* (London and New York: Verso, 2016).
17 Gilman-Opalsky, *Specters of Revolt*, 95.
18 Ibid., 188.
19 Ibid., 234.
20 Raya Dunayevskaya, *The Power of Negativity: Selected Writings on the Dialectic in Hegel and Marx*, edited and introduced by Peter Hudis and Kevin B. Anderson (Lanham, Maryland and Oxford: Lexington Books, 2002).
21 Harry Braverman, *Labor and Monopoly Capitalism: The Degradation of Work in the Twentieth Century* (New York: Monthly Review Press, 1998).

22 Stiegler, *Symbolic Misery*: Vol. 1, 4.
23 Ibid., 10.
24 Ibid., 79.
25 Ibid., 77.
26 For a discussion of the rise of new forms of populist 'folk-thinking' on the left (the 'local and the spontaneous'), see Srnicek and Williams, *Inventing the Future*.
27 Gilman-Opalsky, *Specters of Revolt*, 22.
28 For a defence of the autonomy of the object, see Manuel DeLanda, *Assemblage Theory* (Edinburgh: Edinburgh University Press, 2016), Graham Harman, *Speculative Realism: An Introduction* (Cambridge: Polity Press, 2018), and Timothy Morton, *Humankind: Solidarity with Nonhuman People* (London and New York: Verso, 2017). For a 'transcendental'-subject-based critique of assemblage theory and the de-totalized autonomous object, see Slavoj Žižek, Frank Ruda and Agon Hamza, *Reading Marx* (Cambridge: Polity Press, 2018).
29 See Quentin Meillassoux, *After Infinitude: An Essay on the Necessity of Contingency*, with a preface by Alain Badiou, and translated by Ray Brassier (London and New York: Continuum, 2008).
30 Jacques Camatte, *This World We Must Leave, and Other Essays*, edited by Alex Trotter (Brooklyn: Autonomedia, 1995), 88 and 101.
31 Ibid., 88.
32 Ibid., 154.

Bibliography

Adorno, W. Theodor, and Horkheimer, Max, *Dialectic of Enlightenment*. Translated by John Cumming. London and New York: Verso, 1997.
Adorno, W. Theodor, and Horkheimer, Max, *Towards a New Manifesto*. Translated by Rodney Livingstone. London and New York: Verso, 2011.
Agamben, Giorgio, *Profanations*. Translated by Jeff Fort. New York: Zone Books, 2007.
Agamben, Giorgio, 'Thought is the Courage of Hopelessness: An Interview with Giorgio Agamben', available at: Users/in8500/Desktop/Capitalism%20as%20Religion/Interview%20with%20Agamben.htm
Agamben, Giorgio, *Creation and Anarchy: The Work of Art and the Religion of Capitalism*. Translated by Adam Kotsko. Stanford: Stanford University Press, 2019.
Alliez, Éric, and Lazzarato, Maurizio, *Wars and Capital*. Translated by Ames Hodges. South Pasadena: Semiotext(e), 2016.
Aristotle, *Nicomachean Ethics*. Revised edition, translated and edited by Roger Crisp. Cambridge: Cambridge University Press, 2014.
Augustine, *On the Happy Life: St. Augustine's Cassiciacum Dialogues*, Vol. 11 Translation, annotation and commentary by Michael P. Foley. New Haven and London: Yale University Press, 2019.
Badiou, Alain, *Infinite Thought*. Translated and edited by Oliver Feltham and Justin Clements. London and New York: Continuum, 2005.
Badiou, Alain, *Theory of the Subject*. Translated and introduced by Bruno Bosteels. London and New York: Continuum, 2009.
Badiou, Alain, *The Rebirth of History: Times of Riots and Uprisings*. Translated by Gregory Elliott. London and New York: Verso, 2012.
Badiou, Alain, and Truong, Nicolas, *In Praise of Love*. Translated by Peter Bush. London: Serpent's Tail, 2012.
Badiou, Alain, 'Our Contemporary Impotence', *Radical Philosophy*, No. 181, (September/October 2013).
Badiou, Alain, and Gauchet, Marcel, *What Is to Be Done? A Dialogue on Communism, Capitalism and the Future of Democracy*. Translated by Susan Spitzer. Cambridge: Polity Press, 2016.

Badiou, Alain, and Nancy, Jean-Luc, *German Philosophy: A Dialogue*. Translated by Richard Lambart, edited and with an afterword by Jan Völker. Cambridge and London: MIT Press, 2018.

Badiou, Alain, *Lacan: The Seminars of Alain Badiou, Anti-Philosophy 3*. Translated by Kenneth Reinhard and Susan Spitzer, introduction by Kenneth Reinhard. New York and Chichester: Columbia University Press, 2019.

Baecker, Dirk, ed., *Kapitalismus als Religion*. Berlin: Kadmos, 2009.

Bastani, Aaron, *Fully Automated Luxury Communism: A Manifesto*. London and New York: Verso, 2019.

Beech, Dave, and Roberts, John, *The Philistine Controversy*. London and New York: Verso, 2002.

Benjamin, Jessica, *Like Subjects, Love Objects: Essays on Recognition and Sexual Difference*. New Haven and London: Yale University Press, 1995.

Benjamin, Walter, 'Capitalism as Religion', in Walter Benjamin, *Selected Writings, 1931–1934* Vol. 2. Essay, translated by Chad Kautzer, collection, edited by Walter Jennings, Howard Eiland, and Gary Smith. Cambridge: Harvard University Press, 2005.

Blackburn, Simon, *Mirror, Mirror: The Uses and Abuses of Self-Love*. Princeton: Princeton University Press, 2014.

Boer, Roland, 'Religion and Capitalism', available at: https://www.culturematters.org.uk/index.php/culture/religion/item/2738-religion-andcapitalism.

de la Boétie, Étienne, *Slaves by Choice*. Translated by Malcolm Smith. Egham: Runnymede Books, 1988.

Bookchin, Murray, *The Next Revolution: Popular Assemblies & The Promise of Direct Democracy*. Edited and with an introduction by Debbie Bookchin and Blair Taylor, foreword by Ursula K. Le Guin. London and New York: Verso, 2015.

Bortolotti, Lisa, *Irrationality*. Cambridge: Polity Press, 2015.

Bosteels, Bruno, *The Actuality of Communism*. London and New York: Verso, 2011.

Brassier, Ray, 'Strange Sameness', *Angelaki*, Vol. 24, No. 1 (2019).

Braverman, Harry, *Labor and Monopoly Capitalism: The Degradation of Work in the Twentieth Century*. New York: Monthly Review Press, 1998.

Brecht, Bertolt, *Me-Ti: Book of Interventions in the Flow of Things*. Edited and translated by Anthony Tatlow. London: Bloomsbury, 2016.

Brink, David O., *Perfectionism and the Common Good: Themes in the Philosophy of T.H.Green*. Oxford: Oxford University Press, 2003.

Burke, Edmund, *Reflections on the Revolution in France*. Introduced and edited by Connor O'Brien. London: Penguin Books, 1982.

Callinicos, Alex, *Making History: Agency, Structure and Change in Social Theory*. Cambridge: Polity Press, 1989.

Camatte, Jacques, *Community and Communism in Russia*. [1978] Translated by David Brown, available at: https://libcom.org/files/Jacques%20Camatte-%20Community%20and%20Communism%20in%20Russia.pdf.

Camatte, Jacques, *This World We Must Leave, and Other Essays*. Edited by Alex Trotter. Brooklyn, New York: Autonomedia, 1995.

Castoriadis, Cornelius, *Postscript on Insignificance: Dialogues with Cornelius Castoriadis*. Translated by Gabriel Rockhill and John V. Garner, and edited with an introduction by Gabriel Rockhill. London and New York: Continuum, 2011.

Caygill, Howard, *On Resistance: A Philosophy of Defiance*. London and New York: Bloomsbury Press, 2015.

Chiapello, Eve, and Boltanski, Luc, *The New Spirit of Capitalism*. Translated by Gregory Elliott. London and New York: Verso, 2005.

Chukhrov, Keti, 'Desiring Alienation in Capitalism. Zeal to De-alienate in Socialism', *Crisis & Critique*, Vol. 4, No. 2 (2017).

Cicero, *On the Ideal Orator*. Translated with Introduction, Notes, Appendixes, Glossary, Indexes by James M.May and Jakob Wisse. Oxford and New York: Oxford University Press, 2001.

Cohen, G.A. 'Equality as Fact and Norm: Reflections on the (partial) Demise of Marxism', *Theoria: A Journal of Social and Political Theory*, No 83/84, (October 1994).

Crary, Jonathan, *24/7: Late Capitalism and the Ends of Sleep*. London and New York: Verso, 2013.

Crisp, Roger, *Reasons & the Good*. Oxford: Oxford University Press, 2006.

Davies, William, 'The New Neoliberalism', *New Left Review*, Vol. 101, Second Series, (September/October 2016).

Davis, Mike, *Old Gods, New Enigmas: Marx's Lost Theory*. London and New York: Verso, 2018.

Dean Jodi, *The Communist Horizon*. London and New York: Verso, 2012.

Dean Jodi, *Crowds and Party*. London and New York: Verso, 2016.

DeLanda, Manuel, *Assemblage Theory*. Edinburgh: Edinburgh University Press, 2016.

Deleuze, Gilles, and Parnet, Claire, *Dialogues II*. London and New York: Continuum, 2006.

Deutschmann, Christoph, 'Capitalism, Religion and the Idea of the Demonic', Max-Planck Institute for the Study of Societies, Discussion Paper 12/2, available at, www.mpifg.de.

Dorsey, Dale, 'Three Arguments for Perfectionism', *Nous*, Vol. 44, No. 1 (2010).

Douzinas, Costas, and Žižek, Slavoj, eds., *The Idea of Communism*. London and New York: Verso, 2010.

Dunayevskaya, Raya, *The Power of Negativity: Selected Writings on the Dialectic in Hegel and Marx*. Edited and introduced by Peter Hudis and Kevin B. Anderson. Lanham, Maryland and Oxford: Lexington Books, 2002.

Dyer-Witheford, Nick, *Cyber-Proletariat: Global Labour in the Digital Vortex*. London: Pluto Press, 2015.

Elster, Jon, *Sour Grapes: Studies in the Subversion of Rationality*. Cambridge: Cambridge University Press, 1983.

Elster, Jon, 'Self-Realization in Work and Politics: The Marxist Conception of the Good Life', *Social Philosophy & Policy*, Vol. 3, No. 2 (Spring, 1986).

Endnotes, *Endnotes 4: Unity in Separation*, London and Oakland CA: Endnotes, 2015.

Engels, Frederick, 'On the History of Early Christianity', in Marx and Engels, *Collected Works*, Vol. 27. London: Lawrence & Wishart, 1987.

Fink, Bruce, *Lacan on Love: An Exploration of Lacan's Seminar VIII, Transference.* Cambridge: Polity Press, 2016.

Fiorio, Carlo, V., Simon Mohun, Simon, Roberto, Veneziani, Roberto, 'Social Democracy and Distributive Conflict in the UK, 1950–2010', University of Massachusetts, Economic Department Working Papers, 2013, available at: https://scholarworks.umass.edu/cgi/viewcontent.cgi?article=1154&context=econ_workingpaper.

Fisher, Mark, *Capitalist Realism: Is There No. Alternative?* Ropley, Hants: Zone Books, 2009.

Fleming, Peter, *The Mythology of Work: How Capitalism Persists Despite Itself.* London: Pluto Press, 2015.

Foster, John Bellamy, 'On Fire This Time', *Monthly Review*, Vol. 71, No. 6 (November 2019).

Foucault, Michel, and Deleuze, Gilles, 'Intellectuals and Power: A Conversation between Michel Foucault and Gilles Deleuze', in Michel Foucault, *Language, Counter-memory, Practice: Selected Essays and Interviews.* Edited by Donald Bouchard, and translated by Donald Bouchard and Sherry Simon. Ithaca: Cornell University Press, 1977.

Foucault, Michel, *The Care of the Self: The History of Sexuality*, Vol. 3. Translated by Robert Hurley. London: Penguin Books, 1990.

Frank, Georg, *Okonomie der Aufmerksamkeit: Ein Entwurf.* Munich: Hanser Verlag, 1998.

Frank, Georg, 'The Economy of Attention in the Age of Neoliberalism', available at: http://www.iemar.tuwien.ac.at/publications/Franck_2016b.pdf.

Frankfurt, Harry G., *The Reasons of Love.* Princeton: Princeton University Press, 2004.

Fraser Graham, and Lancelle, George, *Zhirnovsky: The Little Black Book.* London: Penguin Books, 1994.

Freyenhagen, Fabian, 'Honneth on Social Pathologies: A Critique', *Critical Horizons*, Vol. 16, No. 2, (May 2015).

Freyenhagen, Fabian, 'Critical Theory and Social Pathology', in *Routledge Companion to the Frankfurt School*, edited by Hammer, Espen, Honneth, Axel, and Gordon, Peter. London: Routledge, 2018.

Friends of the Classless Society, 'On Communisation and Its Theorists', available at: https://endnotes.org.uk/other_texts/en/friends-of-theclassless-society-on-communisation-and-its-theorists. 2018

Friends of the Classless Society, 'Workers of the World, Fight Amongst Yourselves! Notes on the Refugee Crisis', available at: https://endnotes.org.uk/other_texts/en/friends-of-the-classless-society-workers-of-the-world-fight-amongst-yourselves. 2018.

Fukuyama, Francis, *The End of History and the Last Man.* London: Penguin, 1992.

Gabriel, Markus, Žižek, Slavoj, *Mythology, Madness and Laughter: Subjectivity in German Idealism.* London and New York: Continuum, 2009.

Garcia, Tristan, *The Life Intense: A Modern Obsession*. Translated by Abigail Ray Alexander, Christopher Ray Alexander and Joe Cogburn. Edinburgh: Edinburgh University Press, 2018.
Ghosh, Amitav, *The Great Derangement: Change and the Unthinkable*. Chicago: Chicago University Press, 2017.
Gilman-Opalsky, Richard, *Spectacular Capitalism: Guy Debord & the Practice of Radical Philosophy*. Brooklyn: Minor Compositions, 2011.
Gilman-Opalsky, Richard, *Specters of Revolt: On the Intellect of Insurrection and Philosophy Below*. London: Repeater Books, 2016.
Goldner, Loren, 'Once Again, On Fictitious Capital: Further Reply to Aufheben and Other Critics', available at: dev.autonomedia.org 2003.
Goldner, Loren, *Revolution, Defeat and Theoretical Underdevelopment: Russia, Turkey, Spain, Bolivia*. Leiden and Boston: Brill, 2016.
Gordon, Peter E., *Adorno and Existence*. Cambridge, MA and London: Harvard University Press, 2016.
Gramsci, Antonio, *Selections from the Prison Notebooks*. Edited and translated by Quintin Hoare and Geoffrey Nowell Smith. London: Lawrence and Wishart, 1971.
Green. T.H., *Collected Works*, 5 Vols. Bristol: Thoemmes Press, 1997.
Groys, Boris, *The Communist Postscript*. Translated by Thomas H. Ford. London and New York: Verso, 2009.
Han, Byung-Chul, *Psycho-Politics: Neoliberalism and New Technologies of Power*. Translated by Erik Butler. London and New York: Verso, 2017.
Han, Byung-Chul, *What Is Power?* Translated by Daniel Steuer. Cambridge: Polity Press, 2018.
Harman, Graham, *Speculative Realism: An Introduction*. Cambridge: Polity Press, 2018.
Harvey, David, *Seventeen Contradictions and the End of Capitalism*. London: Profile Books, 2015.
Hegel, G.W.F., *The Philosophy of History*. Translated by J. Sibree, preface by Charles Hegel, and introduction by C.J. Friedrich. New York: Dover Publications, 1956.
Heller, Agnes, *The Theory of Need in Marx*. London and New York: Verso, 2018.
Honneth Axel, 'Organized Self-Realization: Some Paradoxes of Individualization', *European Journal of Social Theory*, Vol. 7, No. 4 (2004).
Honneth, Axel, *Disrespect: The Normative Foundations of Critical Theory*. Cambridge: Polity press, 2007.
Honneth, Axel, *Pathologies of Reason: On the Legacy of Critical Theory*. Translated by James Ingram. New York: Columbia University Press, 2009.
Horkheimer, Max, *Eclipse of Reason*. London and New York: Continuum, 2004.
Hurka, Thomas, *Perfectionism*. Oxford and New York: Oxford University Press, 1993.
Hurka, Thomas, *The Best Things in Life: A Guide to What Really Matters*. Oxford: Oxford University Press, 2011.
Huxley, Aldous, *The Doors of Perception: Heaven and Hell*. New York: Random House, 2004.

Jameson, Fredric, 'The Aesthetics of Singularity', *New Left Review*, No. 92, Second Series (March/April, 2015).
Jameson, Fredric, *An American Utopia: Dual Power and the Universal Army*. Edited by Slavoj Žižek. London and New York: Verso, 2016.
Johnston, Adrian, *A New German Idealism: Hegel, Žižek, and Dialectical Materialism*. New York: Columbia Press, 2019.
Jones, Stephen G. J, *The British Labour Movement and Film, 1918–1939*. London: Routledge, 1987.
Kao, S.J. Karl, ed., *Classical Chinese Tales of the Supernatural and the Fantastic: Selections from the Third to the Tenth Century*. Hong Kong: Joint Publishing Co, 1985.
Kliman, Andrew, *The Failure of Capitalist Production: Underlying Causes of the Great Recession*. London: Pluto Press, 2012.
Kolodny, Niko, 'The Explanation of Amour-Propre', *Philosophical Review*, Vol. 119, No. 2 (2010).
Kristeva, Julia, *The Sense and Non-Sense of Revolt: The Powers and Limits of Psychoanalysis*. Translated by Jeanine Herman. New York: Columbia University Press, 2000.
La Rouchefoucauld, Francois duc de, *Maxims*. Translated and introduced by L.W. Tancock. Harmondsworth: Penguin, 1967.
Lacan, Jacques, 'Du discours psychanalytique', in *Lacan in Italia 1953–1978*. Milan: La Salamandra, 1978.
Lacan, Jacques, *Television: A Challenge to the Psychoanalytic Establishment*. Translated by Jeffrey Mehlman, and edited by Joan Copjec. New York and London: W. W. Norton & Company, 1980.
Lacan, Jacques, *On Feminine Sexuality, The Limits of Love and Knowledge, 1972–1973: Encore, The Seminar of Jacques Lacan*, Book XX. Edited by Jacques-Alain Miller, and translated with notes by Bruce Fink. New York and London: W. W. Norton & Company, 1988.
Lacan, Jacques, *The Ego in Freud's Theory and in the Technique of Psychoanalysis 1954–1955: The Seminar of Jacques Lacan*, Book II. Edited by Jacque-Alain Miller, and translated by Sylvana Tomaselli, with notes by John Forrester. New York and London: W. W. Norton & Company, 1991.
Lacan, Jacques, *The Ethics of Psychoanalysis, 1959–1960: The Seminar of Jacques Lacan*, Book VII. Edited by Jacques-Alain Miller, and translated with notes by Dennis Porter. London: Routledge, 1999.
Lacan, Jacques, *Psychoanalysis Upside Down/The Reverse Side of Psychoanalysis, 1960–1970: The Seminar of Jacques Lacan*, Book XVII. Translated by Cormac Gallagher (2001), available at: https://www.valas.fr/IMG/pdf/THE-SEMINAR-OF-JACQUES-LACAN-XVII_l_envers_de_la_P.pdf.
Lacan, Jacques, *Le Séminaire XVI: D'un Autre à l'autre*. Paris: Le Seuil, 2006.
Lacan Jacques, *The Other Side of Psychoanalysis: The Seminar of Jacques Lacan*, Book XVII. Translated with notes by Russell Grigg. New York and London: W. W. Norton & Company, 2007.

Lacan, Jacques, *My Teaching*, translated by David Macey. London and New York: Verso, 2008.
Lacan, Jacques, *Anxiety: The Seminar of Jacques of Lacan*, Book X. Edited by Jacques-Alain Miller, and translated by A.R. Price. Cambridge: Polity Press, 2014.
Lacan, Jacques, *Transference: The Seminar of Jacques of Lacan*, Book VIII. Edited by Jacques-Alain Miller, and translated by Bruce Fink. Cambridge: Polity Press, 2015.
Lacan, Jacques, *The Sinthome: The Seminar of Jacques Lacan*, Book XXII. Edited by Jacques-Alain Miller, and translated by A.R. Price. Cambridge: Polity Press, 2016.
Lacan, Jacques, *Formations of the Unconscious: The Seminar of Jacques Lacan*, Book V. Edited by Jacques-Alain Miller, and translated by Russell Grigg. Cambridge: Polity Press, 2017.
Lacan Jacques, *… or Worse: The Seminar of Jacques Lacan*, Book XIX. Edited by Jacques-Alain Miller, and translated by A.R. Price. Cambridge: Polity Press, 2018.
Lacan, Jacques, *Desire and Its Interpretation: The Seminar of Jacques Lacan*, Book VI. Edited by Jacques-Alain Miller, and translated by Bruce Fink. Cambridge: Polity Press, 2019.
Lapavitsas, Costas, *Profiting Without Producing: How Finance Exploits Us All*. London and New York: Verso, 2013.
Lasch, Christopher, *The Culture of Narcissism*. New York: W. W. Norton & Company, 1991.
Lazzarato, Maurizio, *Experimental Politics: Work, Welfare, and Creativity in the Neoliberal Age*. Edited by Jeremy Gilbert, and translated by Arianna Bove, Jeremy Gilbert, Andrew Goffey, Mark Hayward, Jason Read, and Alberto Toscano. Cambridge, and London: MIT Press, 2017.
Lifshitz, Mikhail, *The Philosophy of Art of Karl Marx*. Translated by Ralph B. Winn. London: Pluto Press, 1976.
Lordon, Frédéric, *Willing Slaves of Capital: Spinoza & Marx on Desire*. Translated by Gabriel Ash. London and New York: Verso, 2014.
Löwy, Michel, *Fire Alarm: Reading Walter Benjamin's 'On the Concept of History'*. London and New York: Verso, 2005.
Löwy. Michael, 'Capitalism as Religion: Walter Benjamin and Max Weber', *Historical Materialism*, Vol. 17 (2009).
Lyotard, Jean-François, *Libidinal Economy*. Translated by Iain Hamilton Grant. London and New York: Bloomsbury, 2015.
Machiavelli, Niccolò, *The Prince*. Translated with notes by George Bull, and introduction by Anthony Grafton. London: Penguin Books, 2003.
Mackay, Robin, and Avanessian, Armen, eds., *#Accelerate: The Accelerationist Reader*. Falmouth and New York: Urbanomic, 2014.
Macpherson, C.B., *The Political Theory of Possessive Individualism*. Oxford: Oxford University Press, 1962.
Magee, Paul, 'The Scholarly Affair is Self-Love', *Topia*, Vol. 28 (Fall 2012).
Malabou, Catherine, *The Future of Hegel: Plasticity, Temporality and Dialectic*. Preface by Jacques Derrida, and translated by Lisabeth During. Abingdon: Routledge, 2005.

Malm, Andreas, *Fossil Capital*. London and New York: Verso, 2015.
Marazzi, Christian, *Capital and Affects: The Politics of Language Economy*. Translated and with an introduction by Giuseppina Mecchia. Los Angeles: Semiotext(e), 2011.
Marcuse, Herbert, *Eros and Civilization: A Philosophical Inquiry into Freud*. New York: Vintage Books, 1962.
Marshall, Jonathan, *Drug Wars: Corruption, Counterinsurgency and Covert Operations in the Third World*. Forrestville: Cohan & Cohen, 1991.
Marshall, Jonathan, *The Lebanese Connection: Corruption, Civil War and the International Drug Traffic*. Stanford: Stanford University Press, 2012.
Marshall, Jonathan, and Scott, Peter Dale, *Cocaine Politics: Drugs, Armies and the CIA in Central America*. Berkeley: University of California Press, 1991.
Marx, Karl, *Capital*, Vol. 3. London: Lawrence & Wishart, 1972.
Marx, Karl, *Difference Between the Democritean and Epicurean Philosophy of Nature* (1841) in Marx and Engels, *Collected Works*, Vol. 1. London: Lawrence & Wishart, 1975.
Marx, Karl, 'Economic and Philosophical Manuscripts of 1844', in Marx and Engels, *Collected Works*, Vol. 3. London: Lawrence & Wishart, 1975.
Marx, Karl, and Engels, Frederick, 'The German Ideology', in Marx and Engels, *Collected Works*, Vol. 5. London: Lawrence & Wishart, 1976.
Marx, Karl, and Engels, Frederick, *The Holy Family*. London: Lawrence & Wishart, 1956.
Marx, Karl, and Engels, Frederick, 'Preface to the Second Russian edition of the *Manifesto of the Communist Party*', in Marx and Engels, *Collected Works*, Vol. 24. London: Lawrence & Wishart, 2010.
Meillassoux, Quentin, *After Infinitude: An Essay on the Necessity of Contingency*. Preface by Alain Badiou, and translated by Ray Brassier. London and New York: Continuum, 2008.
Menglong, Feng, *Stories to Awaken the World: A Ming Dynasty Collection* (compiled by Feng Menglong, 1574–1646). Translated by Shuhui Yang and Yunqin Yang, and foreword by Robert E. Hegel. Seattle and London: Washington State University Press, 2014. *Monthly Review*, Vol. 71, No. 6, November, 2019).
Morton, Timothy, *Hyperobjects: Philosophy and Ecology after the End of the World*. Minneapolis: University of Minnesota Press, 2013.
Morton, Timothy, *Humankind: Solidarity with Nonhuman People*. London and New York: Verso, 2017.
Muller, Jerry Z., *Capitalism and the Jews*. Princeton: Princeton University Press, 2010.
Nail, Thomas, *The Figure of the Migrant*. Stanford: Stanford University Press, 2015.
Nancy, Jean-Luc, *The Inoperative Community*. Edited by Peter Connor, and translated by Peter Connor, Lisa Garbus, Michael Holland and Simon Sawhney. Minneapolis and Oxford: University of Minnesota Press, 1991.
Negri, Antonio, *The Labor of Job: The Biblical Text as a Parable of Human Labor*. Translated by Matteo Mandarini, foreword by Michael Hardt, and commentary by Roland Boer. Durham and London: Duke University Press, 2009.

Nesbitt, Nick, ed., *The Concept in Crisis: Reading* Capital *Today*. Durham and London: Duke University Press, 2017.

Nietzsche, Friedrich, *The Will to Power*. Translated by Walter Kaufmann and R.J. Hollingdale, and edited with a commentary by Walter Kaufmann. New York: Vintage Books, 1968.

Nora, Pierre, *Realms of Memory*, 3 Vols. Edited by Lawrence D. Kritzman, and translated by Arthur Goldhammer. New York: Columbia University Press, 1996–1998.

'Notes from the Editors', *Monthly Review*, Vol. 71, No. 7 (December 2019).

Noys, Benjamin, ed., *Communization and its Discontents: Contestation, Critique, and Contemporary Struggles*. New York and Port Watson: Wivenhoe, 2011.

Piketty, Thomas, 'Brahmin Left vs Merchant Right: Rising Inequality & the Changing Structure of Political Conflict (Evidence from France, Britain and the US, 1948–2017)', WID, World Working Paper, Series No. 2018/7 (March 2018).

Przeworski, Adam, *Capitalism and Social Democracy*. Cambridge: Cambridge University Press, 1985.

Przeworski, Adam, and Sprague, John, *Paper Stones: A History of Electoral Socialism*. Chicago: University of Chicago, 1986.

Read, Jason, *The Micro-politics of Capital: Marx and the Prehistory of the Present*. Albany: State University of New York Press, 2003.

Read, Jason, *The Politics of Transindividuality*. Leiden: Brill, 2015. https://readingagency.org.uk/about/impact/002-reading-facts-1/.

Reich, Wilhelm, 'What is Class Consciousness?' in *Sex-Pol: Essays, 1929–1934*. Translated by Anna Bostock, Tom DuBose and Lee Baxandall, and edited by Lee Baxandall, and introduction by Bertell Ollman. New York: Vintage Books, 1972.

Reich, Wilhelm, *The Mass Psychology of Fascism*. translated by V.R. Carpagno. Harmondsworth: Penguin, 1975.

Rennwald, Line, and Pontusson, Jonas, 'Paper Stones Revisited: Class Voting, Unionization and the Electoral Decline of the Mainstream Left', available at: https://www.cambridge.org/core/journals/perspectives-on-politics/article/paper-stones-revisited-class-voting-unionization-and-the-electoral-decline-of-the-mainstream-left/A3F8C462B34816E36F9ED7AA3BA766A2.

Roberts, John, *Red Days: Popular Music and the English Counterculture, 1965–1975*. New York and Colchester: Autonomedia/Minor Compositions, 2020.

Roberts, John, *The Reasoning of Unreason: Universalism, Capitalism and Disenlightenment*. London: Bloomsbury, 2018.

Roberts, John, 'The Newest in What is Oldest': History, Historicism and the Temporality of the Avant-Garde', available at: http://www.neme.org/texts/the-newest-in-what-is-oldest 2018.

Roberts, Paul, *The End of Oil*. London: Bloomsbury, 2004.

Rodinson, Maxime, *Islam and Capitalism*. Translated by Brian Pearce. London: Pantheon Books, 1973.

Rosen, Michael, *On Voluntary Servitude: False Consciousness and the Theory of Ideology*. Cambridge: Harvard University Press, 1996.

Rousseau, Jean-Jacques, *A Discourse on Inequality*. London: Penguin Books, 1984.

Rousseau, Jean-Jacques, *Discours sur l'origine et les fondements de l'inégalité parmi les hommes. Discours sur les sciences et les arts*. Paris: GF Flammarion, 1992.

Rousseau, Jean-Jacques, 'A Discourse on Political Economy', in *The Social Contract and the Discourses*. Translated by G.D.H. Cole, with an introduction by Alan Ryan. New York: Everyman's Library, Alfred A. Knopf, 1993.

Rousseau, Jean-Jacques, 'Discourse on the Origin and Foundations of Inequality Among Men', in *The Discourses and Other Early Political Writings*. Edited and translated by Victor Gourevitch. Cambridge: Cambridge University Press, 1997.

Ruda, Frank, *For Badiou: Idealism without Idealism*. Preface by Slavoj Žižek. Evanston: Northwestern University Press, 2015.

Sartre, Jean-Paul, *Being and Nothingness: An Essay on Phenomenological Ontology*. Translated by Hazel E. Barnes, and introduction by Mary Warnock. London: Methuen & Co, 1969.

Schiller, Friedrich, *On the Aesthetic Education of Man*. Translated by Keith Tribe, with an introduction and notes by Alexander Schmidt. London: Penguin Books, 2016.

Schumpeter, Joseph, *Capitalism, Socialism and Democracy* [1942]. London: Routledge, 2010.

Seneca, *On The Happy Life*. North Shore, Auckland: Vigeo Press, 2018.

Shanin, Teodor, *Late Marx and the Russian Road: Marx and the Peripheries of Capitalism*. London and New York: Verso, 2018.

Shukaitis, Stevphen, *Combination Arts: Notes on Collective Practice in the Undercommons*. Colchester and New York: Autonomedia/Minor Compositions, 2019.

Shuster, Martin, *Autonomy After Auschwitz: Adorno, German Idealism, and Modernity*. Chicago: Chicago University Press, 2014.

Solty, Ingar, 'Why is There Now Socialist Politics in the United States?' *The Bullet*, 6 June 2019, available at: https://socialistproject.ca/2019/06/why-is-there-now-socialism-in-the-united-states/.

Spinoza, Baruch, *Theological-Political Treatise*. Translated by Samuel Shirley. Indianapolis: Hackett Books, 2001.

Spinoza, Baroch, *Ethics: Proved in Geometrical Order*. Translated by Michael Silverthorne and edited by Matthew J. Kisner. Cambridge: Cambridge University Press, 2018.

Srnicek, Nick and Williams, Alex, *Inventing the Future: Postcapitalism and a World Without Work*. London and New York: Verso, 2015.

Stavrakakis, Yannis, *Lacan & The Political*. London and New York: Routledge, 1999.

Strauss, Leo, 'The Crisis of Political Philosophy', in *The Predicament of Modern Politics*. Edited by Howard Spaeth. Detroit: University of Detroit Press, 1964.

Stiegler, Bernard, *The Decadence of Industrial Democracies: Disbelief and Discredit*, Vol. 1. Translated by Daniel Ross and Suzanne Arnold. Cambridge: Polity Press, 2011.

Stiegler, Bernard, *The Lost Spirit of Capitalism: Disbelief and, Discredit*, Vol. 3. Translated by Daniel Ross. Cambridge: Polity Press, 2014.

Stiegler, Bernard, *The Re-Enchantment of the World: The Value of Spirit Against Industrial Populism*. Translated by Trevor Arthur. London: Bloomsbury, 2014.

Stiegler, Bernard, *Symbolic Misery: The Hyper Industrial Epoch*, Vol. 1. Translated by Barnaby Norman. Cambridge: Polity Press, 2014.

Stiegler, Bernard, *Symbolic Misery: The katastrophe of the sensible*, Vol. 2. Translated by Barnaby Norman. Cambridge: Polity Press, 2015.

Sünker, Heinz, 'Bildung, Alltag und Subjectivität: Elemente zu einer Sozialpädagogik', in *Studien zur Philosophie und Theorie der Bildung No. 6*. Weinheim: Deutscher Studien Verlag, 1989.

Tafuri, Manfredo, *Architecture and Utopia: Design and Capitalist Development* [1973]. Cambridge: MIT Press, 1976.

Tawney, R.H., *Religion and the Rise of Capitalism: A Historical Study*. Prefatory note by Charles Gore. Harmondsworth: Penguin Books, 1966.

Thoby, Arthur, 'Capitalism as Religion', in *Student Economic Review*, Vol. 26 (2012).

Tillich, Paul, 'The Demonic: A Study in the Interpretation of History', in *Paul Tillich on Creativity*. Edited by Jaquelyn Ann K. Kegley. London: University Press of America, 1989.

Tiqqun, *Preliminary Materials for a Theory of the Young-Girl*. Translated by Ariena Reines. Cambridge: Semiotext(e) and MIT, 2012.

Tomšič, Samo, *The Capitalist Unconscious: Marx and Lacan*. London and New York: Verso, 2015.

Tomšič, Samo, *The Labour of Enjoyment: Towards a Critique of Libidinal Economy*. Berlin: August Verlag, 2019.

Tuck, Richard, *Free Riding*. Cambridge and London: Harvard University Press, 2008.

Vrousalis, Nicholas, 'Capital Without Wage-Labour: Marx's Modes of Subsumption Revisited', *Economics and Philosophy*, Vol. 34, No. 3 (2018).

Vrousalis, Nicholas, 'How Exploiters Dominate', available at: https://ssrn.com/abstract=3388054, 2019.

Wark, McKenzie, *The Spectacle of Disintegration: Situationist Passages Out of the 20th Century*. London and New York: Verso, 2013.

Weber, Max, *The Protestant Ethic and the Spirit of Capitalism*. Translated by Talcott Parsons, with an introduction by Anthony Giddens. London and New York: Routledge, 1992.

Wood, W. Allen, *The Free Development of Each: Studies on Freedom, Right and Ethics in Classical German Philosophy*. Oxford: Oxford University Press, 2014.

Wright, Erik Olin, *Class, Crisis and the State*. London: New Left Books, 1978.

Wright, Erik Olin, *Envisioning Real Utopias*. London and New York: Verso, 2010.

Žižek, Slavoj, *For They Know Not What They Do: Enjoyment as a Political Factor*. London and New York: Verso, 1991.

Žižek, Slavoj, ed., *Lacan: The Silent Partners*. London and New York: Verso, 2006.

Žižek, Slavoj, *In Defense of Lost Causes*. London and New York: Verso, 2008.

Žižek, Slavoj, *First as Tragedy, Then as Farce*. London and New York: Verso, 2009.

Žižek, Slavoj, *Living in the End Times*. London and New York: Verso, 2010.

Žižek, Slavoj, *Less than Nothing: Hegel and the Shadow of Dialectical Materialism*. London and New York: Verso, 2012.

Žižek, Slavoj, *Against the Double Blackmail: Refugees, Terror and Other Troubles with the Neighbours*. London: Penguin, 2016.

Žižek, Slavoj, Frank Ruda and Agon Hamza, *Reading Marx*. Cambridge: Polity Press, 2018.

Index

accelerationism (weak/strong) 2, 6–7, 11–13, 30, 181, 202, 210
adaptive preferences 14, 15, 39, 114, 116–21, 139, 171, 190–2, 197, 199
   Elster's notion of 121–3
   Lordon's model of 123
Adorno, Theodor 11, 53, 63, 69, 73, 139–40, 199
   Dialectic of Enlightenment 25, 61–2, 66
   Towards a New Manifesto 215 n.18
affirmation/affirmationism 30, 46, 91, 100, 103, 164, 202, 207
Agamben, Georgio 46
akratic/akraticism 105
Alliez, Éric 55, 200–2, 206
   Wars and Capital 52
Althusser, Louis 56, 84
   subjectless subjectivations 162
antagonism/antagonistic 8, 44, 89, 97, 127–8
anthropology 36–7, 51, 70, 76, 82, 87, 114
anti-akratic/-akraticism model 105–6, 115–16, 171, 204, 226 n.13
anti-Aristotelian model 115, 226 n.13
anti-capitalist 11, 23, 31, 43, 88, 155, 172, 200–2, 204, 208
anti-egalitarian 146, 150. *See also* egalitarian/egalitarianism

anxiety 11, 28, 30, 56–8, 61, 93, 108, 119, 131–2, 134, 136, 169, 176, 186–7, 191, 199, 210
Aquinas, Thomas 74, 144, 155
aristocracy/aristocratic 67, 68–70, 141, 143–4, 145, 162
Aristotle 73, 105, 142, 143, 145, 148, 155, 164
   Aristotelian model 105, 148, 151, 155, 171 (*see also* anti-Aristotelian model)
   claims on best interest 171
   happy life 144
Artificial Intelligence 30, 208
ataraxy (avoidance of unpleasure) 56, 61, 106
authoritarian/authoritarianism 22, 89, 101, 221 n.67
autolatry 29, 49, 61, 91, 94, 106, 114
automation 3, 6, 13
autonomy 2, 7, 12–13, 18–19, 21, 36, 50, 52, 54, 65–6, 73, 75, 84, 87, 95, 121–2, 125, 139, 158, 166, 169, 190–1, 196, 208
   economic war against 52, 61
   and pleasure 106, 120, 122, 131, 160, 164
   self-directed 173, 175, 176–7, 179
   workers' 128–9

Badiou, Alain 5, 8, 161, 204
Banaji, Jarius 86–7

barbarism 202
Bastani, Aaron 173
  The Third Disruption 13, 172
Becker, Wolfgang, *Good Bye, Lenin!* 93–4, 96, 98, 103
belief(s) 31, 32, 45, 103, 105, 116–18, 129, 140, 168, 189, 191, 229 n.13
Benjamin, Jessica 135
Benjamin, Walter 46, 73
Bensaïd, Daniel 86
best interests 1, 15, 171, 204
Beyoncé 222 n.76
Blackburn, Simon 161
Bolsonaro, Jair 48
Boltanski, Luc 123–4
  systems of confirmation 100
Bosteels, Bruno 33
bourgeois 8, 21, 66–70, 72, 75, 77, 87, 96, 99, 141–3, 145
  cultural authority 63
  egoism 80–1
  European 143, 168
  individuation (Rousseau) 66–8, 73, 80
  petty-bourgeoisie 3, 10, 89
  politics 82–3
  possessive individualism 28
  public culture 99
  utilitarian eudaimonism 143, 145
Braverman, Harry 206
Burke, Edmund 100–1

Camatte, Jacques 211–12
capitalist reason 13, 46, 84, 96–107, 117, 134–5
capitalist reproduction 100, 132
Castoriadis, Cornelius 26, 29, 40, 94, 122
Caygill, Howard, *On Resistance* 39
Chiapello, Eve 123–4
chih-kuai (records of anomalies) 231 n.65
China 9, 41, 45, 182, 187, 230 n.60
Cicero 143
civilization 53, 67, 70, 80, 177, 208, 211
  civilizational struggle 202–7

civil war 4, 53–4, 200
  war for pleasure 54–5, 197
class identity 5, 9, 10, 34–5, 42, 63–4, 82, 84, 89, 115, 147
class interests 8, 44, 118, 121, 142, 190, 198
class struggle 34–5, 53, 84, 87, 90, 97, 101, 147, 157, 177, 181, 203–4
climate change 22–3, 25–6
Cohen, Jerry 147, 215 n.18
collective class consciousness 8, 83, 89–90
collective interests 10, 118, 121, 190–1
collective reason 105, 121
comfort 35, 47, 48, 103–4, 119, 138, 148, 150, 161, 185–6, 198
commodity 10, 15, 36, 40–1, 53, 56, 58, 60, 66, 88, 112, 173
common sense 48, 69, 100, 103, 104, 218 n.21
Communism 45, 156–7, 173, 179
  communist 3, 6, 33, 60, 76, 78, 82, 85–6, 90–1, 169, 178, 202
community 14, 77–8, 81, 83, 85, 145, 187, 195
consciousness of capital 7, 8, 62, 77, 82, 84, 90–1, 147, 170, 181, 199, 212, 233 n.13
consumption 7, 29–31, 34–7, 43, 49–52, 56, 64, 65–6, 104, 111–12, 127, 129–31
  production and (producer and consumer) 1, 29–30, 36, 51, 53, 56, 113, 115, 127, 129, 138
counterculture 64, 162
counter-hegemony 5, 41, 64, 82
Crary, Jonathan, *24/7: Late Capitalism and the Ends of Sleep* 54, 220 n.62
creative destruction 27, 31, 34, 47–9, 54, 104
creativity of capitalism 4, 18, 26–31, 35, 38, 46–7, 49, 51, 60, 97, 99, 173, 189

critical knowledge 99, 101, 169
critical theory 8, 14, 25, 37, 40, 46, 51, 53–4, 63, 112, 117, 171, 197
critique of capitalism 22, 31, 84
culture industry 65, 98–9

Davies, William 99
Dean, Jodi 6, 204
de-attachment 212
   and dis-attachment 199–202
   and perfectionism 207–8
Debord, Guy 28, 39, 63
debt/debtor 46, 50
de la Boétie, Étienne 119–20, 227 n.52
Slaves by Choice 118
Deleuze, Gilles 37, 175, 193, 195, 203
   control societies 1, 52, 55, 83, 91
demand(s) 31, 47, 82, 97, 109–10, 113, 121, 124, 129, 132–6, 138, 147, 160, 162, 167–8, 180, 186, 204–7, 215 n.18
   capitalist/capitalism 50, 56, 130–2
   communicative 27
   emancipatory 147
   for full unemployment 231 n.64
   normative 2, 232 n.5
   perfectionist 2, 142, 158
   subject 210
   of surplus *jouissance* 157, 165
   of wage labour 44
democracy 53, 95, 97–8, 101, 122, 140
   and capital 24, 172, 202
   and freedom 98
   and market allocations 6
   parliamentary 8, 24, 117, 197
   real 94
   social 3, 6–7, 9, 13, 22, 31, 34, 62, 102, 117, 122, 137–8, 146, 156, 200
   Western 9, 51
   workplace 128
demonic-infinite 1, 45–9, 56–7, 88, 221 n.67

de-rationalization 15, 37, 49, 54, 113
Descartes, René 8
desire 105–7, 115–16, 119, 135, 188, 190, 194–5, 196, 206, 212
   advocacy 95, 97, 101
   best reason 49, 116, 122, 170, 227 n.45
   blocked 108, 191, 194, 209
   capitalist 37, 129, 168, 197
   and communication 110
   comparative 160, 161
   conatus (energy of desire) 115
   contingent 116
   crisis of 119–20
   deliberative 158
   dependent/dependency 190–4
   for desire 1, 56–7, 65–6, 94, 108–9, 113, 120, 137, 140, 160, 171, 189, 194, 199
   as detour 108–9, 111–12, 115, 130–2, 138
   emancipatory 103–4
   empty 96, 100, 120
   master's desire 112, 122–34, 140, 144, 158, 163, 168, 172, 182, 190, 197–8
   object of (object *a*) 57, 107–11, 114–15, 131–2, 139
   and perfectionism 192–7
   and pleasure 57, 93–6, 103, 107, 109, 111, 123
   postponement of 190–2
   and subjecthood 110
   worker's desire 125–7
destructive creativity. *See* creative destruction
developmentalism, capitalist 45
Diderot, Denis 74
digital capitalism 18, 50–1
digitalization 24, 27, 51–2, 206
discernment 52, 57, 67–8
ductile/ductility 28–30, 48–51, 104, 128, 131
Dunayevskaya, Raya 39, 205

ecological crisis 2, 6, 12, 21–3, 24–6, 44, 62, 92, 104
egalitarian/egalitarianism 146. *See also* anti-egalitarian
ego/egoism 77–81, 87, 88, 91, 103–4, 139, 195, 224 n.46
ego-ideal 133, 135–6, 138. *See also* ideal ego
electoral politics 24, 121, 215 n.14
Elster, Jon 116, 147, 155
   dissonance reduction 117, 122–3
   notion of adaptive preference 121–2
   Sour Grapes: Studies in the Subversion of Rationality 116
emancipatory politics 2, 4–5, 7–8, 13, 82, 87, 113–14, 121, 137, 156–7, 171, 192, 220 n.62
Endnotes 1, 5, 11, 16, 36, 90
   consciousness of capital 7–8
   'A History of Separation' 9
endocolonization 54
Engels, Friedrich 85, 87, 144
enjoyment, production of 38, 65, 96, 105
Enlightenment 18, 37, 62, 66, 69–71, 72, 74
   anti-Enlightenment 11, 16, 52, 87
   counter-Enlightenment 100
enterprises 124, 126–8
   capitalist 66, 125–6
   joint 124–5
   neoliberal 125
equality 6, 12, 134, 175. *See also* inequality
eudaimonism 141–9, 153–4, 156–8, 169, 175, 189
   'bitter-sweet' 181
   capitalist 158, 171
   modern 174
   non-utilitarian 158, 160, 164, 165, 169, 181
   utilitarian 158, 181, 190
Europe 9, 24, 41–2, 44, 64, 86, 143, 146, 168

exceptionalism 211
exploitation 10, 14, 55, 69, 115, 118–21, 126
exteriority (loss of) 34, 40
   and creativity 26–31
   and crisis 25–6
   internal/interiorized 25–6
Extinction Rebellion movement 23

Fichte, Johann 77
financial bondage of capitalism 47, 115
Fink, Bruce 135
Fleming, Peter, *The Mythology of Work: How Capitalism Persists Despite Itself* 126
fossil capital 23, 26
Foucault, Michel 36, 162, 163–4, 175, 203
   The Care of the Self 162–3
Fourier, Charles 174, 178
Franck, Georg 55
Frankfurt, Harry 164–6
freedom(s) 4, 102, 105, 118–20, 173, 178, 192–4, 197, 205, 207, 211, 213, 232 n.5
   and autonomy 158
   capitalist 16, 38, 98, 197
   and democracy 98
   from exploitation 118, 120–1
   and individuation 4, 73, 98
   voluntarist realization of 120
   walk to freedom 119–21, 194
free-rider theory 121–2, 171, 218 n.23
French Revolution 39, 77, 80
Freud, Sigmund 21, 37, 93, 103, 109, 111, 170
Friends of the Classless Society 43
full-time employment 11, 13, 43–4, 52
fundamental permissiveness 174

Garcia, Tristan 1, 16, 29, 36
Gates, Bill 34
Gauchet, Marcel 217–18 n.19
Gilman-Opalsky, Richard 56, 203–5
   Specters of Revolt 203

Goldner, Loren 45, 86–7
Gorz, André 5
Gramsci, Antonio 39–40
green energy. *See* New Green Deal
Green, T. H., *Collected Works* 229 n.18
Griebel, Otto, *The Internationale* 95
Guattari, Félix 5, 201

Han, Byung-Chul 54
happily dominated 39, 114, 128, 139
'happy life' 144, 152, 158, 173, 176, 189
Harvey, David 23
healing process, capitalist 44–5
Hegel, G. W. F. 61, 73, 80–1
hegemony 16, 26, 40, 53
Heidegger, Martin 8
Heller, Agnes 146
   The Theory of Need in Marx 162
historicism 87, 209–10
   anti-historicism 86, 88
homo economicus 46
Honneth, Axel 51, 66
   on individuation 14–15
   on Rousseau in *Disrespect* 72
Horkheimer, Max 64, 69
   Dialectic of Enlightenment 25, 61–2, 66
   Towards a New Manifesto 215 n.18
human agency 209–10
humanity 8, 21, 38, 49, 51–2, 54, 68, 72, 73, 81, 85, 179, 206, 211
   humanist 23, 63, 84, 98–9, 175, 210, 220 n.62
Hurka, Thomas 2, 193
   elements of 148, 150–1, 153
   Perfectionism 148–59
   radicalism 154
Husserl, Edmund 8
Huxley, Aldous 175
   The Doors of Perception: Heaven and Hell 230 n.60

I-cracy 21, 30–1, 35, 46, 49–51, 56, 67, 112, 130, 136
   production of 96–107, 129

ideal ego 135–6, 138. *See also* ego-ideal
ideal self 132–3, 135, 163
ideal version of capitalism 1, 99, 132–4, 140
immanent 13, 25, 30, 62, 69, 83, 85, 88, 94, 139, 181, 190, 194
immigration crisis in Germany (2017) 43
immiseration 10, 14, 16, 32, 40, 44, 46, 85, 144, 192, 197, 215 n.20
India 41, 45
individualism 2, 17–18
   possessive 28–9, 104, 106
individuation 2, 16–18, 28–31, 35, 37–8, 50, 52, 55–6, 62–5, 70–1, 80, 87, 102, 120, 129, 139, 158, 165–6, 170, 187, 195–6, 199
   abstract 79
   adaptive 14
   capitalist 17, 47–8, 60, 84, 89, 106
   and class reproduction 89–92
   countercultural production of 64
   de-individuation 2, 52–4, 60, 61–7, 73, 81, 84–6, 87–8, 91, 96, 106, 113, 114, 129, 131–2, 137–9, 140, 147, 157, 166, 169, 174, 182, 186, 190, 193, 195–6, 205, 221 n.67
   economic war on 52
   and egoism 77–8, 83
   and freedom 4, 73, 98
   Honneth on 14–15
   human 75–6
   of Marx 73–6
   post-capitalist 90
   production of 18, 55, 64, 113
   of Rousseau (bourgeois) 67–9, 73, 75
   and self-affection 182–8
   social-psychic aetiology of 15
   social/socialized 5, 38, 49, 85, 88, 172, 176–7, 182, 189, 194–5, 195
   subjective 89
   and transindividuation 81–8

inequality 24, 32, 33, 70, 72. *See also* equality
interpellation 46, 55, 101, 113, 125
investment 1, 6, 124, 167, 169
   active 1, 49, 55, 138
   ideological 210
   libidinal 15, 42, 111, 114, 131, 133, 147
   narcissistic 135
   subjective 11, 29, 50, 172, 181

Jameson, Fredric 39, 41, 50, 175, 178, 180–1, 202–3
   An American Utopia: Dual Power and the Universal Army 173
jouissance 1, 14, 17–18, 21, 39–40, 43, 49–50, 55, 56, 66, 81, 88, 91–2, 95–6, 107–8, 111, 116, 124, 130, 134, 140, 166, 169, 181, 210
   capitalist 37, 193
   entropy 111
   of individuation 35, 84
   Lacan's writing on (Seminars) 15, 107, 110–12, 140
   of repetition 111–12
   of self-correction 32
   surplus 1, 37, 47, 49–59, 83, 94, 110–15, 130, 132, 134, 137, 139, 140–1, 147, 157, 160, 165–6, 169–71, 189–90, 199, 205–6, 210, 213, 221 n.67
joyful alienation 36, 39, 40, 49, 55, 91, 106, 124, 156, 197

Kant, Immanuel 74, 160, 162, 164–5, 206
knowledge production 112–13
Korsch, Karl, *Marxism and Philosophy* 224 n.46
Kristeva, Julia 36

labour(s) 4, 37, 68, 72, 84, 96, 114, 118, 128, 154, 172
   alienated 180–1
   and capital 6, 11, 41, 49, 60, 81, 128, 146, 157, 198, 206
   collective 2, 9–11, 34, 83–5, 87, 198, 206, 209
   daily 143
   disaggregation 2, 8, 35, 41, 61, 81, 83, 85, 88, 90, 104
   in electronic sectors 41
   free time 64, 173
   living 7, 25–6, 34, 37, 42, 44, 62, 83, 85, 87, 92, 97, 127, 200, 206
   low-paid workers 10
   necessary 177–82, 213, 231 n.64
   re-temporalization of 179
   self-love and workplace 123–7
   social division of 76, 85, 115, 123, 144, 154–5, 167, 172, 177–8, 206
   and sublimation 177–82
   waged 3, 7, 9, 13, 16–17, 25, 44, 63, 84, 127, 146, 154, 200
   working/non-working day 179
Lacan, Jacques 1, 15, 21, 37, 47, 51, 56, 61, 73, 93–4, 103, 105, 107, 115, 129, 135, 155, 158, 166, 170, 192, 226 n.13
   object of desire 107–8
   The Other Side of Psychoanalysis 110
   production of knowledge 112
   psychoanalysis (*see* psychoanalysis)
   writing on *jouissance* (Seminars) 107, 110
Laclau, Ernesto 5
Lasch, Christopher 49
Lazzarato, Maurizio 54–5, 200–2, 206
   Wars and Capital 52
liberalism, politics of 53. *See also* neoliberal/neoliberalism
liberation 87, 89, 138, 173, 175, 211
   liberationist 203, 205, 207–8
libidinal economy 1–2, 14, 16, 36–42, 44–5, 49, 51–2, 55, 57–8, 60, 62, 88, 93, 96, 98, 103, 105, 109–10, 113–14, 122, 124, 132, 137–40, 148, 155–6, 158, 159, 166, 177, 189, 198, 202, 206–8, 212

Lifshitz, Mikhail 80
 The Philosophy of Art of Karl Marx
  224 n.46
Lordon, Frédéric 1, 17, 36, 39, 41, 54,
  115, 122, 127–8, 147, 155, 157,
  197, 227 n.52
 co-linearization of desire 124–6
 Fleming on 126
 on 'happily dominated' 39, 114, 128
 *Willing Slaves of Capital: Spinoza &
  Marx on Desire* 115, 125, 156
 love of capitalism 16–17, 38, 45–9, 56,
  127, 129–30, 197
  and idealized internal self 132–6
 love of love of self 1–2, 17, 55–8, 90–1,
  103, 106, 114–16, 127, 129–32,
  135, 137, 165, 171, 189, 221
  n.67. *See also* self-love (*amour-
  propre*)
Löwy, Michael 46
Lukács, Georg 46
 History and Class Consciousness 82,
  224 n.46
 theory of reification 15, 40
Lyotard, Jean-François 50, 130, 137–8,
  140, 163, 173–4, 181, 202
 Libidinal Economy 40

Machiavelli, Niccolò 97, 118
Maoism 74
Mao Tse-Tung 39, 192
Marcuse, Herbert 5, 138, 173
market socialism 31, 60
Marxism/Marxist 8, 54, 87, 115, 148,
  171
 analytic 116
 anti-Marxist 82
 orthodox 40, 45, 112, 146, 162, 198,
  224 n.46
 post-68 211
 revolutionary tradition 120
 Western 37, 40, 63, 81
Marx, Karl 2, 31, 34, 37, 39, 50–1, 67,
  73, 83–5, 106, 109, 113, 115–16,
  139, 140, 146, 172, 180, 182, 189,
  192, 195, 211, 225 n.57
 all-roundedness 2, 74, 76, 151, 154,
  156–7, 179, 180–1, 208
 anti-historicism 86–8
 atomism 80–1, 90–1
 bourgeois egoism 80 (*see also* ego/
  egoism)
 Capital (Volume Three) 178–80
 Communist Manifesto 86
 Democritus 78–9
 *Difference Between the Democritean
  and Epicurean Philosophy of
  Nature* 78, 143
 *Economic and Philosophic
  Manuscripts* 77–8
 Epicurus 78–80, 91
 The German Ideology 76–7, 146, 180
 Grundrisse 36, 37, 75, 86, 112
 The Holy Family 78
 individuation of 73–6
 political economy 8
 post-historicist 87
 and Rousseau 73
mass culture 46, 57, 63–5, 97, 172
mature capitalism 2, 14–15, 17, 31,
  39–40, 49–50, 106–7, 129, 137,
  139–40, 154, 157, 177, 192, 197,
  220 n.62, 232 n.5
Menglong, Feng, 'The Old Gardener
  Meets Fairy Maidens' 185–8, 189
Middle East, war zones in 42, 48, 104
migrancy/migrants 42–5
modernity/modernization 43, 45, 71,
  80, 83, 85–7, 143, 182–3, 211
moralism 15, 155, 158, 174–5, 193
More, Thomas 174
Mouffe, Chantal 5

Nancy, Jean-Luc 195
narcissism/narcissistic 2, 17–18, 29, 49,
  71, 95, 133–5, 164
 primordial 51, 220 n.58
narcosis 176, 230 n.60

naturalization 40, 47, 53, 191
Negri, Toni 5, 39, 90, 123
neoliberal/neoliberalism 4, 6, 17, 22, 26, 29–30, 37, 40, 49–51, 54–6, 83, 91, 97, 99, 123–4, 129, 137–8, 140–1, 146, 197, 202
neotony 60, 88, 112, 114, 191
  feminization of 57–9
network culture 50, 55, 60
New Green Deal 6, 23, 26, 34, 233 n.13
new Naming of Things 24, 200–1, 208
Nietzsche, Friedrich 138, 144
nihilism 74, 97, 176
non-human 209–10
non-state actors 98
non-state technocrats 98
non-work/non-workers 12–13, 28, 63, 82, 98, 104, 118, 133, 141, 147, 157, 171, 179, 197–9, 202
North America 41, 64

Other 47, 57, 109–10
overidentification 3, 26, 30, 47

passion/passionate 11, 22, 28, 32, 37, 77, 80, 96, 114, 118–20, 122–3, 128, 135, 144–5, 153, 158, 162, 165, 167, 170, 173–7, 182–3, 190, 208, 210, 231 n.64
  attachments 11, 135, 180, 193
  libidinal 178
  pleasure 180–1
  sad 174
  well-/ill-chosen 175
peace 54, 103, 156
  pseudo-peace 54
perfectionism 2, 18–19, 60, 67, 88–90, 140, 172, 175, 178, 180, 187, 208, 213, 232 n.5
  agent-neutral 151
  anti-perfectionist 173, 175
  and de-attachment 207–8
  and desire 192–7
  egalitarian 146
  and eudaimonism 141–9, 153–4, 156–8, 169, 175, 181
  Hurka's 147–59
  libidinal economy 155, 159
  Marx's 73–6
  moral 73–4, 141, 155–6, 193, 221 n.67, 228 n.11
  non-moral 74
  'peak' achievement 150–2
  perfectionist excellence 152–3, 159, 172, 188, 203
  perfectionist goods 74, 172, 180–1, 189, 193–4, 196, 207, 213
  perfectionist tradition 2, 18, 73–4, 106, 114, 141, 144–5
  and self-love 159–64
  utilitarian 141–2
personal development 51, 112, 130, 197
pleasure(s) 1, 14, 15–16, 31–2, 35–40, 49, 54–6, 57, 62, 66, 85, 90, 103–4, 107, 112, 115, 124, 131, 139–40, 144, 153, 190–1, 197, 221 n.67
  adaptive/non-adaptive 52, 58, 93–4, 157–8, 170
  alienated 62, 105, 128, 143
  and autonomy 106, 120, 122, 132, 164
  continuity of 48, 123, 130, 132, 189
  of critique 22, 143
  dependent 190, 191, 199
  and desire 93–6, 103–4, 107, 109, 111, 123
  displeasure 108–9, 120, 130, 175, 181, 194, 200, 207
  distribution of 59–60
  future 124–7, 130
  good reason 15, 42, 106, 108, 120, 142, 171, 190
  habituated 21
  of individuation 29
  and knowledge 102, 181
  as least resistance 1, 54, 99, 103, 106, 111–13, 119, 122, 129–31,

139–41, 153, 156, 158, 159–60, 170–1, 176, 190
masochistic/masochism 51, 130, 181
and moral theory 157
overt/covert 40
pleasure principle 95, 104, 106, 109, 138, 170, 207
reality principle 138, 170, 177, 182, 187, 197, 200, 207
of repetition 103, 112
unconstrained 98
and unpleasure 94, 104, 130, 158
of unrealistic expectations 47
war for pleasure 54–5, 197
Plotinus 143
political economy 8, 36, 53, 83–5, 88, 113, 154, 158, 197, 201
political Islam, violence of 43
post-68 aestheticism 205
post-capitalism 60, 173–5, 178
post-capitalist politics 7, 18
postmodernism 98, 198
post-work political theory 2, 6, 8, 11–12, 18
poverty 35, 45–6, 48, 212, 216 n.20
progressive anti-progressivist theory 3, 5, 45
proletarians/proletarianization 10, 34–5, 40, 52, 54, 87, 91, 95, 156, 177, 206
cultural 52, 169, 207
against proletarians 42–5
Przeworski, Adam 117, 118–19, 147
psychoanalysis 8, 14, 16, 37, 40, 54, 81, 107, 109–10, 113, 115, 117, 122, 147, 155, 166, 171, 210

race/racism 32, 43, 47, 53
radical permissiveness 173, 176
radical theoretico-political models 3–4, 24
Read, Jason
The Micro-Politics of Capital 38
The Politics of Transindividuality 196

realism 11, 48, 61, 96, 208
biopolitical 93
speculative 210
Real Politik 26
real subsumption 35–8, 40, 52, 62–5, 83, 85, 113, 123, 129, 138, 147, 189, 194, 200
reformism 34, 89
Reich, Wilhelm 171, 197
religion(s)
capitalism as 46–7, 112
Christianity 144, 167, 169, 229 n.13
ecclesiastical 142–3
monotheistic 142
robotics 30, 180
Romanticism 77, 80, 179
Rosen, Michael 105–6, 119, 171
Rousseau, Jean-Jacques 2, 21, 70–1, 73, 75, 77, 144–6, 148, 150, 159, 162, 165, 168, 189
concern on *amour-propre* 71, 75
'A Discourse on Inequality' 69–70, 72
'A Discourse on the Arts and Sciences' 67
individuation of 66–9, 72–3, 75
and Marx 73
völkisch/völkischism/völkism 69, 72, 75, 86, 146, 152

Sartre, Jean-Paul 193
Schelling, Friedrich 77
Schiller, Friedrich 74, 80
On the Aesthetic Education of Man 77
Schmitt, Carl 53
Schumpeter, Joseph 27
Second World War 34, 40, 54, 62, 64, 192
self-affection 2, 12, 17, 159, 161, 164, 169, 170–3, 174, 176, 180–1, 189, 193, 196, 199, 204
and individuation 182–8

self-attention 160, 164–5, 169, 176–7, 182
self-consciousness 79, 81, 178, 190, 198
self-control 50, 72, 112, 127, 131
self-correction system 32, 104
self-cultivation 186, 188
self-development 1, 16, 29, 72, 90, 138, 154, 160, 173
self-differentiation 62, 200
self-discipline 4, 143–5, 149, 168
self-display 50, 54, 68
self-evaluation 71, 160
self-governance 145, 162, 164, 166, 187–8, 190, 194–5
   forms of 167–70
   non-repressive 2, 177, 181, 189, 192, 208, 212
self-idealization 134–5
self-identity 9, 12, 26, 31, 42, 72, 77, 83, 93, 114, 120, 133, 143–4, 161, 165, 232 n.5
self-improvement 150, 177, 229 n.18
self-interests 50, 69, 72, 96, 118, 121, 132, 160, 171, 190–1, 216 n.20, 227 n.52
self-love (*amour-propre*) 2, 17–18, 21, 30, 38, 56, 59–60, 67–73, 88, 90–1, 96, 106–7, 113, 123, 133, 138, 144, 182, 196, 199, 204–5, 208. *See also* love of love of self
   and feminization of neotony 57–9
   forms of 167–70
   and its vicissitudes 114–16
   and perfectionism 159–64
   and selflessness 164–6
   and voluntary servitude 127–30
   and workplace 123–7
self-possession 28–9, 105–6
self-preservation (*amour de soi*) 17, 21, 30, 69–73, 75, 81, 90, 105, 114, 160
self-realization 2, 12, 14–15, 17–18, 46, 50, 65, 68, 71, 73, 75–7, 83, 90, 96, 104, 106, 130, 132–5, 137, 139, 140–3, 146–52, 155–9, 161–3, 165–8, 171–3, 176, 179, 180, 189–90, 193, 196–9, 202, 210, 212, 216 n.20, 232 n.5
self-regard 69–71, 159–60, 169, 186–7
self-reliance 46, 127–30, 137–8, 140, 144, 168, 168, 171
self-transformation 8, 13, 30–1, 74, 120, 134, 176
self-worth 39, 70–1, 73, 134, 159
Seneca 143, 160
shared interests 131
Simmel, Georg 26, 46
social being 77
socialism 24, 31, 59–60, 137–8
socialization 2, 12, 28, 77–8, 81, 84, 103, 109–10, 113, 145, 161, 174, 195
social reproduction 1–2, 4, 9, 13–16, 18–19, 33, 37, 39, 44–5, 49–51, 54, 60, 103, 114–15, 123, 138, 168, 172, 197, 199
Soviet Union, post-1950s 175
Spinoza, Baruch 48
   conatus (energy of desire) 115
Stalinism 25, 33, 45, 74, 82, 104
state of emergency 3–6, 11
St. Augustine 74, 143–4, 148
   On the Happy Life 142, 228 n.13
Stiegler, Bernard 1, 5, 16, 36, 52–3, 63, 156, 170, 206, 212, 220 n.58
   hyper-capitalism 95
   on sublimation 176
   Symbolic Misery 156
   technological crisis of individuation 51
Strauss, Leo 97
subjectivation 13–16, 19, 37–8, 53–4, 57, 61, 62, 67, 83, 107, 113–15, 131, 136, 137, 139, 154, 163, 189, 196, 200–1
   capitalist 13–16, 38–9, 52, 82, 114, 204, 215 n.20, 221 n.67
   class 13, 89
subjectivism 15, 77, 209–10

subjectivity 5, 12, 30–1, 36–9, 49, 51, 53, 77, 107, 113, 115, 131–2, 139, 156, 173, 197–9, 212
   capitalist 218 n.21
   economic war against 61
   human 209
   political 91
   and production 53–4, 61, 64, 67, 113, 115
sublimation 176, 191
   de-sublimation 139, 173, 181–2, 189, 212
   and necessary labour 177–82
survey on employment 17

Tafuri, Manfredo 30
technology 2, 7, 11–13, 31–2, 50–2, 212
   digital 55
   third technological revolution 13, 172
Thomism 74. *See also* Aquinas, Thomas
Tillich, Paul 47
Tiqqun, *Preliminary Materials for a Theory of the Young-Girl* 58
Tomba, Massimiliano 86–7
Tomšič, Samo 1, 16, 36–7, 41, 50–1, 105, 114, 130
trade union 10, 23, 28, 30, 42, 62–3, 89, 97, 200, 215 n.14
transindividual/transindividuality 2, 74, 77, 81, 89, 91, 168, 191, 195–6, 199, 220 n.58
transindividuation 18, 195
   and individuation 81–8
transition 13, 22, 65, 87–8, 94, 138, 155, 158, 171–8, 181, 197
Tronti, Mario 39

underdevelopment 43, 48, 72
unemployment 7, 10–11, 17, 22, 35, 42, 47, 215 n.20

The United States 4, 24, 42
   banking crisis in 2008 104
   US Bureau of Labor Statistics 17
uxoriousness, capitalist 31–6, 39, 45–7, 49, 55, 91
   and neotony 58, 60

value formation process 17, 93–4, 99
Virno, Paulo 5, 39, 90, 123
virtue(s) 29, 31, 69, 72, 75, 141, 143–5, 158, 162–4, 165, 170, 204
   civic 68, 71, 75, 145
   classical 143
   intellectual 145, 149
   Kantian 164
   moral 31, 74, 144, 152, 159
   perfectionist 144, 157–9, 188
   pragmatic/defensive 156
   public 69–70, 145
voluntarism 119–20, 193, 224 n.46
voluntary servitude 15, 39, 114, 125, 156, 171, 197
   and self-love 127–30
von Clausewitz, Carl 53

'walking away' from capitalism 118–23
war footing 5, 53–4
war for pleasure 54–5, 197
war machines 5, 53–4, 200–2
Weber, Max 26, 46
well-roundedness 152–3
workers' movement 4–5, 8–11, 25, 28, 35, 41, 52, 62–4, 82, 88–91, 146, 157, 197
   old 4–5, 11, 27, 63, 89–91, 172
working-class identity 5, 6–8, 34, 40, 42, 64–5, 82–3, 97, 117, 144

Žižek, Slavoj 5, 21, 32–3, 100, 119
zone à defendre (ZAD), France 233 n.13

www.ingramcontent.com/pod-product-compliance
Lightning Source LLC
Chambersburg PA
CBHW060947230426
43665CB00015B/2098